Novelty and Change

New research, ideas, thoughts and interpretation on the British Civil Wars and the military history of the 17th century

---

Proceedings of the 2023 Helion and Company 'Century of the Soldier' Conference

Edited by Charles Singleton

'This is the Century of the Soldier', Fulvio Testi, Poet, 1641

Helion & Company

Helion & Company Limited
Unit 8 Amherst Business Centre
Budbrooke Road
Warwick
CV34 5WE
England
Tel. 01926 499 619
Email: info@helion.co.uk
Website: www.helion.co.uk
Twitter: @helionbooks
Visit our blog http://blog.helion.co.uk/

Published by Helion & Company 2024
Designed and typeset by Mary Woolley (www.battlefield-design.co.uk)
Cover designed by Paul Hewitt, Battlefield Design (www.battlefield-design.co.uk)

ISBN 978-1-804516-28-7

British Library Cataloguing-in-Publication Data.
A catalogue record for this book is available from the British Library.

Contents

Contributor biographies v
Foreword by Professor Malcolm Wanklyn viii
Introduction xv

1 Novelty and Continuity in European Warfare 1618–1721
Peter H. Wilson (University of Oxford) 17

2 'Seats of war'
Current Investigations into ECW fortifications
David Flintham 56
Bibliography 93

3 Marmaduke Rawdon's Regiment of Foot
The Formation of The Regiment, from Colonel Rawdon's Commission to the arrival at Basing House
Andrew Robertshaw 97
Bibliography 122

4 Dragoon Warfare in the Welsh Borders during the British Civil Wars
Andrew Abram 124

5 Locating the Battle of Stow-on-the Wold 1646
Simon Marsh & Sam Wilson 135
Appendix I 161
Appendix II: Military related finds from the Stow battlefield survey 164

6 Countermarch, Caracole and Charge, 1642
Dr Pádraig Lenihan 167

7 Montrose's Armies, 1644–1646
Dr Edward M. Furgol 185
Appendix: Units by General 201
Appendix: Orders of Battle 214

The Century of the Soldier Conference Saturday 15th April 2023

Contributor biographies

Professor Peter Wilson
Professor Wilson is the Chichele Professor of the History of War, All Souls College, Oxford. His research interests are centred on the impact of war in European and World Development, as well as the history of the Holy Roman Empire.

David Flintham
David Flintham is the co-founder and project manager of the King's Lynn under Siege community archaeology project. He is the author of three books (including one for Helion), and more than 60 other papers, essays and articles on mid-17th century fortress warfare, particularly across the British Isles. David is also part of an archaeological research project 're-discovering' London's ECW fortifications. His paper today is a key component of his next book for Helion.

Andrew Robertshaw
Andrew Robertshaw, BA, PGCE, MA, FSA. Head of Education at the National Army Museum from 1988 until 2007, Directs of the Royal Logistic Corps Museum 2007–14, and now freelance historian, film maker and author. Since 2010 advisor to film directors including Stephen Spielberg, Peter Jackson and Sam Mendes.

Dr Andrew Abram
Dr Andrew Abram served in the British Army for sixteen years and in 2007 was awarded his doctorate in History by University of Wales, Lampeter. He was employed there as lecturer in Medieval History until 2015 and subsequently acted as an associate lecturer at Manchester Metropolitan University. He has researched, written about, and taught on medieval and early modern warfare. Andrew is the

author of three books on seventeenth-century warfare published by Helion & Co., whilst a fourth (on dragoons) is due out in 2023.

Simon Marsh, Sam Wilson

Simon Marsh is the Battlefields Trust Research and Threats Coordinator, Joint Chair of the Trust's Mercia Region and managed the Trust's project to rediscover the location of the battle of Stow. He is a researcher on early modern warfare with a particular interest in the British Civil Wars. He published *Battle of London*, with the late Dr Stephen Porter in 2010 and has had two volumes examining the papers of the Earl of Essex's train of artillery published by the Pike and Shot Society (2016 and 2022). He has also contributed to Helion publications, is a regular contributor to the Pike and Shot Society's journal, *Arquebusier,* and has written for the Journal of the Society of Army Historical Research.

Sam Wilson is a Trustee of the Battlefields Trust and its Archaeological Advisor. He has extensive experience of participating in and running battlefield surveys, including leading the fieldwork for the Trust at Stow (1646), Otterburn (1388) and Langport (1645). He also led the fieldwork for a Heritage Lottery Funded project to locate the battle of Barnet (1471) and is one of the archaeologists working with Waterloo Uncovered. He has extensive commercial archaeological experience and in a brief hiatus from archaeology, is currently working as a film armourer for a major Netflix production.

Dr Pádraig Lenihan

Pádraig Lenihan lectures in history at the University of Limerick. His recent publications include *Conquest and Resistance: War in 17th Century Ireland* (2001) and *1690 the Battle of the Boyne* (2003).

Dr Edward Furgol

Completing a D.Phil. in 17th century Scottish history at Oxford University was scarcely a secure route to a career. Fortunately, the Manpower Services Commission funded training opportunities for people in my situation and in 1982 I became the historian at the Pendle Heritage Centre, mainly dealing with the Tudor and Stuart period. In 1984 I left to work for Historic Environment Scotland researching manuscripts containing information on Duff House, creating a still-used resource on the house and a catalogue to the Montcoffer Papers. Then I produced exhibits on Holyrood Park and Mary Queen of Scots. In 1987 I returned to the USA as the curator of the National Museum of the United States Navy, where I retired as managing director in 2017. During that period, I wrote articles, New Dictionary of National Biography entries and reviews covering 17th Scottish military history.

Since retiring, I have revised my *A Regimental History of the Covenanting Armies, 1639–1651,* and written chapters for *'His Majesty's Loyal Subjects': The Scottish Royalist Armies of the British Civil Wars, 1639–1655*, which I am co-authoring with Dr Andrew Lind. *Seats of war*: current investigations into ECW fortifications.

Foreword by Professor Malcolm Wanklyn

After letting it be known far and wide that, having reached the age of eighty, I had decided that family responsibilities must take precedence over making further contributions to the study of the military history of the British Wars, it was a great honour that I could not refuse to be asked to write an introduction to the revised set of papers given at the conference held under the auspices of Helion Press at the University of Worcester in April 2023. In my opinion they can only be described as a forthright celebration of the revival of research since the millennium in what I like to describe as the hard military history of the British Isles in the seventeenth century, namely the study of campaigns, battles and sieges, of strategy and tactics, and of the relationship between theory and practice in offensive and defensive warfare, as opposed to soft military history which focuses on the multi-faceted impact of war on the human condition and the success or otherwise of civilian governments and military administration in providing not only military hardware but also pay, food, clothing, and medical care for army personnel. This change in direction has not, however, been at the expense of soft military history. What I see in the keynote address is clear evidence of a synthesis.

The years immediately following the Second World War had been a false dawn. The publication of C.V. Wedgwood's *The King's War* (1958) and Austin Woolrych's *Battles of the English Civil Wars* (1961) made it look as if the high regard for the contribution of hard military history towards an understanding of the events of the middle years of the seventeenth century established by the writings of S.R. Gardiner and Sir Charles Firth would continue into the future only for a new generation of historians to think differently and in a way that went beyond establishing different priorities for research. In an atmosphere coloured by the Suez crisis, the loss of empire and the evaporation of the dream of the new Elizabethans this aspect of the English revolution had become an embarrassment. The party line was now that hard military history for that period was done and dusted. The historians of the late nineteenth and the first half of the twentieth century had produced the definitive narrative. No further academic research was necessary. Filling in the minor details could be left to retired generals and colonels.

Instead, the focus should be firmly on such neglected areas as the administrative underpinning of war, primarily at the county and provincial level, even though such compartmentalisation had the unfortunate result of missing the wood for the trees insofar as understanding the principal campaigns as they took no notice of such boundaries.

For my own part I was warned that an academic career was out of the question if I persisted in research begun in my MA dissertation on the King's Armies in the West of England, and I duly turned to examining the reasons why members of the gentry and the aristocracy in Cheshire and Shropshire chose, or did not choose, to support King or Parliament at the start of the First Civil War, and then abandoned military history altogether in order to oversee the computerising of the Gloucester Port Books which shed much light on inland trade in the West Midlands and beyond throughout the early modern period. Even so I continued to teach a module on the English Civil War and can well recall at a time when I saw myself as an economic historian pure and simple being told by a student of Charles Carlton's mould-breaking study *Going to the Wars* (1992), and then a few years later seeing the sign of a new dawn in the window of a bookshop in Chancery Lane containing a display publicising John Barratt's *Cavaliers – The Royalist Army at War 1642–1646*. Both works, like their distinguished precursor, Ronald Hutton's *The Royalist War Effort 1642–1646* (1982) stood firmly on the boundary between soft and hard military history, but they helped to open the floodgates. That is not to say that nothing was happening outside the higher education section in the late twentieth century. Interest in moving forward research into the hard side of the British Wars developed amongst the enthusiasts for military history who joined Brigadier Peter Young's secret army *The Sealed Knot*. Their re-enactments of the battles provided practical knowledge of weaponry and how it could or could not be employed, whilst the publications of Partizan Press under the aegis of David Ryan provided a training ground for research and writing for non-academic historians which would give them in due course the confidence to produce scholarly significant monographs.

Since the year 2000 the trickle of new works on the hard history of the civil wars in England and elsewhere in Great Britain has become a flood encouraged first by the publishers Pen and Sword and then by Helion Press whose series *The Century of the Soldier: Warfare 1618–1721* has currently achieved the most impressive total of over a hundred volumes covering not just the British Isles but the whole of Europe with forays into North America and parts of Asia. In overview they are a refreshing mixture of the research of both professional and amateur historians, which has hopefully scuppered the tendency in the dark ages as I remember them of the former ignoring the writings of the latter because of their authors' lack of academic training.

The keynote paper delivered by Professor Peter Wilson was a reflection on the sixty-year long debate about whether or not there was a military revolution in the early modern period. As first conceived by Professor Michael Roberts it was located in the first half of the seventeenth century, but it became bound up with such developments as the *trace Italienne* of the early sixteenth century at one extreme to improvements in field artillery in the eighteenth century at the other. It is therefore scarcely surprising that the concept has been seen as extending over far too long a time period to be described as a revolution. Professor Wilson's approach is a judicious one. In his review of evidence used in the past in support of a revolution he is critical. For example, he sees the degree of continuity as opposed to change in military practice being neglected despite most developments spreading only slowly across west and central Europe during the course of the seventeenth and early eighteenth centuries. Nevertheless, he accepts that armies were in general much larger at the end than at the beginning of the period as evidenced by the increasing number of regiments, and in support of this he supplies very convincing statistical data. He also singles out important corollaries to the expansion in army size that were almost universal. First, provincial armies were merged into national ones. Second, the abandonment of the age-old practice by which regiments were raised for a specific conflict and then disbanded immediately afterwards came to an end. Instead in many cases they remained in being at half-strength or less. As such they would be capable of setting out on campaign almost immediately fighting broke out again with the veterans quickly bringing the new levies up to scratch. Finally, there were important administrative and social consequences of the new way of organising armies which he sees as requiring further research. For example, keeping skeleton units in being created new priorities for governments ranging from building barracks to accommodate the soldiers being retained, providing hospitals for veterans once their state service was over who were incapable of earning their livelihood, and keeping army pay under control by trying to prevent the career rank-and-file from marrying.

Andrew Robertshaw's paper is a move from the macro to the micro but with the attention still firmly fixed on the regiment, namely Sir Marmaduke Rawdon's. As such it fills an important gap by focussing on the first months of the regiment's existence as its contribution towards the successful defence of the exposed royalist garrison at Basing House, home of the Marquess of Winchester, in 1643 and again in 1644 is well known from accounts already in the public domain. Its colonel was a prominent member of the London mercantile community, warden of the Clothworkers' Guild and a trader in wines, with a country seat at Hoddesdon in Hertfordshire. Although Rawdon's royalist sympathies were clear, he did not leave for Oxford until March 1643. Soon afterwards he received a commission to raise a regiment of foot, though in terms of the number of companies that were formed as a result, it was never more than a half regiment. The intention was for the rank and file to be recruited in Oxfordshire, but many of the officers were Rawdon's neighbours in the City, his trading associates, or fellow members of the Honourable Artillery Company, and some of the rank-and-file probably came from there as it was subsequently described in *Mercurius Aulicus* as 'the London regiment'. Documents in the Royalist Ordnance Papers give unprecedented detail about the provisions of arms and ammunition for the newly raised troops, but the absence of muskets causes Robertshaw to speculate that Rawdon had somehow or other brought them from London presumably via Hertfordshire. Initially the regiment was intended to help garrison Oxford, though it became surplus to requirements in mid-July with the arrival of a brigade of Northern infantry regiments. A week or so later Rawdon was ordered to take his men to Basing. This may have been a response to its being in danger through the capture of Reading by the earl of Essex's army, but the two months' gap between the two events looks odd. Possibly the King's spymasters at Oxford had just received intelligence of a forthcoming attack on the marquis's house from Parliamentary controlled Winchester. It was surely more than a coincidence that the first of Rawdon's companies to reach Basing arrived only a few hours before the enemy arrived at its gates.

Andrew Flintham's paper deals with what he describes as the neglected face of the archaeology of British Wars (1642–1651) – fortifications and siegeworks – which he sees as surprising given that the evidence on the ground is far more substantial than it is for battles. Flintham's focus is on three ongoing projects – the defences constructed by the Eastern Association at King's Lynn, the earthworks and forts around London erected by Parliament during the First Civil War, and a register of fortified towns, castles and houses throughout the United Kingdom and Ireland in use in the mid-seventeenth century – and his contribution has been expanded in this volume to include progress made in the year since the Worcester conference. King's Lynn was a town with decayed medieval fortifications but blessed with water features covering most of the approaches. Taking advantage of these it was transformed during the course of 1643 and early 1644 into a veritable fortress, which befitted its position defending the access into Parliamentary controlled East Anglia from the north and wide open to attack from the north by the royalist army commanded by the marquis of Newcastle.

Documentary evidence was very helpful in revealing the various stages in the development of the defences, but their exact location, though it proved challenging, was ultimately rewarding in that the excavation of the earthworks covering the gaps between the water features provided interesting evidence as to how such defences were constructed. In the case of London contemporary administrative sources, fieldwork and excavation have within the last three years overturned many of the claims about the location of virtually all the forts and the lines connecting them. Finally, a collaborative effort has identified 1,104 towns, castles and country houses in all four of King Charles I's kingdoms which were fortified or refortified during the British Wars of which 675 witnessed hostile action of some kind or another between 1642 and 1653.

If the archaeology of war in mid-seventeenth century Britain has recently prioritised the investigation of battlefields, there nevertheless remain uncertainties about the exact location of some of them. The paper delivered by Simon Marsh and Sam Wilson focused on one of these, the last major encounter in the First Civil War at Stow-in-the-Wold in March 1646 in which contingents from the West Midland garrisons on their way to join the king at Oxford were hunted down and destroyed. I am known to be wary about drawing firm conclusions from archaeology that relies on what is discovered by field walking and metal detecting unless the material evidence is overwhelming as, for example, in the case of Naseby and Marston Moor. In this case, after reading the revised paper I am sure that Marsh and Wilson and their volunteers have found the correct site, and in my opinion it could well serve as a model for future studies of the archaeology of early modern battlefields. The most convincing evidence is the failure to discover musket balls or any other military artefacts dating from the seventeenth century at the traditional location for the battle, namely Horsington Hill in Donnington parish. Admittedly, few musket balls were found in what they are careful to describe as the most likely location just to the north of Stow, but their extensive and painstaking appraisal of the documentary and landscape as well as the archaeological evidence explains why this is so.

Dr Andrew Abram's paper is concerned first with briefly explaining the purpose, nature and type of military operations conducted by mounted infantry, or dragoons as they were termed at the time. He then supplements this with a case study of Sir William Brereton's use of dragoons in his campaigns in Cheshire and adjacent counties between the establishment of an army base at Nantwich in January 1643 and May 1645 by which time their tactical role was firmly established in Brereton's mind. As such the paper forms an interesting and informative adjunct to his recently published monographs *More Lions than Men: Sir William Brereton and the Cheshire Army of Parliament 1642–46*, which has a broader remit covering not only command and control but also such administrative matters as recruitment, pay, and military supplies, and *Dragoon and Dragoon Operations*, which discusses their usage in the wars in all three of Charles I's kingdoms for the whole of the period 1638 to 1653.

Dr Padraig Lenihan's closely argued and copiously illustrated paper discusses infantry and cavalry tactics in the first year of the war in Ireland between Protestant settlers and the Irish and Old English Catholics, who I choose to call the patriots, which began with a major uprising in Ulster in October 1641 that overran many of the standing army garrisons in the province and then quickly spread to the rest of the country. Insofar as the infantry were concerned, the government's success in maintaining a strict control over the import of gunpowder meant that the patriots' provincial armies could not use conventional battlefield tactics of the day which were heavily reliant on musketry for both attack and defence. Instead they were forced to fall back on the traditional charge whose success depended upon taking the enemy by surprise and cutting them down with bladed weapons before they could fire their weapons. This achieved some success against untrained levies as at Julianstown in November 1641, but it needed a good measure of luck when against experienced infantry formations. In September 1642, however, substantial quantities of gunpowder supplied by the Catholic powers on the continent arrived in the south coast ports controlled by the patriots thus enabling their provincial armies to change to conventional battlefield tactics. At the start of the war the Protestant generals having copious supplies of powder used the caracole on the battlefield by which their cavalry rode up to the enemy, shot off their pistols to discomfort them, and then retired to reload before advancing again until such time as successive cascades of incoming fire caused the enemy to turn tail and run for their lives. This tactic proved reasonably effective against infantry units but was potentially disastrous when facing cavalry. The patriot generals on the other hand could not spare any gunpowder for their horse, but if their troops survived the first discharge of enemy pistols in good order, they could counterattack by following their assailants ride back to their lines to reload. Thus, on several occasions in the first year of the war the former had the chance to win a cavalry engagement, and at Ballinvegga in March 1642 they might well have done so had not an experienced officer, who had not been involved in the engagement up to that point, stood firm with his troop and forced a melee in which the more experienced Protestants won the day.

The campaigns of the Marquess of Montrose in Scotland in 1644–1646 have received much attention over the years from political and military historians alike, but in his contribution to the Worcester Conference Dr Edmund Furgol provided an interesting and novel perspective on the fighting. Others have focused on the fact that Montrose's armies were to a large extent *ad hoc* formations over which he did not have overall authority because of limitations in the commission he had received from the king, but with only rough details about the numbers involved. Furgol, however, has provided clear numerical evidence via bar charts as to how few were the soldiers in his polyglot armies to whom he could issue mandatory commands beginning with the shilly-shallying over the forces with which he was to invade Scotland in the summer of 1644 and ending with his futile attempts in the winter of 1645–46 to regain the initiative lost after the rout at Philiphaugh. Furgol has also argued convincingly that the principal factor underlying Montrose's failure to build on his string of victories over Covenanter forces in 1644 and 1645 was that there was not a civilian government in Scotland to provide him systematically with men, money and military supplies, and that he showed little interest in establishing one. In consequence he had to fall back on force to maintain the momentum of his campaign whilst allowing the Highland and Irish Catholic elements in his army to pursue their personal agendas at the cost of alienating the civilian population of Scotland and weakening the forces at his disposal at what proved to be critical moments.

When I undertook to write the introduction to the papers delivered at the Worcester conference, I did not expect to find any common themes given the diverse directions taken by recent research into hard military history research of the period. I did not find any or thereafter feel that I was under any obligation to conjure one up. What to my mind was important to mind is that the papers and the discussion that followed them displayed in no uncertain terms a vigour and rigour in scholarship being pursued since the Millennium which is not free-standing or divorced from the military and political, and in Professor Wilson's paper, social history of the seventeenth century. This absolves it from any charge of being antiquarian in content or approach. The papers also clearly show that the flood of new outputs in hard military history is nowhere near exhausting itself.

Introduction

The 2023 Century of the Soldier conference was held the University of Worcester on 15 April.

The theme of the conference was 'Novelty and Change', echoing the words of the Venetian Ambassador writing of his experiences of England in the Republic of the 1650s. Following on from the global pandemic, we used the conference as an opportunity to showcase new research and findings that perhaps had been overlooked and past by during the lockdown period.

The day had a truly international feel as we welcomed speakers from Ireland and America, and delegates from Europe and as far a field as Australia. The conference was a great success, and we received a lot of very positive feedback from those that attended. It was also a day for breaking records. The conference sold over 120 tickets, our best attended conference to date.

I'd like to thank the delegates for their attendance and to acknowledge the support of the conference goers who have made the event the lead in the yearly calendar.

Charles Singleton
Creative Director Antiquity and Early Modern Portfolio, Helion and Company

1

Novelty and Continuity in European Warfare 1618–1721

Peter H. Wilson (University of Oxford)

Change often appears more exciting and interesting than continuity. That was not always the case. Most ordinary people in early modern Europe viewed 'novelty' with suspicion. To them, change usually meant higher taxes and the erosion of 'ancient liberties.' The latter were usually not that old, but popular appeals to preserve rights allegedly 'hallowed by time' further indicates how 'progress' was not universally welcomed. Efforts to 'reform' faith and the church in the sixteenth century had opened deep divisions which showed no signs of resolution after 1600. Human history was understood as bounded by God's divine plan as revealed through the Bible in which change was limited to a cyclical process akin to the natural rhythm of the seasons, of birth, growth, decline, and death. Life would remain fundamentally the same until Judgement Day.

Historians have viewed things differently. Modern historical method has its roots in the era of the Enlightenment and early nineteenth century when change was increasingly viewed positively as 'progress.' Cyclical views of history were displaced by ideas of fundamental change across time, either as a linear modernisation process, or as a succession of distinct epochs, each ushered in by some kind of revolution or fundamental shift in human relations.

These features are especially prominent in the writing of military history which often sees change as a progression through distinct eras, each defined by a 'paradigm army' emerging as model for the others to emulate.[1] This stadial

1 For example, J.A. Lynn, 'The evolution of army style in the modern West 800–2000', *International History Review*, 18 (1996), 505–545.

approach has long historiographical roots and was popularised by Hans Delbrück (1848–1929) whose four volume *History of the Art of War* first appeared in 1900–08.[2] Change is explained as intrinsic to warfare, rather than driven by wider political, social, economic, or other factors. The focus is on the battlefield, and especially weaponry and tactics. For example, the sixteenth and early seventeenth centuries are commonly described as the era of 'pike and shot' which gave way to that of 'horse and musket' persisting into the nineteenth century.

The most influential example of this approach is the Military Revolution thesis, first propounded in 1955. Michael Roberts' original version emphasised the drill and discipline adopted after 1560 to maximise the potential of handguns which in turn transformed tactics, led to armies becoming more effective and larger, transforming strategy and, ultimately, causing war to have a greater impact on state and society. Geoffrey Parker presented a revised version in the 1970s which instead stressed new fortification techniques responding to improved artillery, but otherwise retained Roberts' causal sequence leading to a greater scale and impact of war. In both cases, technological change (or at least changes how weaponry was used) is regarded as triggering a sequence of wider developments which, accumulatively, are believed to have shaped not only the prevailing character of war, but human history more broadly.[3]

Much effort has been spent debating the timing and character of this Revolution, whether it was a singular event, or one of several such periods of change, and whether the explanation can be extended from Europe to include change elsewhere in the world. This debate has undoubtedly expanded our knowledge of early modern warfare. Nonetheless, the focus on weaponry and tactics has led to a neglect of some other important, yet less obvious changes. Moreover, developments were not always interconnected and change in one aspect did not necessarily alter conditions more generally. Indeed, a major reason why there is a debate at all is that the historical record is muddled and confusing and we can find different aspects of warfare (weaponry, tactics, financing, command etc) changing seemingly separately from each other, and at different times.

2 The English translation of the 1920 corrected edition was published in 1990. Fuller discussion of this point in P.H. Wilson, *Lützen* (Oxford, 2018), pp.108–113.

3 This debate has generated an extensive literature. The viewpoints of the original protagonists can be found in C.J. Rogers (ed.), *The military revolution debate: Readings on the military transformation of early modern Europe* (Boulder, 1995); G. Parker, *The military revolution: military innovation and the rise of the West 1500–1800* (Cambridge, 1988). Critique and useful further discussions are offered by J. Black, *Beyond the Military Revolution. War in the Seventeenth-Century* World (London, 2011); H. Carvalhal, A. Murteira, R.L. de Jesus (eds.), *The First World Empire. Portugal, War and Military Revolution* (London, 2021).

This last comment applies directly to the years 1618–1721, the period framing this volume, and which falls in the middle of Parker's longer version of the Military Revolution as lasting from about 1500 to 1800. It is helpful to consider this shorter timeframe on its own terms, as it spans the conventional break around 1648, the year of the Peace of Westphalia ending both the Thirty Years War and the Dutch struggle for independence from Spain. That settlement often taken as a major demarcation point between what is (erroneously) termed an age of religious wars c.1517–1648 which are perceived as violent, destructive, and barely under control, and the 'age of absolutism' 1648–1789 associated with limited war during which change is viewed as modest in contrast to the following French Revolutionary and Napoleonic Wars.

The conventional view of 1648 as a fundamental turning point is open to question. For example, it was only in the 1860s that the Peace of Westphalia was canonised by legal scholars as the 'birth' of the modern international system of sovereign states.[4] Nor, as will be demonstrated shortly, did the end of the Thirty Years War mark the 'birth' of European standing armies. Rather than constituting a fundamental turning point, the mid-seventeenth century was characterised more by a slow evolution of earlier developments. Nonetheless, the century as a whole saw important changes in how armies were organised and structured internally. This chapter will argue that the decades from the 1660s saw a major development which has been partly obscured by the more usual focus on what happened on battlefields: the consolidation of European armies through the establishment of permanent regiments. Whereas many states had maintained forces permanently, in some cases since the fourteenth-century, these had not only fluctuated considerably in size, but had largely lacked internal coherence. That changed during the later seventeenth century, establishing military organisations by the 1710s which remained, in their fundamentals, unchanged into the French Revolutionary era.

The discussion will concentrate on land warfare in western, central, and southern Europe with some reference to developments elsewhere on the Continent, as well as to naval warfare. It opens with a reappraisal of the significance of the technological and tactical changes which have been given such prominence in the Military Revolution discussion. The second section explores the growth in the size of armed forces, arguing that we need to look deeper than total numbers and consider how armies were structured to appreciate the significance of the changes across the seventeenth century. The chapter concludes with a brief outline of the broader impacts of this growth, concentrating mainly on the consequences for military-civil relations.

4 D. Croxton, *Westphalia. The Last Christian Peace* (Basingstoke, 2013).

Weaponry and Tactics

Changes across 1618–1721 were gradual rather than revolutionary, but that is not to say that they were not fundamental. Seventeenth-century armies differed considerably in their organisation, armament, and tactics from their sixteenth-century forebears. The longer-term direction of travel was convergence and standardisation.

Sixteenth-century armies exhibited more numerous and pronounced differences than those a century later which were more alike. These distinctions should not be seen as 'national' in the modern sense as this was not yet an age of nation states. Though some weapons, forms of dress, and tactics did become associated with an emerging sense of national identity, the key distinction in the sixteenth century was that between different troop types. Armies were composed of units, armed, trained and employed differently from each other, with these distinctions gradually smoothed out to create more uniform infantry, cavalry, and artillery as separate branches of service during the seventeenth century.[5]

Certain regions of Europe became famous around 1500 for providing specific kinds of soldiers. A good example is the Swiss heavy infantry who were in fact initially mainly armed with halberds rather than the pikes for which they became famous. Halberds remained the 'national' weapon and were still used in the civil war of 1712, though not by the side that won which instead relied on firepower.[6] Germany was renowned for the Landsknechte, its answer to the Swiss, as well as pistol-armed cavalry known as Reiters who emerged around 1530. Hungary, the Balkans, and Eastern Europe supplied light cavalry, while Italian and Dutch engineers were highly sought after.

These examples could be multiplied, but the key point is that armies were assembled by hiring these specialist troop types, or creating local substitutes, often trained by foreign experts. For example, Sweden created its own heavy infantry during the sixteenth century using German and later Dutch officers. Adopting the prevailing best practice was no guarantee of success, and the remodelled Swedish army was smashed by the Poles at Kirchholm in 1605.[7]

The Italian Wars (1494–1559) and other wider ranging conflicts brought belligerents from across Europe into conflict, often for the first time, or at least after a long period without contact. Encounters with unfamiliar opponents forced

5 For an excellent survey, see J.B. Szabó and P. Fodor (eds.), *On the Verge of a New Era. The Armies of Europe at the Time of the Battle of Mohács* (Budapest, 2021).

6 J.A. Meier, 'Halbarte oder Bajonett? Zur Vorgeschichte des bernischen Sieges in der 2. Schlacht bei Villmergen 1712', *Waffen und Kostümkunde*, 47 (2005), 43–82.

7 M. Neuding Skoog, *I rikets, tjänst: Krig, stat och samhälle i Sverige 1450–1550* (Lund, 2010).

armies to adapt, copy, and innovate. Practice gradually coalesced around 'schools', or combinations of practices which were regarded by their exponents and outside observers as coherent and impressive ways to organise and fight. The label was particularly apt as the leading armies attracted volunteers keen to learn best practice, as well as writers who engaged with Europe's burgeoning print market to sell military manuals and other 'war books.'

The Spanish School was associated with the Army of Flanders formed in 1567 to crush the Dutch Revolt. The success of its opponents in resisting defeat soon also attracted admiration, especially after the military reforms promoted by Maurice of Nassau (1567–1625) and his half-brother and successor as Dutch leader, Frederick Henry (1584–1647).[8] The opposing Spanish and Dutch schools remained dominant into the 1620s, but there were other influential military systems, notably that of the Austrian Habsburgs who were engaged in a long series of conflicts with the Ottomans until 1606. Meanwhile, French armies merged elements of Dutch, Spanish, and German methods with existing local practice during the Wars of Religion 1562–1598.[9]

Sweden combined the earlier influence of the Germans and Dutch with its own solutions once it resumed conflict with Poland after 1621 and had to adapt to fight opponents who had far more numerous and effective cavalry. Though widely admired by British and other foreign volunteers serving King Gustavus Adolphus (1594–1632), these methods were not wholly effective against the Habsburgs and their allies once Sweden entered the Thirty Years War in 1631 and most of the truly distinctive elements, such as the famous 'brigade' deployment in checkerboard blocks, had been abandoned within three years. The armies of the British Civil Wars followed the same pattern. The Swedish methods advocated by officers who had served on the Continent or had learned them from war books were soon abandoned after 1642 as unnecessarily complex.

The experience in the long wars of the first half of the seventeenth century thus accelerated the convergence of military practice, reducing the differences between armies as they adopted similar weaponry, organisation, and tactics.[10] Those that were unwilling or unable to do so, found their operational radius restricted to regions where their own methods retained value. For example, Transylvanian armies remained effective against the Ottomans and Habsburgs when fighting

8 F. González de Leon, *The Road to Rocroi: Class, Culture and Command in the Spanish Army of Flanders, 1567–1659* (Leiden, 2009); O. van Nimwegen, *The Dutch Army and the Military Revolutions 1588–1688* (Woodbridge, 2010), pp.85–116.

9 J.A. Lynn, 'Tactical evolution in the French army 1560–1660' *French Historical Studies*, 14 (1985), 176–191; T.J. O'Brien de Clare, *One Faith, One Law, One King: French Armies of the Wars of Religion 1562–1598* (Warwick, 2021).

10 Neatly summarised in K. Roberts, *Pike and Shot Tactics 1590–1660* (Oxford, 2010).

close to home, but they suffered from their lack of artillery and regular infantry during their interventions westwards into Austria and Bohemia during the Thirty Years War.[11]

Change was gradual and from the distance of both time (our perspective) and when viewing warfare more generally, it can appear evolutionary. However, when examining the micro level of unit tactics, innovation clearly occurred more unevenly and often as an unplanned sequence of ad hoc changes in response to specific events.[12] Developments were neither smooth nor linear. For example, small arms improved with lighter, smaller calibre weapons appearing in the 1620s and 1630s and the shift in tactics towards greater emphasis on infantry firepower was already evident during the Thirty Years War. However, the proportion of infantry declined relative to cavalry, particularly in forces assembled for battle during that conflict's final phase in the 1640s. There were a set of interrelated logistical, military, and political factors behind this which were not fully repeated in subsequent conflicts, during which the proportion of infantry again grew.

By mid-century, most armies employed broadly similar linear tactics, forming their infantry into battalions of between 500 and 1,500 with musketeers flanking pikemen, while the cavalry deployed in squadrons of 150 to 300 and artillery remained relegated largely to a supporting role. Armies usually deployed in two lines, with often no more than a small reserve to the rear, though this could vary depending on the terrain. Change nonetheless continued through technological innovation and the discussion of military practice, both among officers and within print media. The number of ranks in both infantry and cavalry formations was progressively reduced from the 1660s to lengthen the unit frontages. Small numbers of infantry were equipped with grenades after the mid-1660s for use in both battle as well as siege warfare which was already an established arena for this weapon. Grenadiers first appeared in the Austrian Habsburg army in 1663, four years ahead of their introduction in France and seven before their adoption by the Dutch. Most armies included them within infantry formations by 1700, though they were only grouped together in their own companies somewhat later, and finally as separate battalions in the mid-eighteenth century by when they had morphed into elite troops disassociated from their original weapon other than for distinctions in their uniforms.

Other important changes in weaponry included the adoption of flintlocks which increasingly replaced matchlocks around the 1680s as the standard small

11 See the two chapters on the Transylvanian army by J.B. Szabó in G. Kármán (ed.), *The Princes of Transylvania in the Thirty Years War* (Paderborn, 2023).

12 This argument is made in the excellent unpublished thesis by D. Yun, 'Early modern British infantry combat: Realities, perceptions and the question of modernity, 1642–1746', (PhD, University of Exeter, 2021).

arm due to their greater reliability in bad weather. Paper cartridges were adopted in France (1692) and elsewhere, further improving the rate of fire somewhat. The introduction of the plug (1670s) and then socket bayonet (around 1700) was associated with the corresponding phasing out of pikemen, further standardising equipment and tactical employment within the infantry.

Improvements in gun founding meanwhile added to the potency of artillery. The greater willingness of governments to invest in purpose-built warships allowed Europe's maritime powers to exploit this by adding more numerous and heavier guns than could be carried on hired merchantmen. Naval tactics also became more linear and standardised with the adoption of the line of battle in the 1650s.[13] Field artillery in land warfare also became considerably more effective during the later seventeenth century. Thus, war on land and at sea became more linear and reliant on firepower which continued to dominate both the theory and practice of warfare throughout the next century.[14]

These developments feature prominently in the Military Revolution arguments, as well as much military history more generally. However, it is hard to attribute the outcome of individual actions (let alone wars) to such tactical or technological changes alone. Differences between armies remained, but they had become progressively less pronounced after the mid-seventeenth century. Within Europe, it was rare for an army to be defeated through encountering wholly unfamiliar weaponry or tactics. The growing convergence heightened attention on the remaining differences which were discussed ever more intensively in the specialist military literature as authors searched for comparative advantages. Armies which were successful acquired prestige and became objects of emulation. For most of the period between 1660 and 1714, it was France that was the model to follow, and French styles were copied for uniforms in Britain, Sweden, several German territories, and elsewhere.

However, success or failure always involved a multitude of factors, including morale, training, experience, and soldiers' confidence in themselves, their comrades, and their officers. Most officers agreed that performance usually depended on the proportion of veterans in each unit, as well as such external factors as the prevailing level of supply, whether the troops had been paid, the terrain, and the weather. The prolonged conflicts of the first half of the seventeenth century already encouraged efforts to conserve a cadre of veterans in each unit and, where possible, to ensure that new formations were built around men detached from

13 J.D. Davies, *Pepys's Navy. Ships, Men and Warfare 1649–1689* (Barnsley, 2008), pp.248–254.

14 B. Nosworthy, *The Anatomy of Victory: Battle Tactics 1689–1763* (New York, 1990); D. Blackmore, *Destructive and Formidable: British Infantry Firepower 1642–1765* (Barnsley, 2014), pp.8–94. Nimwegen, *Dutch Army*, pp.396–404.

existing formations to provide a solid core. The emergence of true standing armies during the second half of the seventeenth century embedded this as a structural feature, as individual regiments were more likely to be reduced in size, rather than completely disbanded at the conclusion of each conflict, as we shall explore more fully below.

A key element of the Military Revolution thesis is that warfare supposedly became more decisive by about 1600 as commanders sought to use their more effective forces to defeat their opponents in formal, pitched battles. More broadly, it is customary to see this period as an 'age of battles' lasting until at least 1815.[15] Large engagements certainly dominated military thinking and were important to martial culture.[16] Battles also grew considerably in size. An engagement involving around 30,000 combatants would be considered large around 1600, but that threshold was upwards of three times that number a century later.

However, battles remained relatively rare. There were only 48 actions involving more than 7,000 men during the Thirty Years War, and only 21 of these had 30,000 or more combatants with the largest being Alte Veste (1632) involving 89,000 troops.[17] Such numbers were not unknown in the sixteenth century. Charles V and his opponents together mustered 92,000 during the inconclusive fighting around Ingolstadt during the Schmalkaldic War in 1546, while 30,000 men fought in the battle of Mühlberg which ended the conflict in the emperor's favour in April 1547.[18] The real growth occurred during the last third of the seventeenth century, peaking in the battle of Steenkirk in August 1692, involving between 137,000 to 160,000 combatants, or around twice the size of Alte Veste.[19] Nonetheless, such actions were still exceptional, and armies often waged an entire campaign without fighting a battle.

Major sieges were also relatively infrequent. For example, the Dutch conducted 27 major sieges 1591–1646, or roughly one every two years.[20] Like battles, sieges

15 R.F. Weigley, *The Age of Battles: The Quest for Decisive Warfare from Breitenfeld to Waterloo* (London, 1993).

16 Further discussion in P.H. Wilson, 'White Mountain as a Military Event', in K. Keller, P. Mat'a, and T. Winkelbauer (eds.), *Die Schlacht am Weißen Berg 1620* (Vienna, 2024), forthcoming.

17 P.H. Wilson and C. Gantet, 'Battlefields, Images and Cultures of Remembrance in the Thirty Years War', in C. Denys, B. Deruelle, and G. Malandin (eds.), *Après la bataille: Mémoires et Usages* (Villeneuve d'Ascq, 2023), pp.62–91 at pp.80–81.

18 A. Schütz, *Der Donaufeldzug Karls V im Jahre 1546* (Tübingen, 1930); A. Querengässer and S. Lunyakov, *Die Heere des Schmalkadischen Krieges* (Berlin, 2019).

19 J. Childs, *The Nine Years War and the British Army 1688–97* (Manchester, 1991), pp.197–204.

20 Nimwegen, *Dutch Army*, pp.528–529. See also the list of major sieges 1688–1745 in D. Chandler, *The Art of War in the Age of Marlborough* (Tunbridge Wells, 1990), pp.308–310.

were large undertakings but could also last weeks, if not months, and consumed considerable human and material resources. Multiple sieges were beyond the capacity of even the largest armies. Moreover, they were not always necessary as little of Europe was heavily fortified, especially beyond the Low Countries and North Italy. Many towns were defortified during the seventeenth century, for example in the interior of France and across much of Germany.[21] In short, most sieges were of smaller, less well-defended towns and were relatively short and involved fewer resources.[22]

The cliché of limited war presents campaigns being decided through bloodless manoeuvres in the absence of large battles or sieges. Cutting enemy supply lines and other stratagems were indeed favoured options, but campaigns were still bloody even without major actions. Contemporary military theory distinguished between major battles and sieges, and minor operations which could be part of larger scale movements, as substitutes for these or as independent elements of a campaign plan. Minor operations were discussed less extensively, and it is certainly true that a more coherent theory of 'small war' only emerged in around the mid-eighteenth century.[23] However, it would be wrong to assume that earlier armies did not have their own methods, or that specialist units only emerged in after about 1740. Small war was central to seventeenth and early eighteenth-century military practice and involved far more than foraging operations to sustain the main field armies.[24]

Raiding, scouting, and the 'war of outposts' were integral to virtually all campaigns, and not merely those in supposedly 'peripheral' regions like English operations in Ireland. These types of actions were undertaken to screen larger operations, distract or confuse the enemy, deny access, or acquire or destroy resources, attack convoys, and interdict supply lines. Moreover, armies created specialist 'light troops' to conduct them. The most prominent example is the creation of dragoons intended to fight both mounted and on foot for such missions, and to act as skirmishers on the flanks during battle. Most armies also continued to use specialist light cavalry recruited from regions considered particularly skilled in this type of warfare such as Croats and Cossacks. Light infantry were also employed extensively in conflicts in East Central Europe and the Balkans and

21 Y. Mintzker, *The Defortification of the German City, 1688–1866* (Cambridge, 2012).

22 A. Fischer-Kattner and J. Ostwald (eds.), *The World of the Siege* (Leiden, 2019); C. Duffy, *Siege Warfare: The Fortress in the Early Modern World 1494–1660* (London, 1979), and his *The Fortress in the Age of Vauban and Frederick the Great, 1660–1789* (London, 1985).

23 J. Kunisch, *Der kleine Krieg* (Wiesbaden, 1973); S. Picaud-Monnerat, *La petite guerre au xviiie siècle* (Paris, 2010); J.P. Bothe, *Die Natur des Krieges: Militärisches Wissen und Umwelt im 17. und 18. Jahrhundert* (Frankfurt am Main, 2021), pp.179–184.

24 For foraging, see J. Lynn, *Giant of the grande siecle. The French Army 1610–1715* (Cambridge, 1997), pp.538–540.

accompanied Habsburg armies on some of their campaigns in the Holy Roman Empire. France and its opponents in the Low Countries and Rhineland raised so-called free companies for raiding and to levy contributions.[25] Both regular and locally improvised troops were used together in irregular warfare, such as harassing invaders as in the case of the Danish-Norwegian resistance to the Swedish invasion of 1643–1645.[26]

Though often entrusted with missions which would now be the preserve of special forces, none of these troops were considered elite. Attempts to impose more regular discipline and control led to the formation of 'hussar' regiments in the Habsburg army from the 1690s which were soon copied by France and several other powers. However, such units lacked the status of heavy cavalry regiments, and it was not until the mid-eighteenth century that such units and their tactics became more fully integrated with general battle tactics.[27]

Size

Determining army size is far more than an antiquarian pursuit; it is central as a measure of the scale of war and its broader impact. Not only did individual armies become larger, but most seventeenth and early eighteenth century wars were fought between groups of states, rather than bilateral conflicts. For example, what are known as the three Anglo-Dutch wars 1652–54, 1665–57, and 1672–74 were broader than their name suggests.[28] Only the first was a direct contest between

25 B. Sandberg, *War and Conflict in the Early Modern World 1500–1700* (Cambridge, 2016), pp.171–192 on raiding; P.H. Wilson, K. Tkacova and T. Pert, 'Mapping premodern small war: The case of the Thirty Years War (1618–1648)', *Small Wars and Insurgencies*, 34 (2023), 1043–1071; G. Satterfield, *Princes, Posts, and Partisans. The Army of Louis XIV and Partisan Warfare in the Netherlands (1673–1678)* (Leiden, 2003); B. Fonck and G. Satterfield, 'The essence of war: French armies and small war in the Low Countries (1672–1697)', *Small Wars and Insurgencies*, 25 no.4 (2014), 767–783; É. Dosquet, 'Le feu et l'encre. La "desolation du Palatinat". Guerre et information politique dans l'Europe de Louis XIV' (PhD Sorbonne, Paris, 2017), pp.47–247, and her 'Between positional warfare and small war: Soldiers and civilians during the "Desolation of the Palatinate" (1688–1689)', in A. Dowdall and J. Horne (eds.), *Civilians under Siege from Sarajevo to Troy* (Basingstoke, 2018), pp.107–136; Lynn, *Giant*, pp.543–545.

26 O. Bäckström, 'Snapphanar and Power States: Insurgency and the transformation of War in Sweden and Denmark 1643–1645' (PhD, University of Eastern Finland, 2018).

27 M. Rink, *Vom 'Partheygänger' zum Partisanen. Die Konzeption des kleinen Krieges in Preußen 1740–1813* (Frankfurt am Main, 1999), and his 'The Partisan's Metamorphosis from Freelance Military Enterprizer to German Freedom Fighter, 1740–1815', *War in History*, 17 (2010), 6–36.

28 J.R. Jones, *The Anglo-Dutch Wars of the Seventeenth Century* (Harlow, 1996); R. Hainsworth and C. Churches, *The Anglo-Dutch Wars 1652–1674* (Stroud, 1998).

two states. In the second, France backed the Dutch who hired 24,000 German auxiliaries, while England paid the Bishop of Münster to invade the Republic from the east with 30,000 troops. The Third War ran in parallel to the wider Dutch War 1672–79.

Several previous major wars had been waged by loose coalitions, including the Italian Wars and the Thirty Years War. However, alliance systems became more coherent and formalised through the growing standardisation of contracts to hire auxiliaries and to subsidise allies which had developed from the 1620s and were rapidly consolidated with the resumption of prolonged wars in the 1660s.[29] France was considered such a threat by 1667 that the first of a succession of alliances was formed to prevent it overrunning the Low Countries. The Dutch Republic was the initial instigator and primary sponsor of these; a role supplanted by Britain after 1689 and continued until 1815. The succession of Northern Wars between 1655 and 1721 were also waged by coalitions, as were the conflicts between Christian European powers and the Ottoman empire between 1645 and 1739.

Counting soldiers is a difficult, time-consuming, and often frustrating task for historians who have often, albeit understandably, relied on published figures, notably a set of estimates for Europe's leading military powers which first appeared in 1976.[30] This data suggests relatively steady growth in army size across Europe during the era associated with the Military Revolution, but that trend did not in fact apply to all states. The totals commonly accepted for Spain include a peak strength of 300,000 regulars backed by 500,000 militia during Philip IV's reign 16–165, but in fact derive from a boast the king made in 1626. The likely total was around 180,000, and probably less considering that Spain's four main armies combined totalled 145,050 in 1645. Overall strength shrank to 70,000 by the 1670s, before remaining steady at between 80,000 and 100,000 until 1700.[31]

29 P.H. Wilson, 'Mercenary contracts as fiscal-military instruments', in S. Norrhem and E. Thomson (eds.), *Subsidies, Diplomacy and State Formation in Europe, 1494–1789: Economies of Allegiance* (Manchester, 2020), pp.68–92, and his 'Subsidy treaties and troop contracts: A study in Europe's transnational political culture', in A. Nilsson Hammar et al (eds.), *Gender, Materiality, and Politics. Essays on Fine Detail on Great Power in History* (Lund, 2022), pp.359–379.

30 G. Parker, 'The "Military Revolution 1560–1660" – A myth?', *Journal of Modern History*, 48 (1976), 195–214. A similarly influential table of army strengths appeared in A. Corvisier, *Armies and Societies in Europe 1494–1789* (Bloomington, IN, 1976), p. 113.

31 The relevant text is quoted in M. Hume, *The Court of Philip IV: Spain in Decadence* (London, 1907), pp.156–158. For the likely actual totals, see D. Maffi, *En defensa del Imperio. Los ejécitos de Felipe IV y la Guerra por la hegemonía europea (1635–1659)* (Madrid, 2014), pp.169–196; P. Picouet, *The Armies of Philip IV of Spain 1621–1665* (Warwick, 2019), pp.276–285. For strengths after 1665, see C. Storrs, *The Resilience of the Spanish Monarchy 1665–1700* (Oxford, 2006), pp.17–26.

France meanwhile overtook Spain as the power with the largest army. It likewise experienced considerable fluctuations in strength until the 1660s, but unlike the Spanish forces, those of France grew significantly thereafter. French war strength was roughly 40–45,000 men during the first half of the sixteenth century. The civil wars known as the Wars of Religion (1562–1598) saw peaks of 60,000 to 70,000 men, though the main royal field army was rarely over 20,000.[32] The army was doubled by Louis XIII and Richelieu during the war with Spain 1635–1659 to peak at 125,000. A new high of 134,000 was reached during the War of Devolution (1667–68), followed by new peaks of 253,000 during the Dutch War (1672–79) and 340,000 during the Nine Years War (1688–1697). These figures were not matched during the War of Spanish Succession (1701–1714) when the army had a maximum strength of 255,000.[33]

The experience of the Austrian Habsburgs falls between that of Spain and France. The family had around 2,000 field troops at their disposal in 1618, in addition to the 25,000 or so militia and garrison soldiers deployed along Hungary's frontier with the Ottoman empire. The field army expanded rapidly after 1625 to reach a paper strength of over 130,000 men by 1628, with an effective strength of around 110,000. Whilst still fluctuating, thereafter the general trend was a slow decline to 42,300 in October 1648, excluding the troops along the Hungarian military frontier.[34] However, unlike the other princes of the Empire, the Habsburgs did not disband their army at the return to peace, maintaining 33,000 men in 1650, likewise excluding the frontier force. The overall trajectory was now upwards, reaching 137,000 regulars by 1714.

Brandenburg-Prussia, the Habsburgs' later rival, cut its unruly and ineffective army to just 700 men in 1650, but augmented these substantially after 1655 to reach 43,300 during later stage of the Dutch War, with only modest further wartime increases thereafter. The forces of the other German territories combined grew from perhaps 15,000 in 1650 to 120,000 during later 1670s, peaking at around 170,000 during the War of Spanish Succession.[35]

32 F. Lot, *Recherches sur les effectifs des armées françaises des Guerres d'Italie aux Guerres de Religion 1492–1562* (Paris, 1962). J.B. Wood, *The King's Army, Warfare, Soldiers and Society during the Wars of Religion in France, 1562–1576* (Cambridge, 1996), pp.70–74.

33 J.A. Lynn, 'Recalculating French army growth during the grande siècle 1610–1715', *French Historical Studies*, 18 (1994), 881–906, and his *Giant*, pp.32–64. More cautious calculations in D. Parrott, *Richelieu's Army. War, Government and Society in France, 1624–1642* (Cambridge, 2001).

34 See the tables in P.H. Wilson, *Europe's Tragedy: The Thirty Years War* (London, 2009), pp.395, 770.

35 More detail in P.H. Wilson, *From Reich to Revolution: German History 1558–1806* (London, 2004), p.227 and generally in his *German Armies: War and German Politics 1648–1806* (London, 1998).

As this brief survey suggests, growth was not always steady and strength fluctuated considerably during the first half of the seventeenth century and, in several important cases, for several decades more. Growth was steadier in the longer term for France, though the general trajectory conceals several dramatic expansions and sharp reductions. A rachet effect nonetheless set in for France already during the first half of the century. Though the army was still reduced after each conflict, the numbers retained were larger than those present when that war had begun. French paper strength around 1610 was about 10,000, but rose sharply during the 1620s, dropping again, before rising in the mid-1630s. Though reduced after the prolonged conflicts in 1659, the army now totalled a theoretical 72,000 during the early 1660s.[36]

This stage occurred around twenty years later in the Dutch Republic whose army had grown modestly from 25,000 (1587) to 31,000 (1602), then cut slightly in 1609, before rising again after 1621 to peak at 120,000 eight years later, only to drop to half that until 1643 when it was drastically reduced to about 29,000 by 1650, falling to 24,000 by 1661. Caught undermanned in 1664, 1667, and again 1672, the Dutch hired German auxiliaries to increase their forces quickly. Though they reduced their own army again in 1678, it now totalled 40,000. Moreover, the Dutch government ensured that the army retained its internal structure so that it could be expanded again quickly.[37] This combination of national army held as a cadre in peacetime, supplemented by hired auxiliaries in wartime was retained by the Dutch until the end of the Republic in 1795.

When considering army growth, we also should remember that population levels remained broadly constant across 1618–1721, meaning that even modest increases represented a considerable additional burden on society at a time when productivity was low and economic activity generated little disposable surplus. Indeed, the Thirty Years War and parallel conflicts elsewhere in Europe ended a period of sustained demographic growth characterising 1470–1590 and in some areas caused a significant population decline. Most countries only recovered their pre-1618 population levels around 1710. Sustained growth only resumed around 1730 or later whilst army size now remained static or even dropped slightly, other than in Austria, Prussia, and Russia.

For example, French forces fell to around 130,000 after 1715 and though numbers increased again with each new conflict, the largest wartime peak was 390,000 during the War of Austrian Succession (1740–1748), or only modestly larger than the maximum reached under Louis XIV. Mobilisation during the Seven Years War (1756–1763) remained below that under the Sun King, while the

36 Lynn, *Giant*, p.55.

37 Nimwegen, *Dutch Army*, pp.45–47, 406, 510, 525–527.

army ended the Old Regime with a strength of 155,000 in 1789.[38] While Napoleon may have commanded much larger armies than Louis XIV, France's population was at least 25 percent bigger. Army growth after 1714 was primarily restricted to Austria, Prussia, and Russia, all of which expanded territorially, acquiring additional resources. These figures suggest that the period 1618 to 1721 saw the most dramatic increase in both real terms and relative to population, while growth overall became more consistent and sustained from the 1660s.

Navies followed the same general trend but with some significant differences. Together, Europe's maritime powers had fleets totalling around 200,000 tons in 1570. That total was still under 300,000 in 1650 by when it had become more common to construct ships dedicated to war rather than rely on hiring or converting merchantmen. The growth of state navies pushed total tonnage to 441,000 by 1680, while the involvement of the leading naval powers in the great conflicts of the later seventeenth century saw that figure reach 759,000 around 1700. The return to peace prompted a fall to 614,000 by 1720. However, unlike army size, navies continued to increase across the eighteenth century to reach 1,700,000 tons by 1790 thanks to the expansion of European global empires and the conflicts associated with that process. Warships were decommissioned at the end of conflicts, but were still maintained, albeit often poorly, whereas the crews were cut more significantly with most sailors discharged completely. Manpower thus fluctuated more significantly than tonnage.[39]

Army Structure

These figures only tell part of a more complex story. Army structure also changed fundamentally between 1618 and 1721. At the start of that period, armies reflected the political character of Europe where states were composites of distinct elements, each with their own systems of local governance, representative institutions, laws, and finance, often bound together by no more than allegiance to a common monarch.[40] Even supposedly 'absolutist' France was composed of different provinces, many of which had their own assemblies, laws, judiciaries, and finances, while royal rights were not uniform throughout the kingdom. States did not match

38 B.R. Kroener, '"Das Schwungrad an der Staatsmaschine?" Die Bedeutung der bewaffneten Macht in der europäischen Geschichte der Frühen Neuzeit', in idem and R. Pröve (eds.), *Krieg und Frieden. Militär und Gesellschaft in der Frühen Neuzeit* (Paderborn, 1996), pp.123 at p.9.

39 J. Glete, *Navies and Nations: Warships, Navies and State Building in Europe and America, 1500–1860* (2 vols, Stockholm, 1993).

40 J.H. Elliott, 'A Europe of composite monarchies', *Past and Present*, 137 (1992), 48–71.

the ideal defined by nineteenth-century writers as sovereign entities possessing a monopoly of legitimate power uniformly over their territory and inhabitants.

Most armies reflected this through their division into separate establishments, each with their own command structures, organisation, funding streams, and often also area of operations. This did not prevent units and individual soldiers being switched around, but it did complicate administration and inhibit standardisation, as well as encouraging a decentralised approach to strategy whereby governments planned defence against regional threats rather than adopting a single, 'national' coordinated policy.

The most extreme example is Spain which had separate armies of Flanders, Lombardy, Naples, and Catalonia until 1714, as well as for Extremadura and Galicia 1641–1668 and 1703–1713. There were also separate overseas (colonies) forces which persisted long after 1714.[41] Spain's navy also long remained partly decentralised.[42] Denmark was likewise a composite state with separate Danish, Norwegian, and Holstein military establishments.[43] While Sweden had a more uniform structure, the conscription system maintaining the regular Swedish and Finnish regiments was not extended to the Baltic and German lands conquered between the later sixteenth century and 1640s which were guarded by German units recruited from volunteers.[44] Brandenburg-Prussia's forces remained partly provincialized into the 1680s.[45] The Austrian Habsburgs integrated their command structures in the 1640s, though elements of the imperial army retained strong links to specific provinces and the Hungarian military frontier remained administratively separate until 1881.

Britain had separate English, Scottish, and Irish armies, as well as overseas garrisons in Tangiers, North America, and other colonies. Despite the Union of Crowns in 1603, Scotland retained its own Lord High Admiral and issued its own letters of marque to privateers. The Scottish parliament continued to regard itself as sovereign in maritime affairs and periodically fitted out its own warships after

41 G. Parker, *The Army of Flanders and the Spanish Road 1567–1659* (Cambridge, 1972); P. Picouet, *The Armies of Philip IV*, pp.121–138; Maffi, *En defensa del Imperio*; M. del Pilar Mesa Coronado, *Las Fuerzas Terrestres del Reino de Sicilia (1665–1700)* (Rome, 2023); C. Storrs, 'The Army of Lombardy the Resilience of the Spanish Monarchy in the Reign of Carlos II', *War in History*, 4 (1997), 371–397, and 5 (1998), 1–22.

42 R.A. Stradling, *The Armada of Flanders. Spanish Maritime Policy and European War, 1568-1668* (Cambridge, 1992).

43 M. Fredholm von Essen, *Charles X's Wars* (3 vols, Warwick, 2021-3), III 106–132, and his *Charles XI's War: The Scanian War between Sweden and Denmark, 1675–1679* (Warwick, 2019), pp.25–29.

44 G. Tessin, *Die deutschen Regimenter der Krone Schweden* (2 vols., Cologne, 1965–67).

45 C. von Jany, *Geschichte der Preußischen Armee vom 15. Jahrhundert bis 1914* (4 vols., Berlin, 1928), I 308–309.

1627, though shortage of funds resulted in this navy existing largely on paper with only three small, dilapidated vessels afloat in 1707.[46] Lack of funding frustrated various projects for an Irish navy and the Irish parliament was less successful in upholding claims to its own maritime sovereignty. The different establishments persisted until the political unifications 1707 and 1801 which ended the separate military budgets voted by the Scottish and Irish parliaments.[47] Colonial forces meanwhile remained administratively separate into the nineteenth century.

The restructuring of composite forces into single armies across Europe by the early eighteenth century marked an important shift over earlier practice, and reflected the broader process of political consolidation which was underway. Another important change meanwhile occurred at the more granular level of the units composing these armies as regiments became permanent formations, adding greatly to overall coherence. Regimental histories need to be treated with caution as nineteenth-century writers regarded the presence of individual officers as continuity and interpreted the re-formation of previously disbanded formations as an unbroken lineage. Units were frequently reduced to one or two companies at the end of wars into the mid seventeenth century, and it is debatable whether their subsequent use as cadres for new formations indicates genuine stability.

Regimental organisation first appeared between the 1530s and 1550s, but only for infantry which, at that time, fought in large tactical formations of 1,000 to 3,000 men. The absence of stable regimental formations for cavalry reflects their tactical deployment in much smaller squadrons or even companies. French cavalry companies were first grouped into regiments in May 1635, but these were already broken up again in July 1636, before new, more permanent ones were created in January 1638. However, the cavalry's regimental structure remained less stable than that of the infantry, and mounted units were much more likely to be split into individual companies when the army was reduced, as well as still recruited as such. For example, two German officers were contracted in spring 1657 to raise six companies, each of 50 troopers.[48] France's infantry was grouped into regiments much earlier, though these were often so transient that it is impossible to reconstruct their individual stories. At least 22 regiments of foreigners existed between 1535 and 1558, but none lasted beyond 1558, reflecting

46 E.J. Graham, *A Maritime History of Scotland 1650–1790* (Edinburgh, 2015), esp.pp.91–93.

47 See S. Ede-Borrett, *The Army of James II 1685–1688. The Birth of the British Army* (Solihull, 2017), and the three studies by J. Childs, *The Army of Charles II* (London, 1976), *The Army and the Glorious Revolution* (Manchester, 1980), *The British Army of William III 1689–1702* (Manchester, 1987).

48 Contracts dated 23 March and 3 April 1657. These are available online on the French Foreign Ministry website at https://basedoc.diplomatie.gouv.fr/exl-php/recherche/mae_internet traites as TRA16570007 and TRA16570008.

the seasonal character of much sixteenth-century warfare when field forces were raised separately for each campaign.[49]

The French Wars of Religion saw 365 regiments formed between 1562 and 1597, the bulk of which were infantry, with some foreign cavalry units. This period saw the first permanent units, with nine still in existence at the end of the royal army in 1791, while another survived until 1626, but all the others had gone by 1598 and most had lasted no more than a year. Between 1600 and 1629, France was engaged in a series of civil wars, settling issues left over from the Wars of Religion, as well as disputes over royal rule and limited interventions in the Rhineland and Italy. Another 240 regiments were raised for these conflicts, of which 13 still existed in 1791, but only another 21 lasted long enough to fight in the war with Spain 1635–1659, and again the majority were disbanded later in the year they were raised (Table 1. NB the horizontal axis indicates the year a unit was raised, with the year of disbandment indicated on the vertical axis).

Another 64 regiments were raised 1630–1634 for renewed intervention in Italy and the occupation of Lorraine (Table 2). Of these, 18 were disbanded by 1634 followed by another six the next year, despite the outbreak of the war with Spain. A further 26 did not survive till that conflict ended in 1659. Campaign losses only partially explain this lack of permanence which was also due to recruitment difficulties as units often failed to complete and were disbanded or merged with other formations. Financial difficulties or the mismanagement, death, or disgrace of commanding officers were other factors.

The war with Spain coincided with France's direct intervention in the Thirty Years War and entailed a massive military effort, as the discussion of the army's growth has already indicated. A further 458 regiments had been raised by the time France settled with the emperor in the Peace of Westphalia, or an average of 35 new units each year (Table 3). Unsurprisingly, the opening year saw the largest number, with 124 formed in 1635, yet 50 of these did not make it beyond 1636. Altogether, 166 of the 338 regiments formed by 1643 had been disbanded by that point when the army had 139 infantry regiments, plus cavalry. France continued its struggle with Spain for another 10 years from 1649, as well as fighting a renewed civil war known as the Fronde (Table 4). This period saw 316 new units, or about 32 annually. Structural instability continued with up to half the new formations being disbanded in their first year.

Of the 1,443 regiments formed 1562–1659, only 41 survived in 1791. However, these became the core of a more structurally stable army after 1660–1661 as French

49 This and the following discussion are based on analysis of the regimental lists in in G. Tessin, *Die Regimenter der europäischen Staaten im Ancien Reime des XVI. bis XVIII. Jahrhunderts* (vol.1 Osnabrück, 1986), pp.424–524.

forces were reduced and reorganised as four cavalry and 48 infantry regiments, including the guards, plus some individual companies of cavalry. This coincided with the start of Louis XIV's personal rule and more aggressive foreign policy. Having supported the Durch Republic in its second war with Britain (1664–1667), Louis XIV antagonised his former ally by attacking the Spanish Netherlands in the War of Devolution (1667–1668) which revealed the scale of French ambitions. The French army was augmented substantially in 1665 when the cavalry was expanded around the individual companies to give 43 regiments, mostly each only three companies. Another 50 cavalry and five infantry regiments were added in 1667. Overall, 126 regiments were formed 1663–1671, of which 39 survived into the eighteenth century, indicating a greater level of stability (Table 5).

Though 32 regiments were disbanded in 1668 when most of the new cavalry units were reduced to their colonel's companies, most of these units were reraised in 1671 as France prepared to attack the Dutch Republic (Table 6). The ensuing Dutch War (1672–1679) was followed by an aggressive policy of annexations of neighbouring territory in the Rhineland, known as the Reunions. This escalated into renewed war with Spain 1683–1684. These conflicts resulted in another 142 regiments being raised by 1685, of which 72 survived into the eighteenth century (Table 7). Moreover, the rate of wartime disbandment was now much lower, with only 20 units disappearing before 1678, while 43 were dissolved as the war wound down 1678–1679. Five of the disbanded units were subsequently reraised (Table 8).

The army had 68 infantry regiments in 1678 which varied in size according to their seniority. The Régiment du Roi, formed in 1663, had been expanded to six battalions totalling 100 companies. The size of the others depended on their seniority as determined by the date of their foundation. The 11 oldest each had four battalions totalling 70 companies, while the rest had only one or two battalions. Units recruited in France had companies of only 50 men each, whereas those composed of Germans or Swiss had fewer, but larger companies. Subsequent expansions and reductions were increasingly achieved by altering the number of battalions of existing regiments, rather than raising or disbanding entirely new units.

The trend towards stability and permanence continued further during the Nine Years War (1688–1697) when only 16 of the 260 new regiments were disbanded before the end of the conflict, compared to 162 in the general reduction in strength in 1698 while the remaining 82 survived into the eighteenth century (Table 9). Fifteen of the disbanded regiments were reraised for the War of Spanish Succession (1701–1714. See Table 10). The disbandment in 1698 largely affected the 100 infantry regiments which had been formed by embodying militia as single battalion units at the start of the war. This followed the practice emerging since the 1660s of achieving reductions through disbanding the least prestigious regiments in favour of retaining older units, or those commanded by distinguished noblemen. Coherence was strengthened further by the practice since at least the 1660s of retaining veterans whilst discharging newer recruits or men considered unreliable when it became necessary to reduce the army's size. The general reduction of 1698 was also the last to seriously impact the cavalry.

In line with the army's growth, as discussed above, France's effort was less substantial between 1701 and 1714 compared to the Nine Years War. Initial mobilisation was achieved largely by embodying 57 battalions of militia to double that number of single-battalion regular infantry units in 1701. Of the 114 new regiments added in 1702, 100 were raised at their colonel's expense. Only 194 new regiments had entered service by 1709, with no additions during the last five years of the war. If averaged across the entire war, the annual addition of new units was only 15, or around half that of the previous conflict (Table 11). The 194 regiments included 16 from Spain's Army of Flanders that was taken over wholesale in 1707 but returned to Spanish service in 1712, as well as one which served 1706–1709 and three just temporarily in French service in 1709. A major reason behind the lower number of new formations was the army's more stable structure. Discounting the Spanish units, only 16 units were disbanded during the conflict, including several that were lost completely in the disasters at Blenheim (1704) and Turin (1706). Of the rest, 154 disappeared in the reductions across 1713–1715 as hostilities ended, leaving 94 French and 32 foreign infantry regiments, plus cavalry. Compared to the reductions following France's other wars since 1665, those after the War of Spanish Succession were almost total, with only four of the new regiments being retained for service longer into the eighteenth century.

On the eve of its reorganisation by the Revolutionaries in 1792, France's army comprised 183 regiments of which 104 were infantry and the rest various categories of cavalry. Of these, 10 (all infantry units) dated from the sixteenth century, representing 5.4 percent of the total, while four cavalry and 28 infantry regiments (together 17.5 percent) stemmed from 1610–1659. No less than 80 (including 41 cavalry regiments) had been formed between 1663 and 1698, constituting 43.7 percent of the total. By contrast, relatively few new units had been added during the eighteenth century. Only two from the War of Spanish Succession survived in 1791, along with four from 1718–1735, 33 from the 1770s and 14 from the 1780s. The latter two decades had seen major reforms, in which many long-serving units were disbanded or merged to create new infantry and light cavalry formations. Six colonial infantry regiments had been added in 1772 followed by 12 light infantry regiments in 1784–1788.

This analysis reveals that the French army was primarily a creation of the later seventeenth century when the army was expanded after 1663 around a core of units largely dating from 1610 to 1659. Structural coherence was strengthened by the consolidation of the cavalry into permanent regiments which, despite the earlier efforts since the 1630s, was only fully achieved in the 1660s. Only two of the 25 line heavy cavalry regiments in 1791 dated from 1635, compared to 20 formed in 1665–1672, while 14 of the 18 dragoon regiments existing in 1791 had been raised in 1665–1688. Though the two guard cavalry regiments, the Garde du Corps and Gendarmerie, both had their origins in the 1440s, most of the Gendarmerie companies were first formed in the 1660s when both units also acquired a more coherent regimental structure.

Spain's army presents a broadly similar picture with the impermanence characterising the sixteenth century giving way to greater structural cohesion after 1600. Of the 113 regiments raised by Spain in the sixteenth century, only 21 survived into the next, and nine of these were disbanded by 1606. Only two of its famous tercios lasted continuously from the 1530s into the nineteenth century, though another seven regiments raised after 1566 also survived until the old royal army broke up in 1808. At that point, there were 84 regiments. Like France, Spain had reorganised its army in the late eighteenth century adding new units of regular light troops, but the core of its forces stemmed from the later seventeenth century, with 37 of the regiments in 1808 dating from 1651 to 1715 and four others from the first half of the seventeenth century.[50]

England retained a small army when its monarchy was restored in 1660, providing a nucleus for the expansion which set in after 1685. Likewise, Brandenburg-Prussia's army really dates from its mobilisation during the Northern War of 1655–1660 and the Dutch War of 1672–1679 after which many of the new formations were retained. The smaller German principalities followed somewhat later, but by 1700 their armies were largely composed of units raised since the Dutch War of 1672–1679.

Poland-Lithuania was exceptional in being a powerful state which continued to rely on a combination of emergency levies, short-term units, and the private forces of the landowning magnates. There was a small regular army since the fifteenth century to guard the frontiers. This was reorganised in the 1560s, but only totalled about 5,000 men, mainly cavalry, maintained from the crown estates since the 1560s, as well as registers of Cossacks and others who could be summoned when needed. The Grand Duchy of Lithuania only developed permanent forces after 1648, and a few other regular units were added later. However, it was not until the major reorganisation in 1717 that most of these became permanent.[51]

50 Calculated from Tessin, *Regimenter*, pp.695–735.

51 M. Paradowski, *Despite Destruction, Misery and Privations: The Polish Army in Prussia during the War Against Sweden 1626–1629* (Warwick, 2020), pp.11–35, and his *Against the Deluge. Polish and Lithuanian Armies during the War against Sweden 1655–1660* (Warwick,

An important consequence of permanence was the growing bureaucratisation of administration. Custom and what passed as 'common sense' remained important, while officers were still expected to manage their units and to cover deficits and cash-flow problems from their own resources, whilst naturally profiteering from the opportunities created by their autonomy. Nonetheless, larger and more permanent forces posed greater administrative challenges, while the increased costs encouraged rulers to insist on greater scrutiny and accountability.

The Dutch already established tighter checks and routinised paperwork during the 1570s, as well as creating a system of specialist intermediaries who helped officers in their dealings with the civil government and loaned money when official payments fell into arrears – all for a fee, of course. These changes were made directly in connection with the reorganisation of company and regimental organisation, redefining the role of several of the non-commissioned ranks, and abolishing many of the traditional rights claimed by ordinary soldiers. Together, these changes were at the heart of the Dutch reforms associated with the fledgling republic's ability to hold the Spanish at bay.[52] Dutch practice was widely emulated, including their introduction in 1575 of the 'Dutch month' which gave the appearance of raising pay, but spread the new amount across 42 days rather than the customary 30 as an economy measure.

Other states developed their own systems. Bavaria was an early example, already having a model civil administration in the later sixteenth century which supported a comprehensive, though not always militarily effective militia. Bavaria's prolonged and substantial involvement in the Thirty Years War obliged it to expand its military administration and create a system of inspectors to counterbalance the influence and autonomy of regimental colonels.[53] However, development was not always linear. Indeed, in Bavaria's case, the army was largely disbanded as a peace dividend in 1648, and substantial forces were only maintained continuously from the 1670s.

The dramatic expansion and greater permanence of armies from the 1660s added quantitatively and to an extent qualitatively to administrative practice

2022), pp.19–62; V.W. Rospond, *Polish-Lithuanian Regiments 1717–1794* (Point Pleasant, NJ, 2022).

52 P. Groen (ed.), *The Eighty Years War: From Revolt to Regular War 1568–1648* (Leiden, 2019), pp.170–83, 360–77; P. Brandon, Finding solid ground for soldiers' payment: "Military soliciting" as brokerage practice in the Dutch Republic (c.1600–1795)', in S. Conway and R. Torres Sánchez (eds.), *The Spending of States* (Saarbrücken, 2011), pp.51–82; Nimwegen, *Dutch Army*, pp.51–61, 64–9, 330–342. See more generally P. Brandon, *War, Capital and the Dutch State (1588–1795)* (Leiden, 2015).

53 K. Saito, *Das Kriegskommssariat der bayerisch-ligistischen Armee während des Dreißigjährigen Krieges* (Göttingen, 2020). Useful overview of the Bavaria army in L. Spring, *The Bavarian Army during the Thirty Years War 1618–1648* (Solihull, 2017).

which became progressively bureaucratised. One indication of the mounting paperwork was the number of letters received daily by France's war minister, rising from two during the 1630s, three the following decade, but expanding exponentially to 27 during the 1690s, or 10,000 a year.[54] The consolidation into permanent formations fostered distinct institutional cultures and memory, creating a repository of knowledge and 'military customs' which were increasingly codified in written regulations. The organisational structures and administrative methods established by the 1710s remained the basis of most European armies into the nineteenth century.

Growth and greater permanence brought additional challenges. A good example is the greatly enlarged number of officers. By 1690, France had around 24,000 army and 1,000 navy officers, meaning that two-fifths of all French noble families had at least one family member in the armed forces in 1693. The crown relied on regimental and company commanders to manage their own units, and often to invest heavily in raising new formations. It was forced to tolerate extensive patronage networks over which it had little direct control, though Louis XIV did assert greater authority over the senior commanders, who mostly stemmed from the grandees.[55] Other states faced similar problems and, like France, spent much of the eighteenth century trying to impose tighter control over their officers and military administrators within the existing institutions, rather than fundamentally alter how their armies were structured.

Wider Impacts

The growing administrative burden is one reason why many scholars believe war propelled the rise of modern, centralised states. This belief was already expressed in the original Military Revolution thesis which saw state growth as the outcome of the expansion of more effective armed forces. Others have stood this relationship on its head, arguing instead that growing state capacity enabled larger and more prolonged conflicts.[56] There is not the space here to explore this debate further, not least as it remains unresolved, though it is clear there were different kinds of states, while war could retard as well as promote political change.[57]

54 Hanlon, *European Military Rivalry*, pp.122–123.

55 G. Hanlon, *European Military Rivalry, 1500–1700* (London, 2020), pp.125–127; G. Rowlands, *The Dynastic State and the Army under Louis XIV: Royal Service and Private Interest 1661–1701* (Cambridge, 2002).

56 This argument was first put by J. Black, *A Military Revolution? Military Change and European Society 1500–1800* (Basingstoke, 1991).

57 See the useful comparison of Sweden, Spain, and the Dutch Republic in J. Glete, *War and the State in Early Modern Europe* (London, 2002), as well as the discussion in L.B.

Likewise, space constraints preclude a discussion of the economic dimension of the changes in warfare across this period. As with their political repercussions, there is no consensus whether warfare promoted or retarded economic development, though it is likely that it acted as a stimulus only in a few sectors, and then not consistently. Certainly, arsenals and naval dockyards were among seventeenth-century Europe's largest and most complex industrial sites, offering employment to many workers and profits to a few lucky entrepreneurs. In aggregate terms, arms production and sales contributed roughly the same amount to GDP as colonial trade which remains much better studied. However, the demand for weaponry and munitions fluctuated wildly between war and peacetime, while warfare disrupted trade and voraciously consumed money and other resources which could have been invested in greater productivity.[58]

The environmental aspects of the growing scale of warfare are only now being investigated. From preliminary studies, it appears that early modernity was characterised by a greater intensity of the kinds of impacts already encountered during the later middle ages, rather than fundamentally new practices or consequences.[59]

The social consequences are somewhat easier to identify because the growth of permanent units directly affected relations between soldiers and society. The retention of units in peacetime made soldiering a more stable career, though ordinary soldiers lacked 'job security' and could be discharged at short notice if no longer required. Mobilisation necessitated rapid recruitment to bring units up to full war strength which in turn encouraged the limited forms of conscription. As shown above, France increased its infantry in 1688 and 1701 by embodying militia, and several other states also did this. Denmark, Sweden, and many German territories adapted earlier militia systems to create a form of selective service, drafting men directly into regular formations to keep them up to strength.[60]

Kasperson and J. Strandsbjerg (eds.), *Does War Make States? Investigations of Charles Tilly's Historical Sociology* (Cambridge, 2017).

58 Useful studies include K. Boterbloem, *The Dirty Secret of Early Modern Capitalism: The Global Reach of the Dutch Arms Trade, Warfare and Mercenaries in the Seventeenth Century* (New York, 2020); M. t'Hart, *The Dutch Wars of Independence: Warfare and Commerce in the Netherlands*, 1570–1680 (London, 2014); P. Edwards, *Dealing in Death: The Arms Trade and the British Civil Wars, 1638–52* (Stroud, 2000); G. Ongaro, *Peasants and Soldiers: The Management of the Venetian Military Structure in the Mainland Dominion between the 16th and 17th Centuries* (London, 2017).

59 S. Govaerts, *Armies and Ecosystems in Premodern Europe: The Meuse Region, 1250–1850* (Amsterdam, 2021), pp.228–230. See also Bothe, *Die Natur des Krieges.*

60 Summarised in P.H. Wilson, *Iron and Blood. A Military of the German-speaking Peoples since 1500* (London, 2022), pp.176–179.

The retention of more troops in peacetime by the 1660s meant they had to be accommodated. There were few purpose-built barracks before 1700 and soldiers were not fully in barracks until the nineteenth century. Other than guard and garrison units, most soldiers were billeted on civilians with the infantry usually in towns and the cavalry in villages where they had better access to fodder for their horses.

The character of the military changed fundamentally as a result. Sixteenth century wars were often prolonged, but each campaign was seasonal, with most troops raised in the spring and discharged in the autumn when only reduced numbers were retained as garrisons. Though it became more common to retain units continuously in wartime across multiple years from the 1590s, as we have seen, the majority only had a relatively short existence. Even long-serving units lacked a home base, as they were switched to wherever needed. Soldiers and their dependents thus formed an itinerant 'campaign community' into the mid seventeenth century. The retention of more substantial forces in peacetime during the 1660s transformed this into permanent, static 'garrison communities', even if units continued to be rotated between civilian settlements.

These developments created a host of new welfare issues. Armies had long provided rudimentary medical care on campaign, but little effort was made to care for disabled, elderly, or unemployed soldiers once a war ended. The creation of permanent armies made this more pressing because armies were not only much larger, but welfare became an ongoing issue, rather than one only occurring episodically at the end of each conflict. Rulers felt obliged to show their benevolence towards those who had suffered in their service. France responded by building Les Invalides in Paris which opened in 1676 and influenced the construction of similar buildings elsewhere, such as the naval hospital in Greenwich in 1694. Despite its vast size, Les Invalides accommodated only 3,000 veterans, and most assistance was provided in the form of small cash allowances paid to 'out-pensioners' and, occasionally also their widows or families.[61]

The desire to limit state liabilities encouraged a growing restriction on soldiers' marriages from the 1650s, though these measures proved hard to enforce. Now,

61 E. Gruber von Arni, *Hospital Care and the British Standing Army, 1660–1714* (Aldershot, 2006); C. Storrs, 'Health, sickness and medical services in Spain's armed forces c.1665–1700', *Medical History*, 50 (2006), 32–50; A.F. Cormack, *'These Meritorious Objects of the Royal Bounty'. The Chelsea Out-Pensioners in the early Eighteenth Century* (no place, 2017); C.H. Colshorn, *Die Hospitalkassen der hannoverschen Armee. Ein Vorläufer der Sozialversicherung seit 1680* (Hildesheim, 1970).

when armies marched, many of the women were compelled to remain behind, which increased the pressure on an already limited system of poor relief.[62]

The seasonal character of most sixteenth century campaigns had restricted desertion to crises such as logistical breakdown following a defeat. The shift to permanent units transformed desertion into a structural problem since soldiers were no longer free to go home at the end of a campaign and were expected to remain with the colours even when unpaid. The problem was magnified by pressure on military budgets, since armies were now larger and maintained permanently. Governments sought to reduce per capita costs by cutting soldiers' wages to a bare subsistence level by the 1620s, and then struggled even to pay this. Desertion (usually an individual act) replaced mutiny (collective action) as the principal form of disobedience after the 1650s. The changed character of the problem nonetheless indicates the relative growth of state authority which curbed soldiers' collective rights, imposed tighter discipline, made mutinies less common and reduced disobedience to the individual level.[63]

Conclusions

Rather than seeking to identify periods of all-encompassing change, it is more helpful to consider developments as multitrack, where alterations in one or more aspects did not necessarily affect others. Areas of continuity could coexist with more gradual as well as swifter and radical change. The period 1618 to 1721 witnessed a convergence towards common forms of weaponry, organisation, and tactics, along with routinised and standardised administration. As the differences between forces fell away, observers focused ever more closely on the remaining distinctions in their attempts to identify the keys to victory. Slight advantages could still be obtained through modest innovation, and artillery became noticeably more potent during the later eighteenth century. However, the basic forms and practices of European military organisation and the conduct of war established by about 1710 largely endured well into the nineteenth century. Technological change played only a relatively minor role in reshaping warfare until the rapid succession

62 B. Engelen, *Soldatenfrauen in Preußen. Eine Strukturanalyse der Garnisonsgesellschaft im späten 17. und 18. Jahrhundert* (Münster, 2005). See more generally J.A. Lynn, *Women, Armies and Warfare in Early Modern Europe* (Cambridge, 2007); P.H. Wilson, 'Consolidating states, professionalizing armies, and controlling violence in the long-term aftermath of the Thirty Years War, 1600s–1780s', in K. Hagemann et al (eds.), *Oxford Handbook of Gender, War and the Western World since 1600* (Oxford, 2020), pp.74–95.

63 M. Sikora, *Disziplin und Desertion. Strukturprobleme militärischer Organisation im 18. Jahrhundert* (Berlin, 1996).

of innovations which set in during the 1850s, first with small arms, then artillery and naval architecture.

Armies and navies grew significantly in size, though this only became more stable and sustained during the 1660s and 1670s, while the expansion of land forces slowed significantly by 1710, except for Austria, Prussia, and Russia. A rachet effect set in during the early to mid-seventeenth century which saw most European armies larger at the end of each fresh conflict than they had been when it began. More fundamentally, armies became structurally more coherent and stable through the consolidation of different regional establishments into a single force, as well as the establishment of permanent regiments. The structures established by about 1710 would endure for up to a century. The expanded size and permanence had major implications for state, economy, environment, and society.

Table 1: Regiments Raised 1600–1629

	1600	1602	1606	1610	1614	1615	1616	1617	1619	1620	1621	1622	1623	1624	1625	1627	1628	1629	Total
1791				4			3				1				3			2	13
1698												1							1
1673															1				1
1669							1	1											2
1668																	1		1
1666										1									1
1661												1			1				2
1656																2	1	1	4
1653																	1		1
1648																1			1
1645															1				1
1643											1								1
1636														1					1
1635															1				1
1633									1										1
1632																2	3		5
1631															2	2	1		5
1630											2	2				1		2	7
1629										1							9	2	12

1628															1	11	3	x	15
1627															2		x	x	2
1626				1							2	2	4	8	18	x	x	x	35
1625											3					x	x	x	3
1624											1				x	x	x	x	1
1623									3	4	17	25		x	x	x	x	x	49
1622									1	1			x	x	x	x	x	x	2
1621									1	2	2	x	x	x	x	x	x	x	5
1620									6	3	x	x	x	x	x	x	x	x	9
1619								2	1	x	x	x	x	x	x	x	x	x	3
1617						2	1	4	x	x	x	x	x	x	x	x	x	x	7
1616				1	1	12	11	x	x	x	x	x	x	x	x	x	x	x	25
1615						2	x	x	x	x	x	x	x	x	x	x	x	x	2
1614					1	x	x	x	x	x	x	x	x	x	x	x	x	x	1
1610				1		x	x	x	x	x	x	x	x	x	x	x	x	x	1
1606			4	x	x	x	x	x	x	x	x	x	x	x	x	x	x	x	4
1604		4	x	x	x	x	x	x	x	x	x	x	x	x	x	x	x	x	4
1603	2		x	x	x	x	x	x	x	x	x	x	x	x	x	x	x	x	2
1601	6	x	x	x	x	x	x	x	x	x	x	x	x	x	x	x	x	x	6
Total	8	4	4	7	2	16	15	7	13	13	29	31	4	11	29	20	19	7	238

Note: 3 of the 4 infantry regiments raised in 1606 were reraised and disbanded in 1610 (not included in the 1610 figures in the table). Two of the infantry regiments raised in 1610 which survived until 1791 were reraised from units first formed in 1597.

Table 2: Regiments Raised 1630–1634

	1630	1631	1632	1633	1634	Total
1791	1				1	2
1678				1		1
1662			1			1
1661			1			1
1660	2		1		1	4
1659					1	1
1658			2		1	3
1654					1	1
1650				1		1
1649	1	1				2
1648			2			2
1646		1				1
1645				1		1
1643	1		1			2
1642	1				1	2
1641	2					2
1640	3				1	4
1639	1		1		2	4
1638			4			4
1636	1					1
1635	1		3	1	1	6
1634					3	3
1632			7	x	x	7
1631	3		x	x	x	3
1630	5	x	x	x	x	5
Total	22	2	23	4	13	64

Table 3: Regiments raised 1635–1648

	1635	1636	1637	1638	1639	1640	1641	1642	1643	1644	1645	1646	1647	1648	Total
1791	4			1				1		3			1		10
1672			1												1
1665		1													1
1663	1														1
1662	1												4		5
1661	7	2					2		3	1	3	3	2	2	25
1660	4	3	2		1		1	1	1	3	1		2		19
1659	3	1							1	1	1	2	2	1	12
1658	1	1			1					1	1	2	3	3	13
1657	1		2									1		1	5
1656	3			2						1			2	1	9
1655						1				1					2
1654	2	1	1		1	1		1		1		3	2	3	16
1653	2						1	2		1			1		7
1652		3		2						1	1			1	8
1651	11	2	1	2		2				1	1	1	1	4	26
1650	1			1	1		1	1	2		2		3		12
1649	3	1	1	1	2	1			1		3	3		1	17
1648	2	1		2	2		5		4	5	5	1	3	4	34

1647	1			3			1				1	1		x	7
1646	1			2					1	1	1	3	x	x	9
1645	1	3	1			3	3		1		3	x	x	x	15
1644	5	1	1	2					1	6	x	x	x	x	16
1643	8	1	1	3		3	3	7	5	x	x	x	x	x	31
1642	1	2		1	1		1		x	x	x	x	x	x	6
1641	7	1	1	1	1	8	1	x	x	x	x	x	x	x	20
1640	1		1	1	1		x	x	x	x	x	x	x	x	4
1639	7	4		3	2	x	x	x	x	x	x	x	x	x	16
1638		3	2	7	x	x	x	x	x	x	x	x	x	x	12
1637	7	13	7	x	x	x	x	x	x	x	x	x	x	x	27
1636	37	11	x	x	x	x	x	x	x	x	x	x	x	x	48
1635	2	x	x	x	x	x	x	x	x	x	x	x	x	x	2
Total	124	55	22	51	13	19	19	14	21	28	23	21	27	21	458

Table 4: Regiments raised 1649–1659

	1649	1650	1651	1652	1653	1654	1655	1656	1657	1658	1659	Total
1791			2			1		2	2			7
1669											1	1
1668							1					1
1664				1	1							2
1661	1	1	8	13	7		1	1	3	3	4	42
1660		3	4	6	1	3	3	2	6	3	2	33
1659	3	2	1	4	1	1				4		16
1658	1			1	1	1	5	1		5	x	15
1657		1	1	1	8		2			x	x	13
1656	1	1	4	2	3		4	3	x	x	x	18
1655			3	1	3	3	9	x	x	x	x	19
1654	2	2	1	2	3	12	x	x	x	x	x	22
1653	1	3	3	8	3	x	x	x	x	x	x	23
1652	1	4	10	23	x	x	x	x	x	x	x	38
1651		4	5	x	x	x	x	x	x	x	x	9
1650	5	2	x	x	x	x	x	x	x	x	x	7
1649	23	x	x	x	x	x	x	x	x	x	x	23
Total	38	23	42	62	36	21	25	9	11	15	7	289

Table 5: Regiments raised 1663–1671

	1663	1665	1667	1668	1669	1670	1671	Total
1791	1	14	4	2	2	1	3	27
1788							1	1
1761		8					1	9
1714		1					1	2
1684							2	2
1679		5		1			4	10
1678							4	4
1671			1					1
1670					1		x	1
1668		15	50		x	x	x	65
1664	1	x	x	x	x	x	x	1
Total	2	43	55	3	3	1	16	123

One regiment raised in 1671 and disbanded in 1679 was reraised in 1683 and disbanded the following year. For other units reraised, see Table 6.

Table 6: Regiments disbanded in 1668 and later reraised

Raised 1665	Reraised	Disbanded	Raised 1667	Reraised	Disbanded	Raised 1668	Reraised	Disbanded	Total
			1	1689	1698				1
			1	1682	1684				1
			1	1672	1791				1
			1	1671	1791				1
			3	1671	1761	1	1671	1761	4
			1	1671	1713				1
			1	1671	1684				1
2	1671	1679	6	1671	1679	2	1671	1679	10
1	1671	1677							1
			1	1671	1676				1
1	1671	1675							1
			1	1671	1674				1
			2	1671	1673				2
			3	1671	1672				3
			2	1671	1671				2
						1	1669	1791	1
4			24			4			32

In addition, 2 of the regiments raised in 1665 survived until 1679 and were reraised 1684 until 1693. One of the regiments raised in 1668 and disbanded in 1679 was reraised again in 1684 and disbanded the same year.

Table 7: Regiments raised 1672–1685

	1672	1673	1674	1675	1676	1677	1678	1680	1682	1684	1685	Total
1791	6	7	9	3	2	1		1	1	7		37
1775										4		4
1762					1	1	1			12		15
1761	1	1	4									6
1749										7	2	9
1704										1		1
1698			1			1						2
1693									1			1
1684	1				1						x	2
1683	1									x	x	1
1682			1							x	x	1
1679	4	7	11	2	3	5		x	x	x	x	32
1678	5	3	1	1		1		x	x	x	x	11
1677		1	1			3	x	x	x	x	x	5
1676		2	2		3	x	x	x	x	x	x	7
1675				2	x	x	x	x	x	x	x	2
1674		1	1	x	x	x	x	x	x	x	x	2
1673	1		x	x	x	x	x	x	x	x	x	1
1672	3	x	x	x	x	x	x	x	x	x	x	3
Total	22	22	31	8	10	12	1	1	2	31	2	142

See also Tables 6 and 8 for units which were reraised and are not counted in this table.

Table 8: Regiments raised 1672–76 and subsequently reraised

Raised 1672	Disbanded	Reraised	Finally Disbanded	Raised 1674	Disbanded	Reraised	Finally Disbanded	Raised 1676	Disbanded	Reraised	Finally Disbanded	Total
				1	1698	1701	1714					
1	1679	1683	1714	1	1679	1684	1684	1	1679	1684	1684	
				1	1679	1682	1791					
1				3				1				

The regiment raised in 1676 and disbanded in 1684 was reraised again in 1688 and survived in 1791.

Table 9: Regiments raised 1688–1698

	1688	1689	1690	1691	1692	1693	1695	1696	1697	1698	Total
1791	2		5	1	1	1				1	11
1775			1							1	2
1761	4	1								1	6
1749	1	1		1	5	1					9
1715	1		1	2			1			3	8
1714	14	1				6	4	1			26
1713	12	1						1			14
1706	1		1								2
1704		1									1
1699							3				3
1698	17	56	14	12	2	1	58	1	1		162
1697	1				1					x	2
1696	1								x	x	1
1695					1			x	x	x	1
1693	3						x	x	x	x	3
1692	1					x	x	x	x	x	1
1691	1	2			x	x	x	x	x	x	3
1690	3	2		x	x	x	x	x	x	x	5
Total	62	66	23	14	16	8	61	3	1	6	260

See Table 10 for disbanded units which were subsequently reraised.

Table 10: Regiments raised 1688-1693 and subsequently reraised

1688	Disb.	Re-raised	Final Disb.	1689	Disb.	Re-raised	Final Disb.	1690	Disb.	Re-raised	Final Disb.
								1	1698	1705	1713
				1	1698	1702	1714				
1	1698	1701	1714	4	1698	1701	1714	1	1698	1701	1714
				3	1698	1701	1713	1	1698	1701	1713
				1	1689	1692	1698*				
1				9				3			

1692	Disb.	Re-raised	Final Disb.	1693	Disb.	Re-raised	Final Disb.	Total
								1
								1
								6
				1	1698	1701	1713	5
								1
1	1697	1705	1716					1
1				1				15

*The regiment raised and disbanded in 1689, reraised in 1692, and disbanded in 1698 was reraised again in 1701 and finally disbanded in 1713.

Table 11: Regiments raised 1701–1709

	1701	1702	1704	1705	1706	1707	1708	1709	Total
1791					1		1		2
1761						1			1
1756				1					1
1715	2	24		2	9				37
1714	2	75	1	6	16				100
1713		6		9	1		1		17
1712						16			16
1711		1							1
1709		2			1			3	6
1708					1			x	1
1706	2	3		2		x	x	x	7
1705			2		x	x	x	x	2
1704		3		x	x	x	x	x	3
Total	6	114	3	20	29	17	2	3	194

The 16 regiments removed in 1712 were not disbanded, but instead transferred to Spanish service, as were the three raised and removed in 1709, and one of the units from 1706 which was transferred in 1709. See Tables eight and ten for units which had been disbanded but were reraised for the War of Spanish Succession and are not included in this table.

2

'Seats of war'
Current Investigations into ECW fortifications

David Flintham

Sieges dominated the British Civil Wars, a point succinctly made by the late Professor Christopher Duffy, who described the conflict as "a war of trenches, ramparts, palisades, bombardments and blockades". As a result, fortresses were a key aspect of the wars and had considerable influence on the tactics and strategies of all the protagonists.

Historical research uses a myriad of tools and techniques: archaeological investigations make new discoveries, whilst fresh analysis of earlier archaeology allows findings to be re-evaluated and new conclusions to be reached. Then, whilst compiling a database is relatively straightforward (but often time-consuming), the results can be surprising and far-reaching. The paper presented to the April 2023 Century of the Soldier Conference brought together three distinct projects: a community-based archaeological project in King's Lynn, a largely desktop based investigation that re-assesses and re-interprets volumes of existing research on London's Civil War defences, and finally, findings from the Civil War Fortifications Register (CWFR). All three projects have been previously reported elsewhere; but this is the first time that they have been combined into a single paper, and in so doing, discusses how places were fortified, and how the design and construction of Civil War fortifications evolved.

In the eight months since the paper was originally presented to the conference, there has been progress across all three projects. As a result, this paper has been expanded to include developments since April 2023.

King's Lynn under Siege (KLuS) Community Archaeology Project

Conflict archaeology is a relatively new area of archaeology; and in Britain at least, it tends to focus on battles. Yet British battles tended to be relatively short affairs, most lasting just hours. Sieges, on the other hand, lasted for days, weeks, or even months, so here, the archaeological 'footprint' is potentially greater. A decade ago, a group of like-minded archaeologists and historians came together to investigate a Civil War siege-site, and after a few 'false-starts', good fortune ultimately brought them to the Norfolk town of King's Lynn where, in January 2018, Neil Faulkner and David Flintham founded 'King's Lynn under Siege' (KLuS), a community-based archaeological research project.

Not one of England's great walled medieval towns, King's Lynn's defences evolved organically. Situated near the mouth of the River Great Ouse as it enters the Wash, to the west the town was protected by the river, whilst several small rivers and streams provided protection to the east, north, and south. Where there were gaps, earth banks topped with wooden palisades were built, and finally, to control passage in and out of the town, gateways were erected, most notably on the London and Norwich roads. During the latter years of the Middle Ages, these gates were rebuilt in brick and stone (the South Gate is still extant, whilst the East Gate, although demolished more than two centuries ago, retains a short stretch of masonry wall either side of its site). Thus, the defences can be seen as being D-shaped, with the Great Ouse forming its straight-side.

In 1642, the country did not suddenly go from a position of peace to a position of war, and in the months leading up to the outbreak of hostilities towns throughout England took measures to defend themselves in response to the ongoing unrest. In January 1643 King's Lynn was allowed to keep £400 from its subscription to Parliament to improve the town's fortifications, and it is likely that this improvement included the construction of a line of earthworks on the northern edge of the town, along the Fisherfleet. In August 1643, with a Royalist army advancing south through Lincolnshire, a Royalist coup installed Sir Hamon L'Estrange as governor of King's Lynn. Parliament's reaction was swift, and a fleet under the Earl of Warwick was sent into the Wash to blockade the town from the sea, whilst the Earl of Manchester assembled a force with which to besiege the town. Blockaded, under bombardment, and under the threat of assault, and with no relief in sight, on 16 September, King's Lynn surrendered.

Although it had declined since its Hansiatic League heyday, King's Lynn was still important to river and coastal shipping: nine counties could be reached by boat, whilst coastal craft sailed up and down the East coast of England, and the town also traded across the North Sea. Parliament quickly recognised the town's

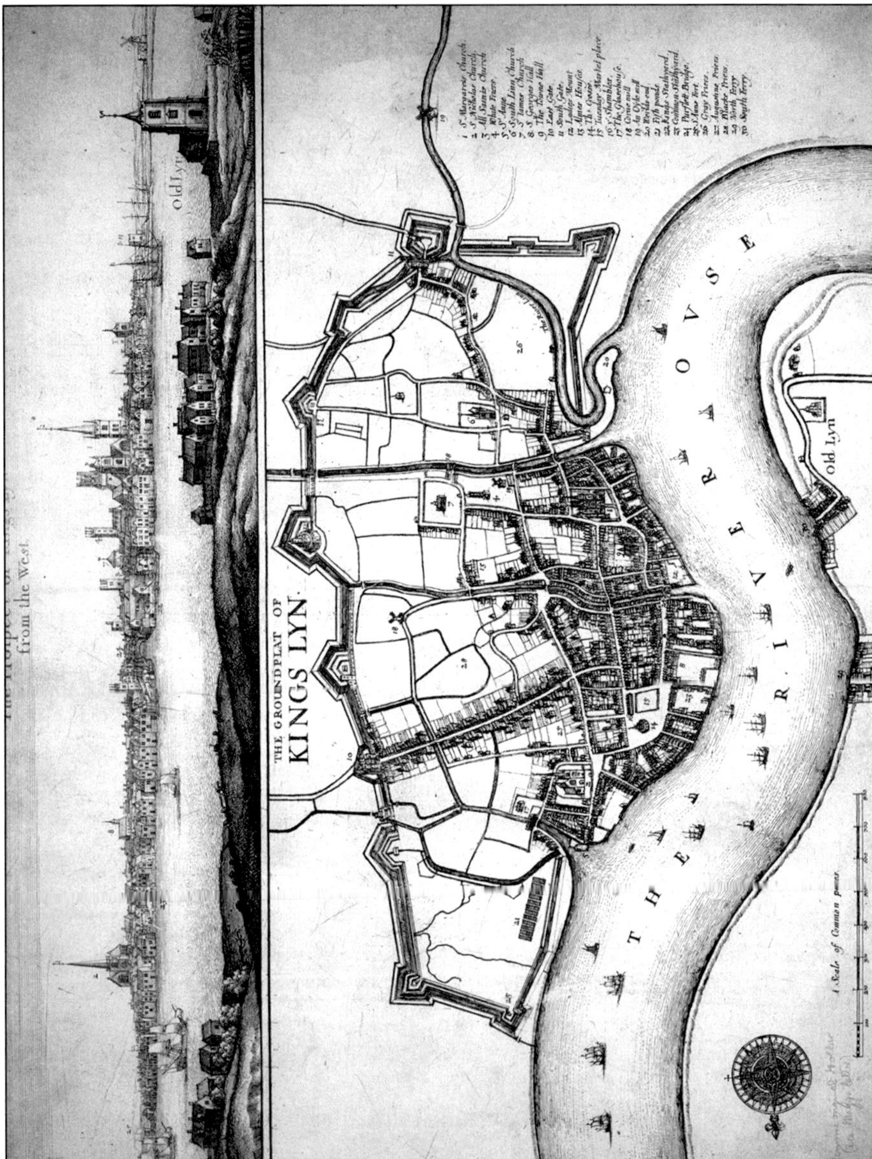

Wenceslaus Hollar's The Groundplat of Kings Lyn (P987b). This shows King's Lynn c. 1645 when the re-fortification was complete. Despite several histories still claiming to the contrary, it does not portray the town at the time of the siege in August/September 1643. With thanks to The Thomas Fisher Rare Book Library, University of Toronto

importance as a logistical hub: for instance, raw materials (including Peak District lead, and local linseed) were brought into the town then shipped to London, whilst weapons and munitions were imported from abroad. Arms, purchased in London, were conveyed by sea to King's Lynn and then sent along the Ouse and the Cam to Cambridge (the headquarters of the Eastern Association)[1]. A wide range of supplies came into the town and were then shipped onto the Army of the Eastern Association as it advanced through Lincolnshire and Yorkshire in 1643–44. King's Lynn supplied the siege of York in 1644, and Cromwell's invasion of Scotland in 1650.

Such a key location would need to be defended. Yet the town's existing fortifications were inadequate – Parliament had actually authorised the re-fortification of King's Lynn in July 1643, but this scheme was interrupted by the siege. Richard Clampe[2], a local physician and mathematician was given the job of designing the new fortifications. Wenceslas Hollar's well-known The Groundplat of Kings Lyn (c.1644–1665)[3], depicts the town following the completion of these fortifications (and not, as several historians state, the town at the time of the siege). Earthwork fortifications were by far the most common type of defences constructed in Britain as they were easier and quicker to construct, and better at resisting artillery fire than masonry walls; one contemporary commented that clay was the 'grave to cannon balls'[4]. Typically, a Civil War fortification was no more sophisticated than a simple earthwork rampart fronted by a ditch. But Clampe planned something very different: his solution was for an earthwork bastioned enceinte (the 17th century equivalent of a town wall punctuated with towers) to completely enclose the town on its north, east, and southern sides. Some 4.35 km in length[5], his design was based on the latest continental methods, utilising the principle of defence in depth, employing multiple layers of ramparts, ditches, and moats. When complete, probably in May 1644[6], the town had been

1 'John Weaver's Account Book, 1644', in Alan Everitt (editor), *Suffolk and the Great Rebellion, 1640–1660*, (Ipswich: Suffolk Records Society, 1960), volume 3, pp. 89–90.

2 David Flintham, 'Richard Clampe, Fortress Engineer, c1617–1696', *Fort*, (Fortress Study Group, 2019), number 46, pp. 3–14.

3 All of Hollar's works referred to in this easy are referenced by their Pennington catalogue numbers (see Richard Pennington, *A Descriptive Catalogue of the Etched Work of Wenceslaus Hollar, 1607–1677*, (Cambridge: Cambridge University Press, 2002). In this case, *P987b, The Groundplat of Kings Lyn*, The Thomas Fisher Rare Book Library, University of Toronto.

4 Balthazar Gerbier, 1592? –1667, *The first publique lecture, read at Sr. Balthazar Gerbier his accademy, concerning military architecture, or fortifications, to the lovers of virtue, come hither to that purpose*, (1649), Oxford Text Archive, http://hdl.handle.net/20.500.12024/A85922 (accessed 31/03/2023).

5 Measurements based on Hollar's plan and where features exist today, Google Earth.

6 TNA SP28/223 Part 5 unfol.

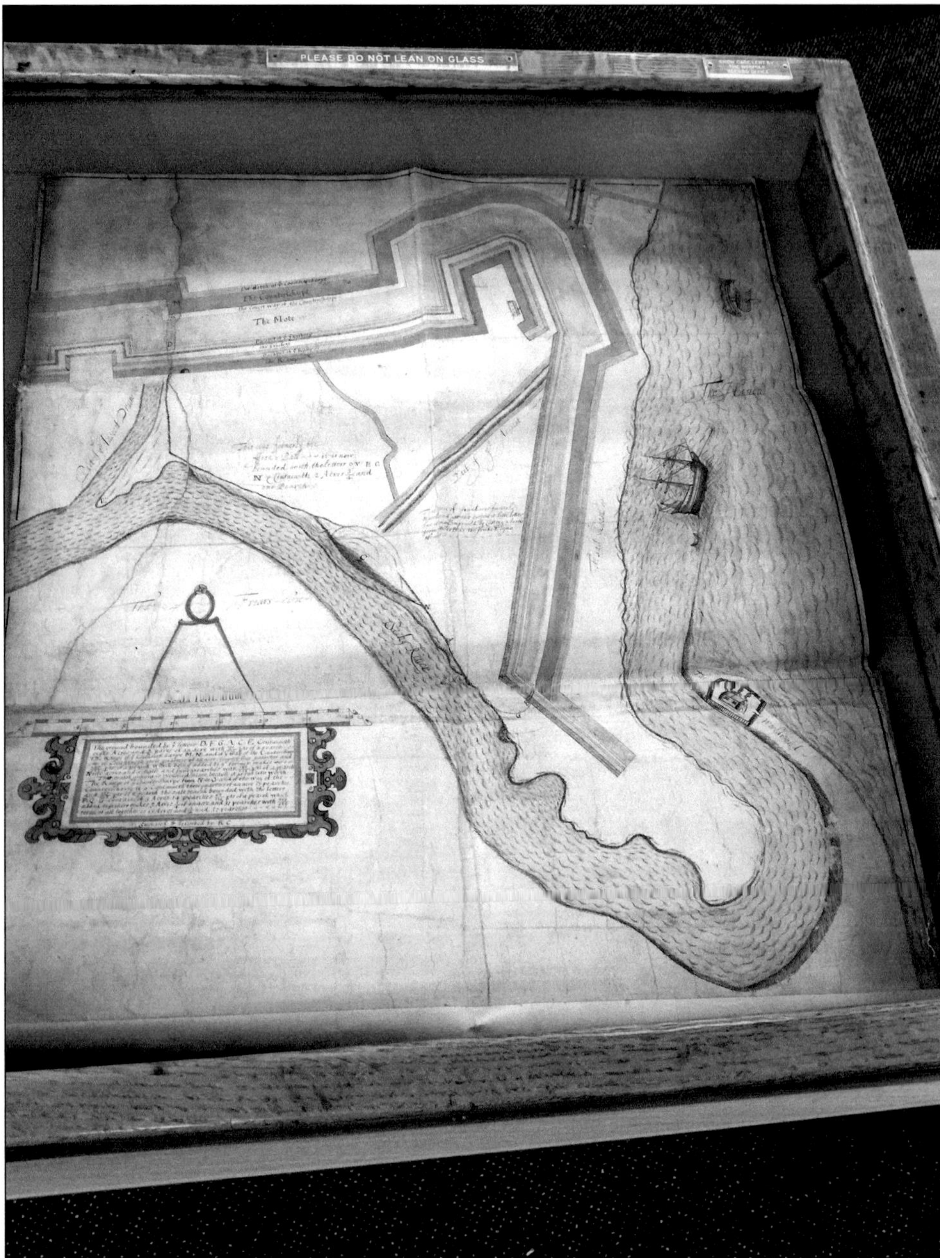

Richard Clampe's plan of King's Lynn's southern defences pictured on display in the town's Archives. This illustrates that the fortifications had a total maximum width of nearly 60m. (King's Lynn Archives/David Flintham)

transformed into not just the strongest fortress in East Anglia, but possibly the most sophisticated fortified place in England.

During the initial research, the project came across Clampe's scaled plan for the south-western bastion[7]. This plan, held in the town's archives, uses colour to set out the various components of the defences, as well as providing width measurements. Yet the south-west bastion itself provided elusive, and a magnetometry survey in May 2019 was inconclusive. The potential offered by the site of the town's north-east bastion was recognised in January 2020, and whilst actual fieldwork was restricted by the pandemic, in early 2021 plans were drawn up to undertake a non-intrusive investigation of the site. Not long after these plans were submitted to the Norfolk Historic Environment Record, Solstice Heritage, the archaeological consultants for Channel 4's *The Great British Dig* programme contacted the project to discuss a televised investigation.

A wooden post is revealed during the Great British Dig excavation. Traces of a wooden cross-piece can be just seen at the base of the trench. Analysis suggested that this was part of the framework for the rampart, a theory corroborated by the discovery of a second post in 2022. (David Flintham)

The resulting dig took place during the first week of September 2021[8]: five trenches were opened, three of which revealed little of interest. However, traces of the glacis were uncovered in Trench 5, a feature shown to be running away from the moat ('the Long Pond'[9]). Trench 3 was the largest and measured 30 m x 1.8 m and running approximately east to west. Here, it was discovered that the moat in this part of the fortifications was wider than that

7 Plan of the fortifications near the Boal, South Lynn, between Sechy River and the Haven. (NRO - King's Lynn Borough Archives, KL/C 48/16 (originally BC 21)) (With thanks to King's Lynn Borough Archives)

8 This was broadcast on *More4* in spring 2022, and is covered in Chloe Duckworth, *The Great British Dig*, (London: Bloomsbury Conway, 2022), pp. 200–213.

9 The 'Long Pond' – this is the best surviving part of Clampe's moat, although until the KLuS investigations, locals considered it to be of Victorian origin.

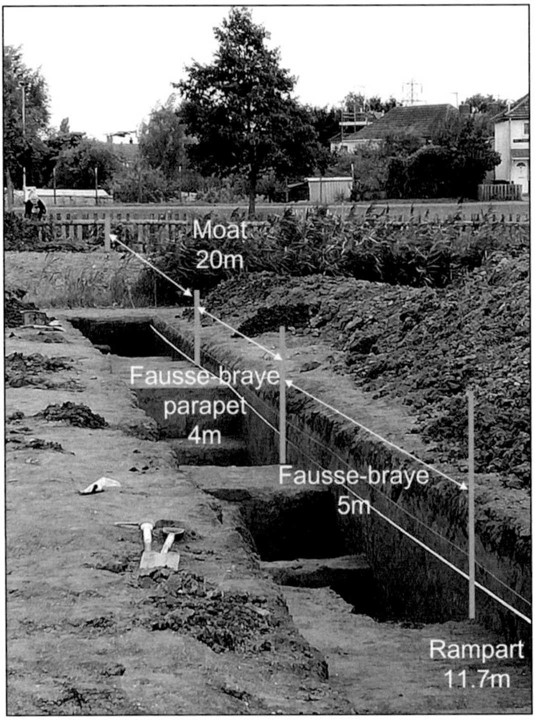

The main Great British Dig trench showing the 'cuts' from the various components of the fortifications. These proved to be very close to the profile developed from Clampe's plan. (David Flintham)

planned for the south-western bastion (20 m compared with 16 m); but the 'cuts' for the fausse-braye and main rampart matched almost exactly. Finally, the discovery of a wooden post and cross-piece at the (outer) base of the rampart suggests that the rampart was constructed around some sort of wooden framework.

KLuS is fortunate that it is just a few miles to the south of Sedgeford, home of SHARP (the Sedgeford Historical and Archaeological Research Project), a community archaeology project founded by Neil Faulkner more than 25 years ago. When the project was generously invited by the landowners to return to site in 2022, it was decided to the run the 'season' under the SHARP umbrella. Tragically, Neil died at the beginning of 2022 and so was unable to see his dream of a Civil War siege project come to fruition. Whilst the 2021 investigation focused on the width of the fortifications, 2022 concentrated on the line of the rampart, both in terms of uncovering further evidence for the construction of the rampart, and also its actual thickness. The project was also curious to learn more about what happened to the fortifications after 1660.

To get things moving, a geophysical survey of the site was undertaken in March 2022, and this informed the plans for the summer. During the July 2022 investigation, initially just a single trench was dug, positioned alongside the line of the 2021 trench (the 2021 rampart post was uncovered once more). A second rampart post was discovered 3.35 m from the first, but still along the line of the foot of the rampart. Both were carefully examined, although it was agreed that nether would be lifted. Three test-pits were then dug to 'chase' further rampart posts, and whilst these were unsuccessful in finding further posts, this did provide

An aerial view of the north-east bastion site during the 2022 excavation. The shape and size of the bastion is clear.
a) is the approximate location of the main 2021 trench
b) is the 2022 trench
c) is the 'glacis' trench from the 2021 dig
d) is the 'Long Pond' – this is the best surviving part of Clampe's moat, although until our investigations, locals considered it to be of Victorian origin.
Photograph thanks to Gary Rossin.

some useful information about the overall site which will be valuable for future investigation[10].

The discovery of two posts in alignment at the foot of the rampart suggest a method of construction of an ECW-period rampart, something which is curiously absent from contemporary accounts. Simply digging a ditch and piling the excavated soil behind it to form a rampart is insufficient to form a structure that would be strong enough or weather-proof. According to Nicholas Stone (who

10 For an account of both the 2021 and 2022 digs, see David Flintham, 'King's Lynn Under Siege', *Current Archaeology*, issue 398, May 2023, pp.42–47. Also see the project's website at <https://www.vauban.co.uk/kings-lynn-under-siege>

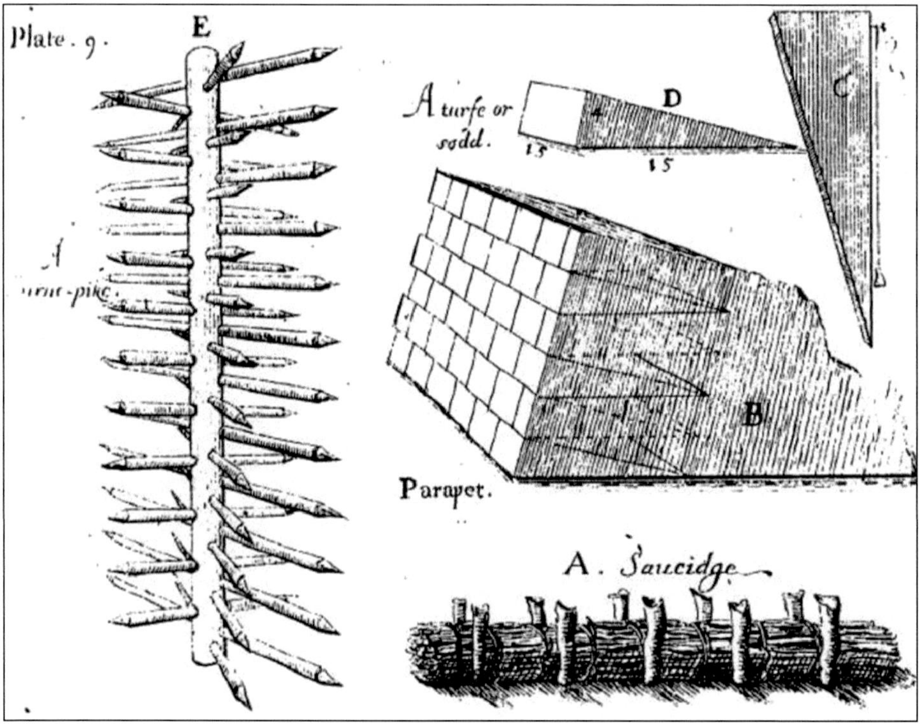

Plate 9 of Nicholas Stone's Enchiridion of Fortification, Or A Handfull of Knowledge in Martiall Affaires (1645) illustrating how turfs were to be cut, and then used to face ramparts. Also shown is the 'saucidge', something that may well have been used to construct a rampart (Author's Collection)

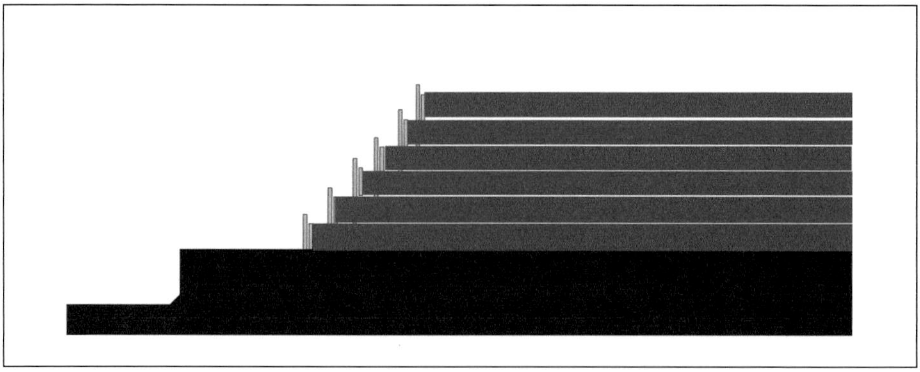

Findings from the project have demonstrated that ECW-period ramparts may have been constructed using 'steps' of hammered clay supported by posts such as those uncovered in 2021 and 2022. (David Flintham)

was Master Mason to both James I and Charles I), the initial foundations of the rampart were secured by using a 'saucidge' ('sausage'): wooden stakes of between 30.48–60.96 cm (one and two feet) in height, tied together with 'brush wood'. Such foundations needed to be specifically secured near the ditch (moat).

Stone wrote:

> First you must drive stakes of a competent length, and at a reasonable distance, as you Saucidges, either for their greatness, or smallness shall require. Either one foot high, one foot and a half, or sometimes two foot in height.
>
> Then between these stakes you must depress bundles of small brush wood, bound fast together: Filling them in the midst with brick-bats, if you would sinke them in a River, but with earth, if you intend them a foundation in a Moat all along the said Work.[11]

Based on an aerial view of the 2022 dig site, this is how the plan of the fortifications would shape across the NE bastion site. Of course, this does present a new problem as here, the fortifications turned by 90°. The exact point that this happened awaits discovery, and will be the subject of a future dig. (David Flintham and Gary Rossin)

11 Nicholas Stone, *Enchiridion of Fortification*, (London: Richard Royston, 1645), p. 34.

Considering this account, and in the absence of evidence of internal frameworks or revetments, the theory is that the rampart was constructed as a series of 'steps' with the posts supporting planking which in turn would support a level of hammered clay. The next level would be added on top of the previous one albeit staggered, and thus forming a slope of approximately 45 degrees). This process would be repeated until the steps had reached the required height, and then a parapet would be constructed atop of the rampart, and the structure covered with the turf which had been removed prior to construction. Sometime in the future, the project would like to test this theory through some experimental archaeology.

Amongst the finds were two sizeable pieces of a late 17th century onion bottle[12], demonstrating occupation of the site during the post-Restoration period, and also linking with the town's role as a wine-importer. The investigations also showed that the fortifications were not removed following the end of the Civil War: more than 70 years later, Daniel Defoe visited the town, noting how strong the fortifications remained[13]. The fortifications, albeit overgrown and weathered, lasted until the end of the 18th century when the clay from the fortifications was harvested to make bricks (mature clay makes better bricks than new clay). William Faden's 1797 Plan of the Town of Lynn[14] shows the existence of a brick kiln, and most of the finds from the western half of the trench, relate to this activity: several mis-fired bricks were found, as well as charcoal and clinker.

Ongoing research is beginning to identify those engineers and overseers who were involved in the construction of the fortifications between autumn 1643 and spring 1644, and also the artillerymen who manned the cannon arming the town's forts and bastions. Overall, the research has demonstrated the consistency between Clampe's plan and subsequent maps of the town, also that his plan for the south-west bastion was indeed repeated around the entire circuit, thus the town's defences were amongst the most sophisticated defences built anywhere during the British Isles during the Civil Wars. Nationally, events in King's Lynn can be seen as a turning point of the Civil War, and the design and construction of its fortifications after the siege are very much 'of national importance'.

12 Similar bottles have been found at the wreck of the *Gloucester* (see <https://www.newscientist.com/article/2363164-relics-illuminate-the-wreck-of-hms-gloucester-a-17th-century-warship/> (accessed 31/03/2023), and <https://the-past.com/feature/the-gloucester-piecing-together-the-story-of-a-royal-wreck/> (accessed 04/12/2023).

13 Daniel Defoe, *A Tour through the Whole Island of Great Britain*, (London: Penguin Books, 1986), p. 97.

14 William Faden, *Plan of the Town of Lynn* from *Norfolk in six sheets* (1797).

Civil War Defences (CWD) of London Project

Whilst London's continual post-war development has enabled archaeologists to uncover much of its past, there is one major feature which is elusive: the 18 km circuit of fortifications constructed during the English Civil War to defend the capital. These evolved from an initial ad hoc construction in the autumn of 1642 to become, in 1643, the largest defensive system constructed during the entire Civil War period, comprising of at least 20 forts and batteries connected by ramparts, ditches and trenches. Decommissioned in 1647, over subsequent centuries they have almost completely vanished, and it is only through archaeology that the fortifications can be rediscovered. Generally, however, remains are encountered more often by chance than by design: the scarcity of contemporary mapping makes targeted investigation difficult, and when potential features are encountered, they are easily misinterpreted. What follows is not intended to provide a detailed history of the planning and construction of these fortifications[15], but instead it will present the recent research that is making archaeologists and historians reconsider long-accepted understandings of the fortifications, particularly in respect of their locations.

In February 1643, the City of London's Court of Common Council specified the location of individual forts, rather than a single encompassing fortified circuit. These forts were of a variety of designs and types, which suggests the hand of more than one engineer. The pragmatic approach to the challenges of fortifying London taken by these engineers is becoming even more apparent because of a ground-breaking archaeological project.

Virtually every study of London's fortifications has been based on George Vertue's Plan of the City and Suburbs of London as fortified by Order of Parliament in the years 1642 and 1643 which appeared in William Maitland's 1738 History of London[16]. Cromwell Mortimer FSA claimed that this plan was 'copyed from Wenceslaus Hollar's map of England'[17], a claim that has never been substantiated.

15 For the design and construction of London's fortifications, readers are referred to Simon Marsh, 2013, 'The Construction and Arming of London's Defences 1642–1645', *Journal of the Society for Army Historical Research* (2013) 91, pp. 275–298, and David Flintham, *Civil War London: A military history of London under Charles I and Oliver Cromwell*, (Solihull: Helion and Company, 2017), pp. 65–71.

16 William Maitland, *The History of London from its foundation by the Romans, to the present time*, (London: Samuel Richardson, 1738). Norman Brett-James noted that when it came to the inclusion of Vertue's plan, Maitland 'unlike his usual custom, gives no indication as to the source of his material' (see Norman Brett-James, *The Growth of Stuart London*, (London: George Allen and Unwin Limited, 1935), p.284).

17 George Vertue, *Plan of the City of London as fortified by Order of Parliament in the years 1642 and 1643*, (1738), Amended by Cromwell Mortimer M.D. in 1746, Kings Topographical Collection, Vol. XX, No. 16.

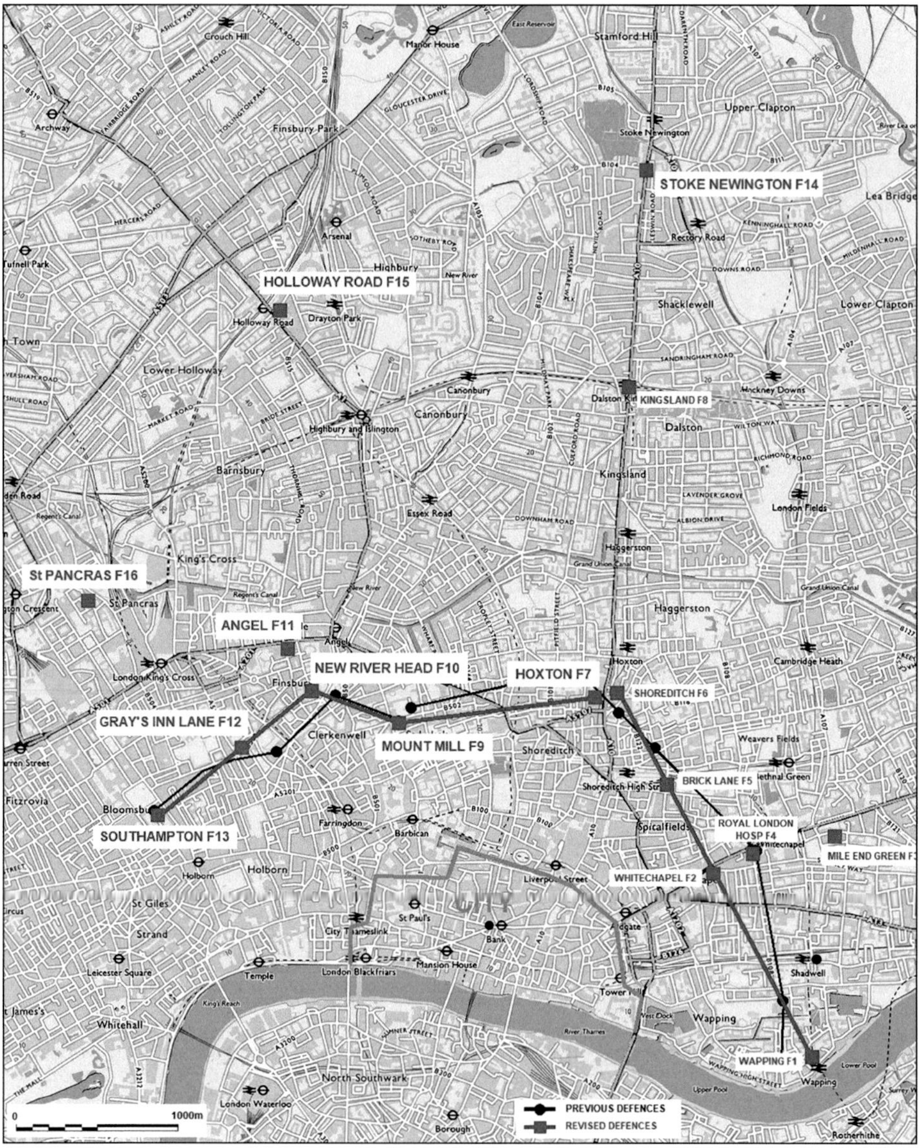

Current research has revised the location of London's Civil War fortifications. This map illustrates the results of Study Areas 1 and 2 (shown in red) with the previous suggested defensive line (shown in black).
Thanks to Peter Mills (Mills Whipp Projects)

Suspicions about Vertue's plan extend beyond this: it doesn't match London's seventeenth century geography, nor does it correlate either with the official order for the fortifications or a contemporary description. In addition, Vertue has been implicated in several forgeries. Therefore, at best, Vertue's plan must be considered very unreliable, whilst at worst, it is a fake, deliberately intended to mislead. Unfortunately, Vertue's plan has long influenced the study of London's fortifications, including the location of the fortifications indicated by the Historic England Record (HER). It has become clear that there was a major discrepancy between the suggested locations of the fortifications indicated by the HER and other documentary evidence. A fresh evaluation of locations was called for, not only for the benefit of historians, but also to identify sites to be designated as Greater London Archaeological Priority Areas (APA), and to be a significant planning tool for Historic England's Greater London Archaeological Advisory Service (GLAAS), to assist them in assessing planning applications in sensitive areas. Thus, the Civil War Defences (CWD) of London project was born[18].

The project has divided the fortifications into five sections: Wapping to Hoxton, Hoxton to Bloomsbury, Bloomsbury to Park Lane, Park Lane to the Thames opposite Vauxhall and finally, Vauxhall to Rotherhithe. To date, the project has covered the Wapping to Bloomsbury, as well as Vauxhall to Rotherhithe sections.

London Archaeologist [19] has already reported the findings for the area defined by the City of London's Court of Common Council resolution dated 23 February 1643:

> That a small Fort conteyning one bulwarke and halfe and a battery in the rear of the flanke to be made at Gravel [Wapping] lane end. A hornworke with two flankers to be placed at Whitechapell windmills. One redoubt with two flankers betwixt Whitechapell Church and Shoreditch. Two redoubts with flankers neere Shoreditch Church with battery. At the windmill in Islington way, a battery and brestworke round about. A small redoubt neere Islington pound. A battery and breastwork on the hill near

18 This project is the mastermind of Mills Whipp Projects (<https://www.millswhipp.com/>), who have been responsible for both re-evaluating existing evidence, and also unearthing a mass of unknown or previously overlooked evidence. Civil War fortress historians and archaeologists owe Mills Whipp an enormous debt of gratitude.

19 Peter Mills, 'The Civil War defences of East London reviewed: preliminary results', *London Archaeologist*, Volume 16, number 3, (London: Winter 2021), pp. 73–81, and Peter Mills, 'The Civil War Defences of north London reviewed: Hoxton to Bloomsbury', *London Archaeologist*, (London; The London Archaeologist Association, 2023), Winter 2023, Volume 16, Number 11, pp. 283–294.

Unlike a number of other towns, there is no known contemporary plan of London's fortifications, despite it being the largest defensive scheme constructed during the entire Civil War period. This extract from Hollar's Quartermasters Map (1644 – P654) is probably the only contemporary map of London's fortifications. Unfortunately, it is just a sketch and measures no more than an inch across. But despite this, it provides a reasonable/likely representation of several forts, including Southampton Fort [a], and St. George's Fields [c]. More curious is the six-pointed star-fort at Tothill Fields [b]. Thomas Fisher Rare Book Library, University of Toronto, and Peter Mills

Clerkenwell towards Hampstead way. Two batteries and a brestworke at Southampton House".[20]

The project has undertaken fresh analysis of the evidence, combining a careful reading of contemporary documents and a re-examination of archaeological records. The study has also tentatively quantified conceivable archaeological survival at the locations of the fortifications. Overall, the results of the research have been dramatic, virtually all of the forts have been relocated and the central emphasis shifted by between 200 m and 400 m.

In May 1643, William Lithgow[21], a Scottish traveller, visited London and followed the course of the fortifications in an anti-clockwise direction although at the time, the defences south of the River Thames were still under construction. He published a 22-page account of his journey, providing a detailed description, one which has been provided to be largely accurate in terms of location, but possibly exaggerated in term of artillery strength, perhaps for propaganda purposes.

There is no known detailed contemporary plan of London's fortifications (the nearest being part of Hollar's Quartermasters Map of 1644[22], but unfortunately, this extract measures only 25 mm (1inch) across). A breakthrough was the discovery of a map drawn by Frederik de Witt in 1666[23] showing the devastation of the Fire of London[24]. Although this map is of no great consequence in itself, between 1666 and 1680, someone added a sketch line showing the Lines of Communication, as the fortifications became known, to the east and north of the City. As the lines were used as a physical definition of London's monetary liabilities during the later seventeenth century, it is presumed that the annotator was providing a visual aid

20 *Journals of the Court of Common Council*, Journal 40, folio 52.

21 The version of William Lithgow, *The Present Surveigh At London*, referred to is that reprinted in Lieut.-Colonel W.G. Ross, R.E., 'Military Engineering during the Great Civil War, 1642–1649', *Professional Papers of the Corps of Royal Engineers*, 1887, Volume XIII, (Chatham: W. J. MacKay & Co., 1888), pp. 160–168.

22 Hollar's works are refenced by their Pennington catalogue numbers, in this case Pennington 654. See Richard Pennington, *A Descriptive Catalogue of the Etched Work of Wenceslaus Hollar*, 1607–1677 (Cambridge: Cambridge University Press, 2002).

23 Frederik de Witt 1666 Map showing extent of the Great Fire. The Lines of Communication and some Forts have been added in pencil, probably to show the City tax limits. (© British Library). This map is also referred to as '*the anonymous annotator's sketch lines on the map produced in 1666 showing the extent of damage in the Great Fire*', and the shorthand term 'Great Fire map'.

24 During the wars with the Dutch, there was a general understanding that neither side would attack each other's civilian coastal towns. However, on 20 August 1666, in a breach of this understanding, the English burnt West-Terschelling. Understandably outraged, the Dutch prepared to retaliate, but news of the Great Fire just three weeks later convinced the deeply Calvinist Dutch that God Himself had punished the English, thus averting reciprocal attacks. Hence, the Fire of London was something of great interest to the Dutch.

for tax purposes. This map demonstrated the wide difference between the lines visible following the Great Fire and those Vertue depicted.

This new research has radically revised the location of the forts and the lines, and has identified archaeological evidence for several of them. One of the most striking findings concerns the location of the fort in Whitechapel, where traditional thinking places it close to the Royal London Hospital. However, the location stated in the City Orders was for 'A hornworke with two flankers be placed at Whitechappell windmills.'[25] Seventeenth century Whitechapel was a linear suburb between Aldgate and modern Fieldgate Street/Greatorex Street (and not the area surrounding the 'modern' Whitechapel station)[26]. The Faithorne and Newcourt map of 1658[27] also places the Whitechapel fort closer to Aldgate, straddling the main road, its southern flank standing roughly on the site of the former Whitechapel Bell Foundry on Whitechapel High Street (this was also the site of the windmill). John Rocque's 1747 map also depicts irregular boundaries, probably reflecting vestiges of the fort [28].

During the autumn of 1642, several Members of Parliament rode out to review:

> the several watches and guards at the outworks and trenches from St James to Hide Park Corner, Piccadilly, St Giles in the Fields, Pancras Fields, Grayes Inn Lane, Holloway Rode, Newington, Hogsden and thence into the several gates of the City[29].

Hoxton Fort, located near the junction of Kingsland Road and Old Street was subsequently upgraded and included in the defensive circuit ordered in February 1643[30]. Three months later, Lithgow visited: 'Hogston, where I found a quadrat

25 *Journals of the Court of Common Council*, Journal 40, folio 52.

26 The area further east, near the Royal London Hospital, and now called 'Whitechapel', was called Mile End in the seventeenth century, having its own common, Mile End Green. This is an example of the migration of place names which is in a large part a fairly recent result of the Underground Stations being named from areas not necessarily immediately adjacent.

27 William Faithorne and Richard Newcourt, *An exact delineation of the Cities of London and Westminster and the suburbs thereof, together wth ye Burrough of Southwark* ..., surveyed in 1643–1647 and published in 1658

28 John Rocque, *A Plan of the Cities of London and Westminster and the Borough of Southwark*, (1747), reproduced as *The A to Z of Georgian London*, (London: London Topographical Society, 1982), p. 6.

29 Simon Marsh, 2013, 'The Construction and Arming of London's Defences 1642–1645', *Journal of the Society for Army Historical Research*, 2013, volume 91, pp. 275–298. 5 Nov 1642 Tract quoted on p. 279.

30 *Journals of the Court of Common Council*, Journal 40, folio 52

Fort, well pallosaded and planted with five Cannons at the two field corners: The strength is double ditched'[31].

Within the so-called Commonwealth Exchequer Papers is a document recording the monies paid to the artillerymen serving at London's forts during 1643 and 1644 which importantly identifies the forts by name. The fort at Hoxton is referred to as 'Pimlico'[32], the name most probably taken from a then famous tavern which lay to the north-west of the fort. It is likely that the fort was so known by its garrison as the tavern was the nearest landmark. About 1.5 km west of Hoxton Fort, at the junction of modern Goswell Road and Lever Street, stood one of the major fortifications of the defensive circuit, Mount Mill Fort. According to Lithgow:

The Malignants Cartoon depicts in a series of frames the attempted Waller Plot of August 1643. In the foreground stands Mount Mill Fort, in the background is the circular New River Head Fort with its overflow pond. Thanks to Peter Mills (Mills Whipp Projects)

> Mount mil-hill, Fort, … where being arryved I found it standing on the high way near to the Red Bull: This is a large and singular Fortification, having a Fort above and within a Fort … The upper Fort standing circular is furnished with eleven pieces of Cannon reall … and upon the bosome top of all standeth a Windmill. The lower bulwarks, are first pallosaded round about, … and three Redoubts of

31 Lithgow in Ross, p. 162.
32 TNA, SP28/198 Part 2: (June 1643–December 1645).

lesser importance, yet all defensive. This is one of the chief Forts about the city and first erected[33].

The Red Bull, a well-known tavern and theatre was actually 400 m to the west of the fort. In addition to the documentary evidence there is a rare image of the fort from a pamphlet detailing an attempted Royalist coup in 1643. In a 'cartoon' style sequence of pictures, the fort is shown bristling with defences.

According to the Dutch method of fortress design, a second ditch (known as a 'cunette') would be dug in the middle of the main ditch, along its entire length. In addition to providing an additional obstacle to any attacker, the cunette would help drain a dry ditch. But the concept of a 'double-ditch' seems to have been misunderstood by the builders of London's fortifications who interpreted this as two narrow parallel ditches. The Huguenot engineer David Papillion complained

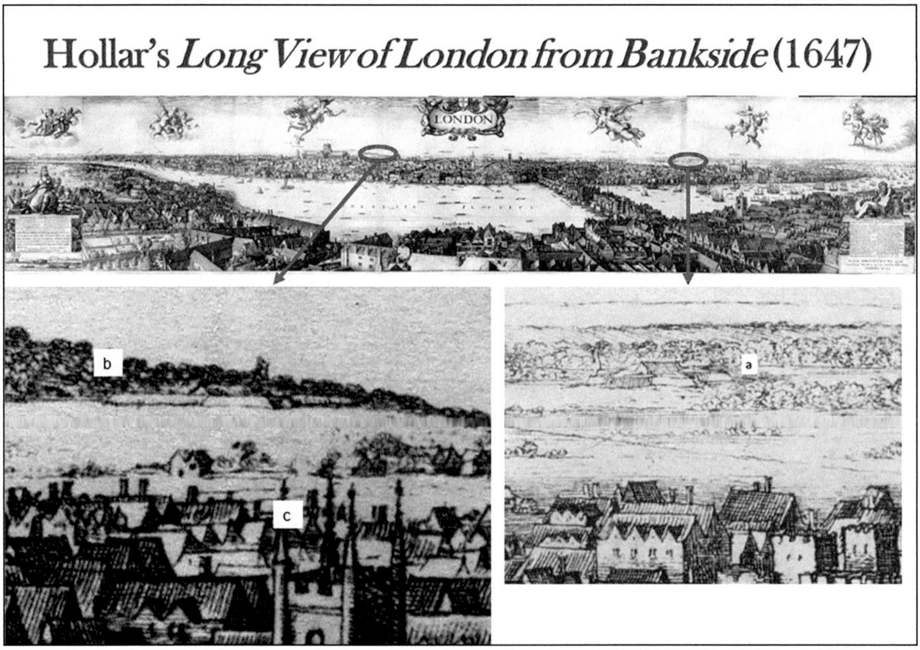

The Angel Fort ('b'), the New River Head Fort ('c'), and the citadel at Whitechapel Citadel ('a' – referred to as Royal London Hospital Fort) from Wenceslas Hollar's Long View of London from Bankside. (1647 – P1014). Thomas Fisher Rare Book Library, University of Toronto

33 *Journals of the Court of Common Council*, Journal 40, folio 52. The papers also make reference to soldiers at *Pimlecoe Foarte* and *Hougsdon Pasage;* Lithgow in Ross, p. 162.

about: 'these small double ditches, having a bank of earth some two foot broad left between them, turfed and erected about the London Redoubts'[34].

Archaeological evidence of the double ditch was uncovered by excavation on the north side of Sebastian Street ,on the western side of Goswell Road revealed two parallel, flat-bottomed ditches of mid-seventeenth century date and running parallel to Goswell Road, cut into the brickearth. Lithgow also observed this feature at Hoxton Fort, Southampton Fort, and Tothill Fort[35].

Modern Sebastian Street probably follows the line of the fortifications as they headed north-west from Mount Mill, and here Lithgow noted: 'Thence [from Mount Mill Fort] footing along the Trench dyke (which is three yards thick, and on the ditch side twice as high) I courted Islington'[36]

Pictured in the background of the Mount Mill Fort cartoon is a distant view of the next fort, located at the New River Head. Known to contemporaries as 'Waterfield Fort', or 'Dead Mill', the fort was included by Hollar in his 1647 panorama, Long View of London from Bankside. Nearly two decades later, Hollar would depict the remains of the fort in his By Islington series of etchings[37]. Although the latter can only hints at what the fort would have looked like, the fortifications in the areas were certainly far more sophisticated than those misinterpreted in a 2010 study of European urban fortification[38].

The highest point of the entire circuit was where Lithgow headed next:

> A little further (about ten paire buts) [c.400 m] I approached to Islington hill, where there is erected a most rare & admirable Fortification, called Strawes Fort, but now Fort Royall. It hath eight angles, and a spacious interlarding distance, between each of the cornerd bulwarks: This Fort is marvellous perspicuous and prospective both for City and country ..., The Northeast cornerd Bulwark is double altified above the rest of the worke ... and the East promontoriat corner adorned with three whole Cannon[39].

At some 40 m (130 ft) above sea level, this fort, also referred to as 'Islington Hill'[40], was also described by Papillon in 1645: 'The Royall Fort neare Islington is much

34 David Papillon, *A practicall abstract of the Arts of Fortification and Assailing, etc*, (London: 1645), p. 29.
35 Lithgow in Ross, pp. 162–164.
36 Lithgow in Ross, pp. 162–164.
37 Pennington 1014; Pennington 916–919.
38 Martha Pollak, *Cities at War in Early Modern Europe*, (Cambridge: Cambridge University Press, 2010), pp.°224–225.
39 Lithgow in Ross, pp. 162–163.
40 TNA, SP28/198 Part 2: (June 1643–December 1645).

after this manner [square], only the face of his Avant guards are square, and doe not extend themselves farre enough into the field, and therefore not so regular, nor so defensible as this'[41].

Hollar also included this fort in his 1647 panorama, depicting it as a massive quadrate structure with an interior building and a flag flying. On De Witt's map there is also a sketch of the fort, and from this, measured 162.4 m x 115.32 m, covering an area of 1.87 ha. In comparison, Newark's Queen's Sconce occupied are area of 1.4 ha[42].

Between Gray's Inn Fort and Southampton Fort, the lines zigzag to avoid a pond and a stream, suggesting a quick solution to avoid this boggy area during the rapid construction of the defences. They are clearly shown on the Richard Daynes map of 1643, and when combined with the John Daynes map of 1665 it is possible to overlay the seventeenth century defences on a modern map with considerable accuracy. Southampton Fort itself probably survived on the south side of Russell Square until early in the nineteenth century. The fort was remarkable for two reasons: firstly, the mapping evidence which has enabled the fort to be studied in some detail[43], and also the finesse of the fort's apparent design which has more in common with contemporary Continental design than anything else in London. This adds a further piece of evidence to the theory that London's forts were designed by several different hands. Lithgow is slightly confused in his description, referring to Southampton Fort as 'Northampton Fort': 'Abandoning the place and shoaring along the Trench a little further to Longfield, I presently rancountred with North Hampton Fort, consisting of two divided quadrangled bulwarks'[44].

Lithgow's description implies that the line of the fortification in this area consist of a trench fronted by a parapet, although the tenants of the Rugby Estate complained of 'Breastworks' across the land[45]. The accepted norm for Civil War fortifications was a ditch-fronted rampart, and it was accepted that London's defences followed

41 Papillon, p. 32. *Fort Royal* is a term given to the very largest of forts, its name denoting its size, not regal status. In the same way, the largest cannon were referred to as 'Cannon Royal'.

42 <https://vauban.co.uk/civil-war-fortifications-register-(cwfr)>

43 Rosemary Weinstein, 'Southampton House and the Civil War', in Joanna Bird, Hugh Chapman, and John Clark (editors), *Collectanea Londiniensia*, (London and Middlesex Archaeological Society, Special Papers, 1978), volume 2, pp. 329–345. As part of her 1978 study, Dr. Weinstein produced an overlay which had the line of fortifications joining the fort directly on the NE bastion. In military terms this is very unlikely, so the interpretation is likely to be erroneous. The revised overlay developed as part of the CWD of London project varies slightly from this, and the Lines meet Southampton Fort at its south-eastern side.

44 Lithgow in Ross, p. 164.

45 Weinstein, p. 334.

Earl of Essex on Foot (P1401) by Wenceslas Hollar. Note the yet unidentified fortress (left background). Thomas Fisher Rare Book Library, University of Toronto

this pattern. But Lithgow is quite precise in his description, and in places identifies trenches instead of a typical rampart and ditch. There are several other accounts mentioning trenches, but Lithgow also refers to 'the trench dyke' in several other locations. From this, it can be concluded that instead of London's forts being entirely connected by ditch-fronted ramparts, dependent upon the terrain, in some places they were connected by trenches, probably fronted by a low parapet; although this could equally be interpreted as a reference to some sort of covered way where the ditch in front of the rampart was used both as a defensive obstacle, and also as a protected route for soldiers to move up and down the lines.

The CWD project has also identified several smaller forts outside the main circuit which were constructed guarding northern approaches to London. These included Kingsland, Stoke Newington, on the Holloway Road and at St Pancras[46]. The project also suggests a further phase of fortress construction that took place between the First and Second English Civil Wars. The site long-known as Whitechapel Mount being part of the 1643 scheme has now been dismissed, and instead, is probably linked with the events of the second half of 1647 and the New Model Army's occupation of London, when, in August, Sir Thomas Fairfax ordered the slighting

46 This was located by the Old St. Pancras Church which Stukeley may have inadvertently recorded. Stukeley had decided that the earthworks at St Pancras Church where the remains of the Roman camp where Julius Caesar met the British tribal chieftains.

An extract from Wenceslas Hollar's equestrian portrait of the Earl of Essex (P1400) depicting the Lord General's military successes in 1642–1643 (the full portrait is shown as an insert). The fortifications of Gloucester ('Gloster'), London, and Reading ('Reding') are depicted, but notably, Oxford is shown completely undefended.
Thomas Fisher Rare Book Library, University of Toronto

of the London's fortifications, but laid the foundations of 'three citadels to bridle the city'[47]. In the background of his Long View of London from Bankside[48], Hollar also included what appears to be a star-shaped fort on the future site of the Royal London Hospital, and so it is concluded that the fort at the Royal London Hospital is one of these three citadels. This was noted by Christopher Wren in 1673, and its remains would later become a notable local landmark.

The CWD London project has put the works of Wenceslas Hollar under the microscope with some unexpected results. As previously mentioned, his Quartermasters Map features a tiny representation of London's fortifications (and might be a clue to 'Wenceslaus Hollar's map of England' that Cromwell Mortimer referred to in 1746). His equestrian portrait of the Earl of Essex also features London's defences in the background, whilst as previously noted, his 1647 Long View … depicts three forts along the far horizon. His portrait of the Earl of Essex on foot shows a yet to be identified fortress in the background[49]. Hollar was not alone in depicting fortresses as a backdrop to portraits: the c.1642/3 portrait of Sir John Hotham features part of Hull's defences for example.

There is another aspect of Hollar's works that is striking: his ECW-period views of Parliamentarian-held towns (King's Lynn, Kingston-Upon-Hull, Plymouth), and the sketches of Gloucester, Reading, and London all depict their fortifications,

47 A. B. Hinds (editor), *Calendar of State Papers Venice*, volume 28, (London: His Majesty's Stationery Office, 1927), p. 23.
48 Pennington 1014.
49 Pennington 654, 1400, 1014, 1401.

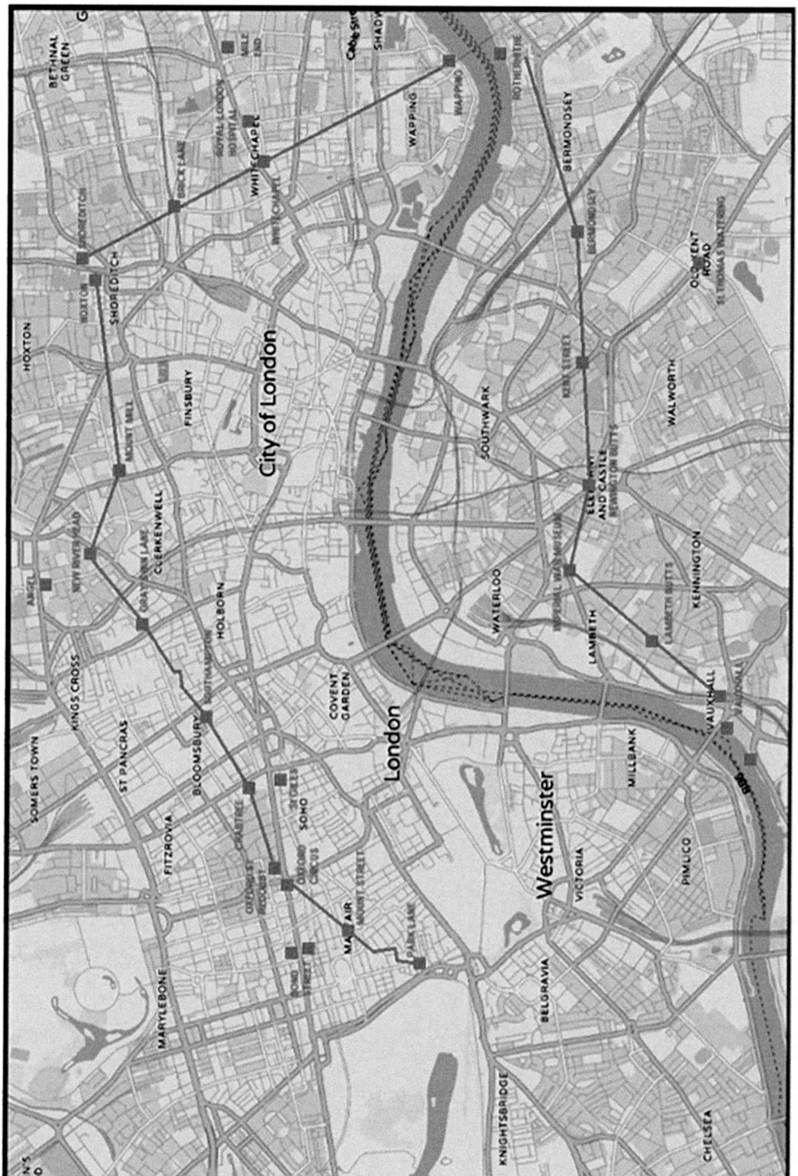

0 2km

The CWD project is significantly re-drawing the map of London's Civil War defences. At the end of 2023, the CWD project have completed its investigations into phases one, two, three, and five, although even here new findings continue to be made so future revisions are possible. This plan depicts the position of the fortifications prior to the commencement of phase four, and this 'missing' western section of the fortifications will be investigated during 2024–2025. Therefore, this plan should be taken as a work in progress. Thanks to Peter Mills (Mills Whipp Projects)

but his 1643 view of the Royalist capital of Oxford[50] does not. This could be that his depiction of Oxford is a pre-war view that was reissued when Charles I made the city has his capital. Alternatively, there could be a darker reason, with Hollar recording the fortifications of Parliamentarian towns, but deliberately withholding those of Royalist towns.

This paper has presented the first two phases of the CWD London project; since April 2023 the project has progressed at pace: the findings from phase five (Vauxhall to Rotherhithe) have now been submitted to Historic England, whilst at the time of writing (December 2023), the report for phase three (Bloomsbury to Park Lane) is in production. Summaries of both phases will appear in future issues of *London Archaeologist*. Ultimately, it is hoped to publish the complete findings (including any revisions – new discoveries continue to be made) in a single volume. Should a second edition of the author's recent *A Town Well Fortified*[51] be possible, it would include the findings for all five phases.

Civil War Fortifications Register (CWFR)

The impact of the Civil Wars was felt right across the British Isles. Even if an area was fortunate enough to escape any actual fighting, the sight of armed men would have been a common one, and who knew where they might turn next. The countryside would be stripped for supplies, and once gathered, these would need to be transported. Coastal districts might be subject to the attention of opposing navies or privateers, or occasionally foreign warships too. The propogandists of all sides were not slow to report, and often exaggerate, the activities of the enemy, describing atrocities in gruesome detail, occasionally even inventing them. So regardless of its strategic importance or loyalty, places up and down the country protected themselves, and hundreds of towns, castles, and houses were fortified during the Civil War. But in some locations, this might have been counter-productive, and actually attracted the warring parties: 'The slight retrenching and garrisoning of many towns of no great strength by nature and situation, though it may by nature and situation, though it may serve for the present securing of particular counties, and particular men's estates from plundering parties, yet they are prejudicial to the public, and to the main of the wars'[52].

50 Pennington 987b, 984, 554, 654, 1055; see also David Flintham, 'His Majaestie's Scenographer: the Military Art of Wenceslaus Hollar', in Serena Jones (editor), *Home and Away – The British Experience of War, 1618–1721*, (Warwick: Helion and Company Limited, 2018), pp. 150–188.

51 David Flintham, *The Town Well Fortified*, (Warwick: Helion and Company Limited, 2023).

52 Joshua Sprigge, *Anglia Rediviva. England's Recovery*, (London: 1647), reprinted (London: Ken Trotman, 1984), p. 14.

The remains of the fort of at Inverlochy (subsequently known as Fort William). Built during the 1650s, it was rebuilt in stone during the 1690s, although the sally port dates from the original Cromwellian fort). (David Flintham)

Included as part of the UK Fields of Conflict (UKFoC) database is a supplementary list of sieges, and whilst limited to England, it does identify 245 sieges between 1642–1649, which equates to 194 individual siege sites. Glenn Foard and Richard Morris themselves identified 242 sieges in England, of which 223 occurred during the first Civil War and nineteen during the second Civil War. As some places were besieged more than once, this identifies 189 actual siege sites. This compares with 30 major battles in England between 1640 and 1651, and so demonstrates that for every major battle which took place in England between 1642 and 1651 there were eight sieges[53]. But as research carried out by the British Civil Wars Project shows, this represents but a fraction of the actual fighting as for every battle there

53 Glenn Foard and Richard Morris, *Archaeology of English Battlefields*, (York: Council for British Archaeology, 2012), pp. 7–8, 127, 175–179; Richard Jeffrey Leese, *Siege Archaeology of the English Civil Wars: Establishing a methodology to unlock the archaeology of attack and defence at early modern siege sites*. Doctoral thesis, (Huddersfield: University of Huddersfield, 2020) pp. 45–46.

were numerous skirmishes and other minor actions[54]. The same applies to sieges, and for every major siege there would have been several other types of actions including the forced surrender of a garrison, a surrender resulting from an action elsewhere, or the fall of a town following a battle outside its walls. Then there were the places that were fortified but were spared any actual fighting (London is a good example). Unfortunately, whether a place was besieged or not largely seems to be the determining factor whether a fortress was included in histories of the period. Added to this, most studies overlook the number of citadels and forts constructed across Ireland and Scotland (and parts of England too) during the 1650s.

The need to identify every place that was fortified during the Civil Wars, covering both Great Britain and Ireland led to the creation of the Civil War Fortresses Register (CWFR). Five years into the project, its initial results are ready to be published. Overall, the register lists 1,104 places that were fortified[55], of which 675

Overlooking Killeany Bay on Inish Mor, Fort Arkin (Caisleán Aircín) dates from the 1580s, but and was rebuilt during the Cromwellian occupation of the 1650s. (David Flintham)

54 *British Civil Wars Project*, <www.Wiki.bcw-project.org>, (first accessed on 06/12/2015).

55 <https://vauban.co.uk/civil-war-fortifications-register-(cwfr)>, and as of 01/05/2023. Any figures and analysis based on the Civil War Fortresses Register (CWFR) is taken at this date. In April 2023, the overall figure stood at 1,095 fortresses, demonstrating that the CWFR is an on-going project, with the reported data being revised continually.

Wenceslas Hollar's etching of the Siege of Plymouth (P554) in 1643 shows the original rampart and ditch defences surrounding the town, together with the shore-line Tudor blockhouses. To the north of the town is a line of triangular redoubts connected by a line of ditch-fronted ramparts. Thomas Fisher Rare Book Library, University of Toronto

(61 percent) witnessed some sort of hostile 'action'. Breaking this down by country, there were 662 fortified places in England, of which 393 (59 percent) saw some sort of action. In Ireland the figure was 231 and 109 (47 percent), for Scotland it was 117 and 94 (80 percent), and in Wales, there were 73 fortified places, of which 58 (79 percent) saw action.

235 towns, cities, and ports across England, Ireland, Scotland, and Wales, were fortified, a figure which represents 21 percent of the total number of fortresses. England contributed two-thirds of this with 157. 18 percent (42) of Irish fortresses were towns or ports, whilst in Scotland it was 14 percent (17), and 26 percent (19) in Wales[56]. Whilst demonstrating the importance of the urban-based garrison in England, it also shows that the nature of the fighting in Ireland, Scotland, and Wales was generally different from that in England. There are of course exceptions

Tantallon Castle has a key stronghold overlooking the main coast road towards Edinburgh from the east. As a result, it was besieged by an English Army under General Monck in 1651. This view from the castle walls clearly shows the ravelin constructed by its defenders. (David Flintham)

56 https://vauban.co.uk/civil-war-fortifications-register-(cwfr).

to every rule, but generally, sieges on towns were rare in Scotland, and Wales, and also in Ireland until the Cromwellian conquest in 1649–1653. The Royalist uprising in Scotland during 1644–1646, for example, witnessed several occasions where towns and cities were occupied (albeit temporarily) by the Royalists, but this was usually only after the respective Government forces had been defeated outside the town's walls.

During the sixteenth century, the focus shifted from internal security to coastal protection, resulting in a significant number of fortifications being built along the coast from Cornwall around to Suffolk (and beyond), whilst in Ireland, during the forty years following the Spanish Armada of 1588, some 16 artillery forts were constructed. But come the Civil Wars, the trend was temporarily reversed, with seven (out of ten) of the most heavily defended English counties being landlocked.

With several fortified ports along its two coastlines, Devon was the county with the most fortified towns and ports in England with 11. This represented a quarter of the county's total number of fortresses (42). Adding these to those in Cornwall and the Isles of Scilly (32), Dorset (21), and Somerset (16), gives the West Country a total number of Civil War fortresses of 111. This compares with the three Severn Valley counties (Gloucestershire, Shropshire, and Worcestershire) combining to give a total of 87, whilst Northeast England (Durham, Northumberland, and Yorkshire) had a total of 77. The Eastern Association (Cambridgeshire, Essex, Hertfordshire, Lincolnshire, Norfolk, and Suffolk) had a combined total of 81 fortresses, of which 63 were in Cambridgeshire and Lincolnshire.

Castles were the most dominant fortress type in Ireland, Scotland, and Wales. In England, their construction was predominately a rural phenomenon, although in the immediate post-Conquest period, most of the towns in England that had been centres of Anglo-Saxon regional administration had castles imposed upon them, numbering some 48 places across England by the early 12th century. By the end of the sixteenth century, England might have contained as many as 1,474 castles (this figure includes both urban and rural castles, mottes, ringworks, late-medieval tower houses, and Tudor artillery forts). But by the time of the Civil Wars, most castles had long outgrown their usefulness as defensive structures, and many were ruinous (and had already started to become quarries for the local neighbourhood). But the Civil Wars did not bring about the sudden end of the castle, and instead, the Civil Wars could be seen as the swansong of the castle, a time when this decay and decline was briefly paused, and many castles were pressed back into service, despite the fact that 'not all castles were fit for use at this time; indeed the majority had undoubtedly passed beyond that stage.'[57].

57 Oliver. H. Creighton, *Castles and Landscapes*, (London: Equinox Publishing Limited, 2005), pp. 52, 133–4; M.W. Thompson, *The Decline of the Castle*, (Cambridge: Cambridge

Cambridge was the headquarters of the Eastern Association, and its castle was incorporated into the city's fortifications in 1643. This view shows the remains of the motte, and the edge of the east bastion (to the left). (David Flintham)

Ruthin Castle in Clwyd was described by a local Parliamentarian commander as 'ruinous' (the Royalist garrison were occupied with repairs), whilst Lucy Hutchinson wrote of Nottingham Castle: 'the buildings are very ruinous and uninhabitable nether affording rooms to lodge soldiers or provisions'. Those that had retained a degree of architectural integrity might have walls that: 'are standing very strong without any decay, only the roofs and leads have been taken down'[58]. Other castles were transformed into domestic country houses with the result that their defensive capabilities were neglected. At the outbreak of the war, many castles, even those in a ruinous state, were re-occupied and garrisoned, such as Goodrich Castle in Herefordshire, and Restormel Castle in Cornwall, and later Haverfordwest in Pembrokeshire. In some instances, the internal fabric of the castle

University Press, 1987), pp. 138, 156–7.

58 *Calendar of State Papers, Domestic Services*, 29 October 1644; J. Sutherland (editor), *Memoirs of the Life of Colonel Hutchinson, by Lucy Hutchinson*, (Oxford: Oxford University Press, 1973), p. 83; A 1595 description of Pembroke Castle quoted in Peter Harrington, *English Civil War Archaeology*, (London: B.T. Batsford, 2004), p.°36.

The strength of Pembroke's medieval castle (and town walls) was demonstrated by its resistance to two Royalist sieges during the First Civil War, and was only captured by Cromwell after an eight-week siege during the Second Civil War. (David Flintham)

was repaired, strengthened, or improved: at Chepstow Castle, for instance, musket loops were cut into existing walls, and embrasures for cannon added. Musket-loops were cut into the walls at Raglan Castle, gun-platforms were constructed at Restormel, whilst an internal bastion-shaped earthwork was constructed at Corfe Castle to provide a view across the village below. But all sides took steps to refortify or reuse them, regardless of their state. There are many examples, including Cambridge (whose castle had been abandoned in the fifteenth century) where the Parliamentarian governor wrote in 1643: 'our town and castle are now very strongly fortified being encompassed with breast-works and bulwarks'[59].

In total, in England during the Civil Wars, some 116 rural and 26 urban castles were refortified. Of these, 79 rural and 17 urban castles were subject to attention by hostile forces. Elsewhere (and the figures for hostile attention are bracketed), in Ireland, the figures were 64 (26) rural and seven (five) urban castles, Scotland it was 68 (58) rural and one (one) urban castles, and finally in Wales it was 29 (23) urban and 10 (eight) rural castles. The oldest site to be transformed into a fortress during the Civil Wars was the neolithic henge site of Maumbury Ring's at Dorchester. Modified during the Romano-British period, during the Civil War, a gun platform was added

59 F.J. Varley, *Cambridge during the Civil War*, (Cambridge: Cambridge University Press, 1935 (Partizan Press reprint)) p. 104.

The Tower of St. Mary at the Walls church in Colchester was used as an observation post and probably a sniper position by the Royalists during the siege in 1648, and according to local legend is where the nursery rhyme Humpty Dumpty originates from (although the siege of Gloucester is a more likely origin for the rhyme). The stone-built tower was damaged during the siege and as can be seen here, was subsequently rebuilt in brick. (David Flintham)

to the southwest, and possibly to the southeast and northwest too[60].

By the end of the sixteenth century, those English counties with the most castles were Northumberland with 233, Yorkshire with 124, and Shropshire with 112. Only a small percentage of these were actually re-fortified during the Civil Wars: just eight in Northumbria, whilst the figures for Yorkshire and Shropshire were 16 and 14 respectively. The Irish counties with the most refortified castles were Tipperary (10), Cork (eight), and Antrim, Donegal, and Dublin with four each. In Scotland, both Aberdeenshire and Argyllshire had 13 refortified castles each, followed by Lothian with 11. Finally, in Wales, Pembrokeshire had seven, Monmouthshire had five, and Carmarthenshire, Denbighshire, and Flintshire with four each. The regional distribution of these castles seems to have more to do with their medieval origins than anything else: the borders between England and Scotland, and England and Wales for instance, and important coastlines as well generally had a more castles compared with other areas. The

60 <https://historicengland.org.uk/listing/the-list/list-entry/1003204?section=official-list-entry> (accessed 09/04/2023)

number of castles in Yorkshire can probably be explained by the geographical size of the county (although at the end of the Middle Ages, Yorkshire had one castle for every 48.9 square miles, compared with one castle for every 8.7 square miles in Northumberland, and one for every 12 square miles in Shropshire). Churches were also fortified: there was nothing new in this (during the twelfth century Anarchy, for example a number of churches became defensible strongpoints), and during the Civil Wars, 24 English churches were transformed into places of strength[61].

Of all the country houses besieged during the Civil Wars, probably none are better known than Basing House. This is a view of one of the gun platforms built by the Royalist defenders, and mounts a replica Saker. (David Flintham)

Like castles, country houses could be of considerable strategic importance, but as they tended to be owned by the leaders of the respective sides, they might be targeted simply because they belonged to a member of the opposition. Yet despite occupying properties built for peace rather than for war, many did try to defend their homes, and where the existing brick and stone walls seemed inadequate, reinforcing them with earthworks. Yet, as one study highlights, the very act of fortifying a country house would draw attention to it, and, as the Committee of Both Kingdoms remarked in November 1644: 'We are informed that the enemy is fortifying two houses near Salisbury, viz at Wilton and Goldbourne, which if they are perfected will be of great prejudice to those parts.'[62] Of the 662 English fortresses, 177 were fortified houses (and there are a further four houses listed in contemporary documents

61 Creighton, pp. 52, 121; <https://vauban.co.uk/civil-war-fortifications-register-(cwfr)>
62 Harrington, *Archaeology*, p. 60.

Ballachurry Fort, Isle of Man (also known as Kerrogarroo Fort, and Fort Loyal). Built on the orders of the Seventh Earl of Derby, this is one of the best-preserved sconces to be found anywhere across the British Isles, and covering an area of approximately 1.49ha, is probably larger than the more famous Queen's Sconce. With thanks to the Estate Manager, Bishopcourt Estate

which have yet to be identified[63]). The counties with the highest number of fortified houses were Gloucestershire (with 17), Oxfordshire (13), and Cheshire (12). These were amongst the most fought-over counties in England, and that each contained a city that was subject to particularly significant sieges is no coincidence. Fortified

63 *A perfect list of all the victories obtained by the Lord General Cromwel from the time that his excellency was made Captain General and Commander in Cheif of the Parliament forces in England, Ireland, and Scotland, (against Charles Stuart King of the Scots, and his forces in the three nations,) to this present time,* (London: Printed for Robert Ibbitson, 1651); *Englands remembrancer: in two parts. Or, A catalogue of all or most of the severall victories, and strong holds obtained (through Gods blessing) by the Parliaments forces since the armies rising from before Oxford in June last, 1645. to the generall thanksgiving, Octob. 2. 1645. As also since that time to this present thanksgiving of the Parliament, city of London, and parts adjacent. March 12. 1645. All within the time of 8 moneths. Published of purpose to draw forth Englands thankfulnesse, unto the Lord of Hoasts at all times, but more especially upon her dayes of thanksgiving,* (London: Printed for Tho. Underhill at the Bible in Woodstreet., March 11. 1645 [1646]).

manor houses were of far less significance elsewhere in the British Isles. Wales and Ireland had 10 fortified houses each, whilst Scotland had six.

In England there is another pattern to the spread of fortified houses since, generally speaking, those counties with a high number of fortified houses tended to have a lower number of castles: for instance, whilst Gloucestershire had 17 houses, only three of its castles were refortified. Oxfordshire had three refortified castles and 13 houses, whilst in Cheshire, it was 12 houses and two castles. Conversely, North Yorkshire had 12 castles, but just the one fortified house. This is probably evidence of a change in the rural landscape from the fifteenth century where landowners moved away from the defensible castle in favour of the more comfortable country house, a transition that had significant consequences during the Civil Wars. The glaring exception is Shropshire which not only came second in the list of refortified castles with 14, but was also fifth in the list of fortified houses with 10. The county's location, on the Welsh border, with Chester to the north, the Midlands to the east and with the River Severn passing through it made the county strategically important to both sides. Thus, it was a heavily contested country and whilst it avoided a major battle, it witnessed numerous smaller actions as both sides attempted to exercise control over the county from the garrison towns of Bridgenorth, Ludlow, Oswestry, Shrewsbury, and Wem[64], and with these towns came various satellite garrisons.

The CWFR has also looked at the multi-bastioned artillery-forts constructed during the Civil Wars, especially the (largely) square four-bastioned type known as the 'sconce'. To date the CWFR has identified 56 of these[65], which, whilst synonymous with the Civil Wars, are Dutch (or perhaps German) in origin. There was no standard size for the sconce, and here, as in most things, the Civil War military engineer reacted to conditions and available resources. As a result, their size varied considerably, from the smallest (Finnea, Westmeath, Ireland covering an area of approximately 0.12 ha) to the largest (Angel Fort, Islington, London, covering an area of approximately 1.87 ha). They could also vary in the same location; for instance, of the five sconces (so far investigated) built by the defenders of Newark, Sandhill's Sconce was the smallest (0.25 ha), whilst the Queen's Sconce, at 1.40 ha, was the largest. These findings have been published as part of The Town Well Fortified[66].

64 Jonathan Worton, *To settle the Crown: Waging Civil War in Shropshire, 1642–1648*, (Solihull: Helion and Company, 2016); Richard Israel, *'Cannon Played from the Great Fort': Sieges in the Severn Valley during the English Civil War, 1642–1646*, (Warwick: Helion and Company Limited, 2021), pp. 69–83, 98–114.

65 Defensive sconces only. There are a number more built by besieging armies, but these are currently outside the scope of the CWFR.

66 David Flintham, *The Town Well Fortified*, (Warwick: Helion and Company Limited, 2023).

These three projects are together revealing a fortified landscape previously only previously glimpsed through various town or country-based studies, or those looking at individual sieges. However, it is obvious that there is still much more investigation and study to be done. Fresh discoveries continue to be made in archives and libraries, whilst existing accounts are re-examined and can be re-considered in the light on new research. Specialist, and local histories continue to contribute to the national picture, and it is hoped that the CWFR will initiate new research into individual sites, and raise their profiles locally. The findings of all of these projects will continue to enhance and increase knowledge of this extremely significant aspect of the Civil Wars, and in so doing, raise the importance of the Civil War fortress amongst historians and public alike.

Civil War Fortifications Register (CWFR) - Some results

	England	Ireland	Scotland	Wales
Total number of fortified sites	652	231	116	71
Subject to Hostile Intervention (%age)	59%	47%	80%	79%
Town/port/village versus other types of fortress (%age)	26%	18%	14%	23%
Most common type of fortress (top three)	Country House / Farm (27%) Towns etc. (26%) [illegible]	Castles (31%) Forts (29%) Towns (18%)	Castles (31%) Towns (14%) Forts (8%)	Castles (55%) Towns (23%) Country House / Farm (10%)
Most heavily fortified county (top three)	Yorkshire (51 sites) Devon (37 sites) Gloucester (37 sites)	Cork (32 sites) Wexford (15 sites) Tipperary (14 sites)	Argyllshire (21 sites) Aberdeenshire (18 sites) Midlothian (10 sites)	Pembrokeshire (16 sites) Monmouthshire (11 sites) Flintshire (10 sites)

A sample of results from the Civil War Fortifications Register. For a more detailed analysis see the author's The Town Well Fortified (Warwick: Helion and Company Limited, 2023). (David Flintham)

Bibliography

Primary

Archives, Libraries and Museums
The National Archives
SP28/198 Part 2: (June 1643–December 1645).
SP28/223 Part 5 unfol.

British Library
Thomason Tracts, E572 (5), *The First Publique Lecture, Read at Sir Balthazar Gerbier His Accademy Concerning Military Architecture, or Fortifications, 1649.*

Guildhall Library (London)
Journals of the Court of Common Council, Journal 40, folio 52.

Other Collections
Calendar of State Papers
Domestic Series, Charles I.
Venetian Series.

Books
Papillon, David, *A practicall abstract of the Arts of Fortification and Assailing, etc* (London: 1645).
Sprigge, Joshua, *Anglia Rediviva. England's Recovery* (London: 1647), reprinted (London: Ken Trotman, 1984).
Stone, Nicholas, *Enchiridion of Fortification* (London: Richard Royston, 1645).
Sutherland, J. (ed.), *Memoirs of the Life of Colonel Hutchinson, by Lucy Hutchinson* (Oxford: Oxford University Press, 1973).
Ward, Robert, *Animadversions of warre; or a militarie magazine of the truest rules, and ablest instructions, for the managing of warre* (London: 1639).

Journals, Pamphlets etc. (bound and unbound)
A perfect list of all the victories obtained by the Lord General Cromwel from the time that his excellency was made Captain General and Commander in Cheif of the Parliament forces in England, Ireland, and Scotland (against Charles Stuart King of the Scots, and his forces in the three nations,) to this present time (London: Printed for Robert Ibbitson, 1651).
Englands remembrancer: in two parts. Or, A catalogue of all or most of the severall victories, and strong holds obtained (through Gods blessing) by the Parliaments forces since the armies rising from before Oxford in June last, 1645. to the generall thanksgiving, Octob. 2. 1645. As also since that time to this present thanksgiving of

the Parliament, city of London, and parts adjacent. March 12. 1645. All within the time of 8 moneths. Published of purpose to draw forth Englands thankfulnesse, unto the Lord of Hoasts at all times, but more especially upon her dayes of thanksgiving (London: Printed for Tho. Vnderhill at the Bible in Woodstreet., March 11. 1645 [1646]).

Lithgow, William, *The Present Surveigh At London* (1643).

Long, C.E. (ed), *Diary of the Marches of the Royal Army During the Great Civil War; Kept By Richard Symonds* (Cambridge: Cambridge University Press, 1997).

Maps, Plans and Drawings

Faithorne, William and Newcourt, Richard, *An exact delineation of the Cities of London and Westminster and the suburbs thereof, together wth ye Burrough of Southwark …*, surveyed in 1643–1647 and published in 1658.

Hollar, Wenceslas: P554, P652–657, P916–919, P984, P987, P1014, P1055.

De Witt, Frederik, 'the anonymous annotator's sketch lines on the map produced in 1666 showing the extent of damage in the Great Fire'.

Secondary

Books

Bubenik, Andrea, and Thackray, Anne (eds), *Perspectives on Wenceslaus Hollar* (London: Harvey Miller Publishers, 2016).

Bull, Stephen, The Furie of the Ordnance: Artillery in the English Civil Wars (Woodbridge: The Boydell Press, 2008).

Creighton, Oliver, and Higham, Robert, *Medieval Town Walls: An Archaeology and Social History of Urban Defence* (Stroud: Tempus Publishing Limited, 2005).

Creighton, Oliver. H., *Castles and Landscapes* (London: Equinox Publishing Limited, 2005).

Defoe, Daniel, *A Tour through the Whole Island of Great Britain* (London: Penguin Books, 1986).

Duckworth, Chloe, *The Great British Dig* (London: Bloomsbury Conway, 2022).

Duffy, Christopher, *Siege Warfare: The Fortress in the Early Modern World 1494–1660* (London: Routledge and Kegan Paul Limited, 1979).

Ede-Borrett, Stephen, and Flintham, David (eds), *'Batter their walls, gates and Forts': The Proceedings of the 2022 English Civil War Fortress Symposium* (Warwick: Helion and Company Limited, 2023).

Edwards, Peter, *Dealing in Death: The Arms Trade and the British Civil Wars, 1638–1652* (Stroud: Sutton Publishing Limited, 2000).

Everitt, Alan (ed), *Suffolk and the Great Rebellion, 1640–1660* (Ipswich: Suffolk Records Society, 1960), volume 3.

Flintham, David, *The Town Well Fortified* (Warwick: Helion and Company Limited, 2023).

Foard, Glenn, and Morris, Richard, *Archaeology of English Battlefields* (York: Council for British Archaeology, 2012).

Gaunt, Peter, *The Cromwellian Gazetteer* (Gloucester: Alan Sutton, 1987).

Harrington, Peter, *English Civil War Archaeology* (London: B.T. Batsford, 2004).

Harrington, Peter, *English Civil War Fortifications, 1642–1651* (Oxford: Osprey Publishing, 2003).

Jones, Serena (ed), *Home and Away – The British Experience of War, 1618–1721*, (Warwick: Helion and Company Limited, 2018).

Kenyon, John R., *Castles, Town Defences and Artillery Fortifications in the United Kingdom and Ireland, A Bibliography 1945–2006* (Donington: Shaun Tyas, 2008).

Kenyon, John, and Ohlmeyer, Jane (eds), *The Civil Wars: A Military History of England, Scotland, and Ireland, 1638–1660* (Oxford: Oxford University Press, 1998).

Maitland, William, *The History of London from its foundation by the Romans, to the present time* (London: Samuel Richardson, 1738).

O'Neil, Bryan H. St J., *Castles and Cannon* (Oxford: Clarendon Press, 1960).

Osborne, Mike, *Cromwellian Fortifications in Cambridgeshire* (Huntingdon: The Cromwell Museum, 1990).

Osborne, Mike, *Sieges and Fortifications of the Civil Wars in Britain* (Leigh-on-Sea: Partizan Press, 2004).

Pennington, Richard, *A Descriptive Catalogue of the Etched Work of Wenceslaus Hollar, 1607–1677* (Cambridge: Cambridge University Press, 2002).

Pepper, Simon, and Nicolas Adams, Nicolas, *Firearms and Fortifications: Military Architecture and Siege Warfare in Sixteenth Century Siena* (Chicago: The University of Chicago Press, 1986).

Pollak, Martha, *Cities at War in Early Modern Europe* (Cambridge: Cambridge University Press, 2010).

Porter, Stephen, *Destruction in the English Civil Wars* (Stroud: Alan Sutton Publishing Limited, 1994).

Saunders, Andrew, *Fortress Britain: Artillery Fortification in the British Isles and Ireland* (Liphook: Beaufort Publishing, 1989).

Thompson, M.W., *The Decline of the Castle* (Cambridge: Cambridge University Press, 1987).

Varley, Frederick John, *Cambridge during the Civil War* (Cambridge: Cambridge University Press, 1935 (Partizan Press reprint)).

Worton, Jonathan, *To Settle the Crown: Waging Civil War in Shropshire, 1642–48* (Solihull: Helion and Company, 2016).

Journals and Other Published Works

Flintham, David, 'King's Lynn Under Siege', *Current Archaeology*, issue 398, May 2023.

Flintham, David, 'Richard Clampe, Fortress Engineer, *c.* 1617–1696', *Fort* (Fortress Study Group, 2018), volume 46.

Harris, John, 'Karlovac: the Renaissance Ideal City in Central Europe', *Fort*, (Fortress Study Group, 2010), number 38.

Marsh, Simon, 'The Construction and Arming of London's Defences 1642–1645', *Journal of the Society for Army Historical Research* (2013), vol. 91.

Mills, Peter, 'The Civil War defences of East London reviewed: preliminary results', *London Archaeologist*, Winter 2021, Volume 16, Number 3.

Mills, Peter, 'The Civil War Defences of north London reviewed: Hoxton to Bloomsbury', *London Archaeologist*, Winter 2023, Volume 16, Number 11.

Ross, Lieut.-Colonel W.G., R. E., 'Military Engineering during the Great Civil War, 1642–1649', *Professional Papers of the Corps of Royal Engineers*, 1887, Volume XIII (Chatham: W. J. MacKay & Co., 1888).

Weinstein, Rosemary , 'Southampton House and the Civil War', in Joanna Bird, Hugh Chapman, and John Clark (eds), *Collectanea Londiniensia* (London and Middlesex Archaeological Society, Special Papers, 1978), vol. 2.

Reports (published and unpublished)

University of London, Law School, Sebastian Street, London EC1, Post-excavation assessment. (Site code SEN16) (Museum of London Archaeology, 2019).

Unpublished Works and Lectures

Leese, Richard Jeffrey, *Siege Archaeology of the English Civil Wars: Establishing a methodology to unlock the archaeology of attack and defence at early modern siege sites.* Doctoral thesis (Huddersfield: University of Huddersfield, 2020).

Maps, Plans and Drawings

Faden, William, *Plan of the Town of Lynn from Norfolk in six sheets* (1797).

Rocque, John, 'A Plan of the Cities of London and Westminster and the Borough of Southwark, (1747)', reproduced as *The A to Z of Georgian London*, (London: London Topographical Society, 1982).

Vertue, George, *Plan of the City of London as fortified by Order of Parliament in the years 1642 and 1643*, (1738), Amended by Cromwell Mortimer M.D. in 1746, Kings Topographical Collection, Vol. XX, No. 16.

Websites

https://biography.wales/

https://canmore.org.uk/

https://coflein.gov.uk/

https://excavations.ie/

https://historicengland.org.uk/

https://www.newscientist.com/article/2363164-relics-illuminate-the-wreck-of-hms-gloucester-a-17th-century-warship/_

https://vauban.co.uk/civil-war-fortifications-register-(cwfr)

https://www.vauban.co.uk/kings-lynn-under-siege

https://www.Wiki.bcw-project.org

3

Marmaduke Rawdon's Regiment of Foot

The Formation of The Regiment, from Colonel Rawdon's Commission to the arrival at Basing House

Andrew Robertshaw

Marmaduke Rawdon was a prominent London Merchant and Master of the Cloth Workers Company, a ship owner and wine trader. He served as a member of the Honourable Artillery Company from 1613 and by 1642 was Lieutenant Colonel in the Red Regiment London Trained Bands. He had almost certainly faced the army of King Charles at Turnham Green in November 1642 as a member of the Parliamentary forces defending London, commanded by the Earl of Essex. However, by the spring of the following year he had decided to use his wealth and influence to support the King. He left his country home in Hoddesdon, Hertfordshire, in early March 1643. The sixty-mile journey, avoiding such Parliamentarian garrisons as Aylesbury, would have taken at least three days to complete and he arrived in Oxford on the 12th or 13th. Rawdon presented himself to the King at Christ Church which had now become the Royal residence. The King may have been aware of Rawdon's plans and: 'knew him well & was very glad to see him & knowing him to be a popular man thought a great part of the Citizens (of London) wd follow him & indeed many honest citizens did come & serve under him'[1]. He received a commission to raise a regiment of foot two weeks later. In August of that year, he became the governor of the Royalist Garrison of Basing House and in early 1644 was then sent to garrison the town of Faringdon where he died in April 1646.

1 H. F. Killick, (ed.), *Memoirs of Sir Marmaduke Rawdon Kt*, p.319.

At the time of the outbreak of war, a full regiment of foot theoretically consisted of 1,200 rank and file, plus non-commissioned officers and officers, who were organised into ten companies. The Colonel's company was the largest consisting of 200 men, his Lieutenant Colonel had a company of 180, the Major had 120, and the captains each a company of 100 men. Royalist regiments rarely reached anything like full establishment and Rawdon's would be no exception. Each company was split into pikemen and musketeers and the proportion was, in theory, one pike to every two musketeers. This ratio was rarely achieved in any Royalist unit because of the expense of muskets compared to pike. Each company officer had a lieutenant, in the case of the Colonel's company he was styled Captain Lieutenant and had seniority over the other Lieutenants. As each company had a colour, there was also an Ensign who showed the position of the commanding officer and would usually be protected by the pike body. To convey orders each company had one or more drummers who were sometimes used as messengers. Within each company there would be one or more sergeants whose weapon, the halberd, was also their symbol of rank. Corporals and other non-commissioned officers carried either a pike or musket[2].

Having received his commission[3] Rawdon needed a number of competent officers for his regiment and these he sought amongst his acquaintances, London business associates and friends in the Honourable Artillery Company. A number of these individuals were, like Rawdon, officers in the London Trained Bands and others, including the Parliamentarians Denzil Holles and John Hampden, were satisfied to obtain the services of such 'trained' men.

It is likely, but not provable, that contact with these people was made before they all left London for Oxford in the winter and early spring of 1642–1643. It is also possible that they travelled together as a party with their own servants from Hoddesdon on 9 March 1643[4]. There is evidence that Thomas Johnson arrived in Oxford in January[5] and it would appear likely that Robert Amery joined the King earlier having fled London before the Battle of Edgehill in October 1642.[6]

It is possible to establish, with some certainty, the links between this group of Londoners. Some were members of the wine trade, others lived close to Rawdon in the parish of All Hallows, others were in the Honourable Artillery Company, and others were associated with Robert Peake and had connections with printing and artistic endeavour. The final connection is medicinal as two officers were

2 S. Reid, *All The King's Armies*, (1998), pp. 4–9.
3 Brit., Lib., Harl MSS 6804, f 50.
4 H.F. Killick, (ed.), *Memoirs of Sir Marmaduke Rawdon Kt*, p.319.
5 J. Foster, *Alumni Oxonienses, The Members of the University of Oxford, 1500-1714*, Vol. II, (1891), p.816.
6 *Calendar(s) of State Papers, Domestic Series*, Charles II 1660/61, Vol. XXV, p.439.

Apothecaries. Two members of the Vintners Company were captains in Rawdon's Regiment, Thomas Fletcher who lived in Seething Lane, in the same, All Hallows, parish, as Rawdon[7] and Robert Amery[8], who was also a member of the Honourable Artillery Company[9].

Another member of the Artillery Company who also joined the Regiment was Robert Peake[10], a print seller, who had a shop at the bottom of Snow Hill, near Holborn Conduit. Peake appears to have brought with him several of the most famous artists and engravers of the day, of whom one at least served in his company. These Civil War forerunners of the Artists Rifles included the painter William Dobson and the engraver William Faithorne who became his ensign, (both had been his apprentices) and Wenceslaus Hollar who may have been at Basing for a brief period.

It is quite possible that Inigo Jones, the King's surveyor, and designer of the Queen's masques, went with this group. He was amongst the prisoners when Basing House was stormed in 1645 but is not mentioned in any other source[11]. A famous man from the same parish was Thomas Johnson the herbalist. He had his physic garden at Snow Hill[12] and was a member of the Trained Bands[13], which may account for his acquaintance with both Peake and Rawdon. It is likely that William Rosewell who later became Lieutenant Colonel joined the regiment as a friend of Johnson, for he was also an apothecary living in the Old Bailey[14].

From the same area also came Thomas Langley of Paternoster Row[15] and an ensign, known simply as Mr Lucas who was a 'silk dyer in the Old Bailey'[16]. Two other men both from the same family provide a link between many of the others and indicate that many of the officers knew each other well before leaving for Oxford. Isaack Rowlett, a scrivener lived next door to The George at Holborn[17] and a member of the Honourable Artillery Company[18], who later became a captain in the Regiment along with his brother. He is known simply as Lieutenant

7 Vintners' Company's Court Minute Book, 1629-38.
8 Vintners' Company's Court Minute Book, 1629-38, p.23.
9 G.A. Raikes, (ed.), *The Ancient Vellum Book of the Honourable Artillery Company* (1890), p.31.
10 G. A. Raikes, (ed.), *The Ancient Vellum Book* (1890), p.100.
11 M. Edmond, *Limners and Picturemakers*, Walpole Soc, Vol. XLVII, p.131.
12 *Dictionary of National Biography.*
13 G. A. Raikes, (ed.), *The Ancient Vellum Book* (1890) p.16.
14 CCC, p.1507.
15 T. Dale, (ed.), *The Inhabitants of London in 1638*, p.122
16 B.L., Thomason Tracts, 'A great Victory obtained by Col Norton ... against Col Roydon', E50 (13).
17 Ibid.
18 G. A. Raikes, (ed.), *The Ancient Vellum Book of the Honourable Artillery Company* (1860), p.56.

Rowlett[19]. Another member of the family Abraham Rowlett, who was probably their father, lived in Water Lane just a few yards from Rawdon's house.[20] A fourth Rowlett, Thomas, sold Faithorne's prints of Dobson's paintings at his 'shopp neere Temple-Barre'[21].

The number of Londoner officers in the Regiment made the unit a curiosity, especially to the Royalists. After the first major action in November when the Marquess of Winchesters regiment was still in embryonic form the Oxford newsletter *Mercurius Aulicus* reported of Waller's assault 'he came on confidently but was so bravely welcomed by the noble Marquesse and the *London* Regiment, who plyed the Rebels thicke with shot of all sorts ....'[22]

If the bulk of the Regiment's officers were from London it would appear that the rank and file were a mixture of men who arrived with Rawdon and his fellow officers. Preserved among the papers of Sir Edward Walker (Charles's Secretary at War) there is the draft of a letter: 'To the High Sheriffe of our Co. [County] of Oxford' which commands him to summon: 'about 300 able men, unmarried fitt and willing to do this service to be ready on Thursday next at ten of the clock at our city of Oxford to enter themselves to the list of that Regiment under ye command of Col. Rawdon who will be ready to entertain them arm them and discipline them'[23]. As the letter is only a draft and undated it is not possible to be certain of the Thursday in question, but Rawdon who was present in Oxford between March and September collected 25 pikes, six halberds and three skeynes of match form the New College magazine on Friday 21 April 1643 a month after he received his commission[24]. It is possible that these weapons were intended to equip the first group of recruits who had arrived on the previous day. If so the halberds would have been to arm the newly appointed Sergeants of whom there were, in theory, two per company.

There is no mention of muskets at this time. Rawdon may have supplied his musketeers with their weapons from his own sources as none are issued from the Oxford magazine. The proof that muskets were available is the issue of 10 pounds of powder and slow match on the same day.[25]

It would appear from the historical evidence that Rawdon had been planning to raise this regiment before he left London and it is possible to see what he planned from his actions before January 1643. A very wealthy man by the standards of

19 B.L., Thomason Tracts, '*A great Victory obtained by Col Norton* ..., E50 (13)
20 T. C. Dale, *The inhabitants of London in 1638*, Vol I (1931) Soc of Genealogists, p.5a.
21 M. Edmond, *Limners and Picturemakers*, Walpole Soc, Vol. XLVII, p.131.
22 *Mercurius Aulicus*, Nov 1643, Week 45, p.641.
23 Brit. Lib., Harl Ms. 6804, f. 50.
24 The National Archive WO55/457 027831.
25 The National Archive WO55/457 027831.

the period, Rawdon was faced with the problem of getting his money out of the City and at the same time acquiring as much military equipment as possible. Some of this equipment must have been in his own armoury, every gentleman interested in warlike matters had one, yet more arms could be obtained from the Clothworkers Company's own armoury. On 1 September 1642 by order of Parliament, the Clothworkers Company sent sufficient arms for twenty pikemen and forty musketeers to the Guildhall.[26] This represented only part of the stores held by the Company and was obviously to be used against the King. As Master of the Company Rawdon was in a good position to divert these weapons to his own use, a position that improved in early September when Rawdon persuaded the Clothworkers Company to appoint his son-in-law, Lieutenant Colonel Edmund Foster, as Deputy Master: 'for as much as his occasions might call him out of town'. Shortly before Rawdon was elected Master, he had taken the lease of the two great vaults at the Clothworkers hall.

In 1640 he had removed his wine from the same cellars at the hall because he refused to pay for the repairing of the pavement of the yard, which was occasioned by the rolling of: 'hogs heads, pipes or butts of wine upon the said pavement to or from the said cellar'. A month after the Battle of Edgehill, Rawdon was instructed to clear the cellars under the parlour and: '... his lease for the great cellars was sealed'[27]. Whatever was removed from the cellars in November 1642 would have been taken by cart from Mincing Lane to Rawdon's warehouse on Thames bank, a route that would have passed his house in Water Lane. This would have provided an opportunity to remove any military equipment or money Rawdon required. Once in the warehouse it could have been loaded into barges and sent upriver via Reading, to await his arrival at Oxford. It is difficult to explain how Rawdon was able to supply his Regiment with so much of its equipment without recourse to the magazine at Oxford unless something of this nature did take place. Evidence for this is the number of muskets received into the magazine from Rawdon's officers to be 'repaired' or 'fixed', that is, 'assembled'. These muskets had not been issued by the magazine and can only have been brought from London or purchased locally. It was normal practice in the seventeenth century for musketeers to learn their initial drill by simply priming and 'flashing the pan' not loading with ball; this would explain why shot is not issued until 4 June, six weeks later.[28]

An unusual factor about this first issue from the New College magazine is that Rawdon contracted with the Office of Ordnance to return the arms or pay for them

26 Court Records of the Clothworkers Company.
27 Court Records of the Clothworkers Company.
28 Brit. Lib., WO 55.458, PT 65, f. 28.

personally, the first occasion on which such an indenture was used.[29] Certainly because he was expected to pay for the equipment, rather than receive it as an issue, Rawdon was able to be unusually specific about which items of weaponry and equipment that he felt his regiment required. On 26 May 1643 he received sixty brown bills There was no shortage of pikes in the Royalist army at this time, indeed an inventory of the magazine at Oxford taken on 8 May records that a total of 1,386 'longe pikes' were in store on that date.[30] It does however seem to have been normal practice to issue bills to regiments in garrison or involved in siege work. 600 bills were sent to the army at Culham camp prior to the storming of Bristol and the siege of Gloucester.[31] These eight-foot-long axe-headed weapons were of more practical use in the confined spaces of a parapet or trench than were pikes of sixteen or eighteen feet in length. Thus, it is quite possible that the regiment was raised it was intended for garrison rather than field services. This is reinforced by the wording of the letter to the Sheriff of Oxford calling for recruits 'for the defence of our city and county of Oxford to have in rediness a regiment of this county only for that purpose'[32].

The musket rests are more unusual, as their use had generally declined during the period leading up to the Civil War. It is possible that the muskets he had obtained were old fashioned and therefore required the use of a rest. The issue of forty musket rests suggests that the regiment was using older and heavier muskets. Stephen Ede-Borrett has indicated that other units received rests in 1642 and 1643 but this practice ended by 1644. This suggests that muskets were then made to the newer 'lighter' pattern or even 'remade'.

Initially, the regiment consisted of three companies; later increased to five. It is possible to trace their formation of through the issues from the magazine and commissions received by the company commanders. The first, formed on 21 April, would appear to be the Colonel's company and that of Lieutenant Colonel Peake. The six halberds issued on that day would be sufficient to provide three companies with two sergeants each.[33] Peake's company was certainly complete by early June and a warrant issued on the 5th of that month states that Peake had 'raised mustered and Armed' his company and that 'his Ensign and all other inferior officers and soldiers' were to receive seven days' pay.[34] Presumably, the other companies were also paid at the same time, but it is significant that in the light of Peake's later role that his company had assumed a quite separate identity as early as this. According

29 I. Roy, *The Royalist Ordnance Papers*, Pt. 2, Oxon Record Society, (1975), p.475.
30 *Royalist Ordnance Papers*, Ed. I. Roy, p.227.
31 ibid., p.240.
32 Brit. Lib., Harl Ms. 6804, f. 50.
33 The National Archive, WO55/457 027831.
34 Brit. Lib., Harl MS 6852, f. 77.

to another warrant issued by the King on the same day each 'private soldier' in the Royal foot was to receive 'Three Shillings a peece' each week and victualls 'to the value of Twelve pence a man in Bread and Cheese'[35], we can assume that Rawdon's Regiment was also paid at this rate but perhaps from his own rather than the King's pocket. The next company raised was that of Thomas Johnson, who would later become the Regiment's Major but who was referred to as Captain when he is first mentioned on 27 April[36]. We can assume that Rawdon's Regiment was also paid at this rate, but perhaps from his own rather than the King's pocket. Another officer who drew equipment for use by the Regiment was Captain Thomas Langley, who is first referred to on 4 June and who must therefore have been commissioned about this time.[37] One officer whose commission does exist is Captain William Rosewell[38], who received his commission on 16 July. This date is perhaps not coincidental, for on the previous day, 15 July 1643: 'all the common soldiers then at Oxford were new apparelled, some all in red, coates, breeches and mounteroes; and some all in blew'[39]. Rawdon's men undoubtedly received their first issue of uniform about this date; until then the Oxfordshire labourers who formed the Regiment's 'rank and file' would have worn their normal working clothes. There is no contemporary reference to the colour of the coats worn by the Regiment, but it is reasonable to assume that they were red. Rawdon had served in the Red Regiment of the London Trained Bands and red formed a significant part of Rawdon's coat of arms, from which a Colonel would often select the coat colour of his regiment.

Of course, Rawdon only had the choice between red or 'blew' when uniforms were issued to the Oxford Foot. Heraldic precedent and his experience must have made this a simple task. The four or five thousand coats that were issued were of a uniform pattern, cut out in the School of Music and made up by tailors within ten miles of Oxford.[40]

The Regiment was now virtually ready for service although some of its new members would still need time to learn their drill, while others had been training for more than two months. The final company to be formed was that of Robert Amery, which received its first equipment on 26 July. Like Rawdon's own company, among the first items issued were halberds[41], in this case only two, for each of the sergeants. The company seems to have been completed in mid-August

35 Brit. Lib., Harl MS 2752, f 216).
36 Brit. Lib., WO 55.457.62.
37 Brit. Lib., WO 55.458, PT 65, f 28.
38 Brit. Lib., SP 16/497 110.
39 A. Clarke, (ed,), *Anthony Wood- The Life and Times,* (1891), Oxon Hist. Soc. p.102.
40 A. Clarke, (ed,), *Anthony Wood- The Life and Times,* (1891), Oxon Hist. Soc. p.102.
41 The National Archive., WO 55, 1661, Pt 1, f. 236.

immediately prior to the Regiment leaving for Basing[42]. However, one nameless officer of the regiment was drawing bandoliers and swords for the Regiment on the 18th of September.[43]

It is possible to calculate the strength of the Regiment at this time from the issues of equipment made to it and various contemporary documents relating to its raising and early service. In April and May the Regiment received 120 pikes and sufficient bandoliers or powder bags were issued for 132 musketeers, although records exist for just 31 muskets.

It would therefore seem that the maximum number of the rank and file members of the Regiment at this time was 260 men, plus sergeants and officers a little below that called for in the King's letter to the Sheriff of Oxford. This figure is supported by an account of the events at Basing House when the regiment was present, which records that Rawdon's Regiment arrived at the house in two parties, one of 100 and the other of 200 men, although the writer doubtless discounted the officers in his calculations.

One officer of the Regiment who first appears on 26th July is Captain 'Hen' or 'Henn'. (His role is unclear as although he is giving muskets to the New College magazine to be 'fixed', he does not appear in the later succession of company commanders in the Regiment. He is however referred to as 'Capt. Henry Henn' Rawdon's 'Captain Lieutenant' in his troop of horse[44].

On 27 April 1643, the Royalist Garrison of Reading surrendered to the army of the Earl of Essex. This surrender meant that a number of houses in the region which had previously felt themselves secure from the advance of Parliament's forces realised they were now exposed and under-defended. The most important of these was Basing House, situated on the road from London to the West Country. The owner was John Paulet, the fifth Marquess of Winchester, a Roman Catholic who had initially elected to stay and manage his estates in peace rather than join the King at Oxford. Well before the siege of Reading the Marquess had recognised that his house could be attacked and wrote to the King at Oxford:[45]

> Most gratious Sovvereigne
>
> Since by Commande your maties forces at Basingstoke are drawing of, and ye enemy now lying wthin lesse then ten miles of this place, I concsance this Castle to be in apparent danger and cannot be long kept

42 The National Archive., WO 55, 1661, PT I, f 124.
43 B. L., *Description of the Siege of Basing Castle*, TT Vol. 191, (E27), No.5, p.174.
44 WO55, PT1, f 116.
45 Brit. Lib., *Description of the Siege of Basing Castle*, TT Vol. 191, (E27), No, 5., p.174.

> without some assistance from your maties army, for from this country no reliefe is to be expected it standing for want of your presence and some authority to commande it devided in itself. If this house be anawayse considerable for your maties service and advantage, be pleased to take it into your consideration and protection lest Ibe necessitated to leave it to the will of the enemy I refer more particulars to the relation of this bearer in case your maties will vouch safe to speak with him
>
> My duty and affection to your maties service occasssions this addresse from
>
> Basing this 2 of Dec:bre 1642 — Your Maties most faithful and Loyal Subject
>
> (Signed by the Marquess of) Winchester

Neither troops nor aid were forthcoming and he was forced to take responsibility for the defence of the House; 'with his Gentlemen Armed with six Musquets (the whole remainder of a well-furnished Armory) he did so well that twice the enemies attempts proved in vain'[46]. Luckily the 'attempts' by the Marquess's enemies amounted to little more than raids by the local Parliamentarians, for he would have stood little chance of holding the house in the face of a determined assault. Such an attack by part of Parliament's field army now became more probable and the Marquess appealed for assistance again, travelling to Oxford to see the King personally.

This time help was granted; Charles and his advisors must have realised the strategic position of Basing House and determined to garrison it. Whether Rawdon's Regiment had already been selected for garrison work or not, and almost certainly it was not raised 'for' Basing. When the decision was made at Oxford to garrison the house, with the bulk of the field army now involved in the campaign to take Bristol, Rawdon's was one of the few units available for such a task. Even when the decision was made time was running short for Basing House and it was decided to send, by forced march, an initial force of one hundred musketeers under the command of Lieutenant Colonel Robert Peake to garrison it until the remainder of the regiment could arrive. It is not possible to be certain of the precise date of this event; the Marquess's *Siege Diary* states that the musketeers arrived on Monday 31 July 1643.[47] On 27 July Captain Thomas Langley had received one

46 Brit. Lib., *Description of the Siege of Basing Castle*, TT Vol. 191, (E27), No, 5., p.174.
47 Brit. Lib., *Description of the Siege of Basing Castle*, TT Vol. 191, (E27), No, 5., p.174.

hundredweight of powder, shot and match, twice the usual rate of half a pound of powder per musketeer and therefore the sort of amount that would be issued to 100 musketeers.[48] Thus equipped and supplied, the one hundred musketeers set out with Peake in command and Langley as the second in command. Marching with 'speed and secrecy' the force arrived just a few hours before Colonel Norton from Portsmouth supported by horse and/or dragoons from London under the command of Colonel Harvey, attempted a surprise attack on what they believed to be a weakly defended house. However, instead of meeting limited resistance from the Marquess's gentlemen, they had to face the fire of Peake's musketeers.

Lacking the force necessary to overcome this surprising opposition the Parliamentarian commanders withdrew their forces to Farnham that night and sent a message to London informing Parliament of a new, and dangerous, royalist garrison in Hampshire.[49]

In Oxford, Rawdon continued to prepare the remainder of the Regiment for the march to Basing and there was a steady build-up of arms and munitions in order to establish a magazine at the house. On 1 August, Sergeant Major Thomas Johnson received from the magazine at New College 75 'Powder Baggs with girdles and hangers for Musketeers' and 25 bandoliers, sufficient items of powder carrying equipment for the one hundred musketeers.[50] The same number of men who had arrived at Basing House the previous day. On 2 August Rawdon received three hundredweight of powder and match, specifically for 'the defence of the Lord Marquis of Winchester his house at Basing'.[51] Henry Percy, the General of Artillery, appointed a conductor, a member of the train of artillery responsible for the transport of munitions, to accompany the three barrels of powder and to establish the magazine.[52] At the end of the month, just before the Regiment left Oxford, three light cannon were assigned for the defence of Basing House. These cannon, two brass six pounders and a three poundor, had formed part of the Queen's train when she arrived in Oxford from Bridlington with the arms and equipment she had purchased in the Netherlands.

That the Marquess was a Roman Catholic was well known and may well have influenced Henrietta Maria's decision to send these guns for the defence of Basing House, called by its enemies; 'a nest of popery'. With the guns were sent three gunners, John Lasby, John Gilbert and James Brown, who each received a pole-axe for their defence, while the 20 matrosses, assistants to the gunners, each had a brown-bill. It would seem that these guns formed part of Rawdon's small force

48 The National Archive, WO 55, 458, Pt 66, f. 19.
49 British Library Thomason Tracts Vol 191 E 27 (5).
50 The National Archive, WO 55, 458, Pt 66, f. 19.
51 *Royalist Ordnance Papers*, Ed. I. Roy, p.277.
52 The National Archive, WO 55, 458, Pt 65, f. 49.

for its march to Basing because on the original warrant from Henry Percy for the dispatch of the guns, Major Thomas Johnson's name is noted along with his lodgings. He would appear to have been quartered on 'Mrs Davis, Bookseller Behinde Alhallowes'[53]. As the Regiment's most senior officer other than Rawdon remaining in Oxford much of the administrative and organisational work must have fallen to him and the officers of the ordnance would have needed to contact Johnson in his quarters.

A few days later the remaining 160 members of Rawdon's Regiment, mainly pikemen but with a few musketeers from Rosewell's recently raised company, left Oxford. The breakdown of this force was 120 pikemen, eight or ten sergeants with halberds and the remainder, 30 or so musketeers. With them went a small train of artillery pieces, a single cart containing the powder and shot, at least four pack horses and whatever horses and carts the Regiment's officers had managed to provide for themselves. If this is the case then the Regiment was at this time least 260 strong until Rawdon arrived at Basing House to find that Lieutenant Colonel Peake had left the Regiment with '50 armed men'[54].

The Regiment's last duty before it left Oxford was to stand guard on the city's defences, a duty it undertook on 13 August 1643. As was normal practice, the City's Governor, Colonel Sir William Pennyman, appointed an officer to receive the ammunition for the task. Captain Rosewell, the most junior company commander in the regiment, was appointed for the task. This event marks the date on which the Regiment as a whole undertook active service for the first time, although the musketeers had already seen service at Basing.

53 *Royalist Ordnance Papers*, Ed. I. Roy, p.277.
54 Hampshire Record Office, 40M93/1.

Documents

I

(To the High Sheriffe of our County of Oxford)

Trusty and well beloved we greet you,
Whereas we lately commanded out of the Inhabitants within this our county there should be summoned to appear before us at our Citty of Oxford all such of able body as were fit for our service in our present Army our purpose then being to make choyce of such a number as were necessary for ye defence of our Citty and County of Oxford whilst we were removed from thence in our own person and then finding that we were otherwise well supplied from other parts and so might spare them for the present we dismissed those who appeared to their owne homes againe and forbare to send for others who appeared not. But we do now find that we do want about 300 able men to compleat a regiment for our service that we have need for the defence of our Citty and County of Oxford to have in rediness a regiment of the inhabitants of this county only to that purpose we do hereby will and require you to warne out of the several parishes within this our county 300 able men unmarryed, fitt and willing to do this service to be ready on Thursday next at tenne of the clock at our City of Oxford to enter themselves to the list of that Regiment under ye command of Colonell Rawdon who will be there ready to entertain ym, arme them and discipline them. And as We shall thank them for their rediness to do ts service so We are assured that they will have cause to thank us for our particular care of their well usage and the whole County will have cause to thank us for our general care of them and the protection of their wifes children and Estates in these times of danger. And we also require you to return the names of a thousand others of the inhabitants who shall at that time and place shew themselve with arms and weapons to be a guard for the said city and county and such as shall want fitt weapons we shall take car to furnish them with such as shall be necessary. And because the choice of thes men of either sort may be with the more indifferency we desire and advise you that you will so dispose your warrants which shall be sent out to yt purpose, that every part of the County may afford some able bodyes thereat the rest may better attend their husbandry and trades and others their private affairs
Given [April 1643?]

Harl MSS 6804, f. 50

II

21th Apll: 1643

Oxon. Receaved out of his Maties: stores for the prsent vse of my Regiment accordinge to his Mats: Commission to mee directed bearing date ye 13th: day of this instant Aprill. And hereby signifyed by Sir John Heydon Knt: Leivetennt: genrall of Thordinance, for ye same (Wch: I doe hereby ablidge myselfe toretourne in specie or to pay for the same according to ye vsuall rates given by his Matie: Vizt

Longe Pikes Headed.................................11)
more Longe Pikes Headed ....14) 25
Halberts.. 6
Powder..10 ll
Match.. 3 skeynes

Marmaduke Rawdon

27 Apll: 1643

Delivered to Thomas Johnson Captaine for the vse of Collonell Rawdons Regimt:

Long Pikes..............................12
Bandeleers..............................12

19 Maij 1643

Delivered to Thomas Johnson Captaine for ye vse of Coll Rawdons Regimt.

Long Pikes..............................83
Match.................................. 3 skeynes

Thomas Johnsonne
26 Maij 1643.

Receaved out of his Mats: stores ffor the vse of my Regimt:

Browne Bills................................60
Rests for Musketts......................40

M: Rowdon

WO 55.457.62
Royalist Ordnance Papers pp. 217–218

III

Col Rawdon According to a warrant to me directed from the

> Lord Generall. These are to will and require you that you forthwith issue out of his mats: magazine fifty pound of Powder wth match and Ball proportionable. And the samne to delever to this bearer Captaine Langley for the prsent supplying of the Regiment of Foote of Colonell Roydon. And for yor soe doing this shall be yor warrant. Court att Oxford the 4th. of June 1643.

Hen. Percy

To Sir John Heydon Kt:

Oxon 4° die 1643

Received out of his mats. stores according as is required by this warrant

Powder..50 lb
Match..50 lb
Muskett Shott...............................50 lb

Tho: Langley.

WO 55.458, Pt 65, f. 28

IV

5th June 1643

Whereas Robert Peake Lieutant Colonell of the Regiment of Colonell Marmaduke Rawdon hath raysd mustered and Armed one Company of foot in that Regiment Our will and pleasure is that you pay unto him seaven days pay for his Lt: Ensign and all other inferior officers and soldiers of his Company being this day of his Muster Roll and this our Warrant together with acqutance for the same shall be your sufficent discharge given this 5th June 1643

To Mathew Bradley Esq Payst:
General of Or Army

Harl MS 6852, f. 77

V

6 Junij 1643

Of Coll: Retou'ned fro Wm. Stannight &c.
Rawden Muskett fixt, & reped...................14
WO 55, 1661 [5]

R.O.P. p. 102

VI

8o Julij 1643

Col	Received into his Mats: stores
Rawdon	from Colonell Rawdon to be fixed
	Musketts...2

WO 55, 1661, Pt I, f. 107
R.O.P. p.105

VI

13th July 1643

Received into his Mats stores from Colonell Rawdon to be fixed

Musketts......................5
Barrells........................2
Locks...........................2

WO 55, 1661, Pt I, f. 110

VII

16th July 1643

Charles R
Charles by ye Grace of God King of Great Britain, France & Ireland, Defender of ye Faith etc. To our Trusty & Well beloved William Rosewell, Greeting.
We doe hereby constitute & appoint you to be Captaine of one Company of foot under ye Regiment of Our Trusty and Well beloved Collonel Marmaduke Rawden, wich Company by Vertue of this Our Commission you are fortwith to impress & retayne of such as are willgly & voluntarily serve Us for Our Pay, & for defence of Our Royal Person, ye two Houses of Parliament, ye Protestant Religion, ye Law of ye Liberty & Property of ye subject & Priviledges of Parliament, to bring these to Our Royal standard, and to cause these to be duly exercised in Armes Commanding all inferiuor Officers & Soldiers of your said Company you to obey as their Captaine according to this Our Commission hereby given unto you. And you yourself also to observe & follow such Order and Direction as from time to time you shall receive from Ourselfe, Our General of Horse, Our Lieutenant General, your Collonel or others your Superiour Officers accding to occasion & ye disciple of Warre. And in all things to governe yourselfe as unto your duty & Place of Captaine of a Company of foot doth of right apperteyne & belong.
Given under Our Signe Mannual at Oxford this 16 July 1643. in ye 19th yeare of Our Reigne

SP 16/497 110

VII

19th July 1643

Col Rawdon dd out of his Mats Stores for the use of Colonell Rawdon his Regmet of Foote beinge formerely broughte in to be repaired

Muskettes....................11

WO 55, 1661, Pt I, f. 231

VIII

24th July 1643

Sr John Heydon

Colonell These are to advise you to cause deliver to this Rawdon bearer one of Colonell Roydon's Captaines 25ll of Powder wiht Match and bullet proporcionable for the use of there Regmt for which doinge this shalbe yor warrant dated at Oxford this 24th of July 1643

fforth
ffor Sr John Heydon

By vertue of this Order from my Lord Generall you are to deliver for the Regmit of Colonell Roydon the Powder, Match, and Shott, thereby appointed

Jo: Heydon

To the officers & clerkes
of his Mats Stores at Newe College

26th of July 1643

Received out his Mats Stores for the use of Colonell
Rawdon his Regimt of ffoote

Powder........................75 ll)
Match..........................75 ll) weight
Muskett Shott.............75 ll)

Thomas Langley Capt:

WO 55, 458, Pt 66, f. 17

IX

26o July 1643

Col Rawdon

Received from Captain Hen of
Col Rawdon's Regimt

Musketts............7

WO 55, Pt I, f. 116

X

26o July 1643 dd out of his Mats Stores to Captaine Emore of Colonell Roydons Regimt
Col Rawdon

Halbertes...........2

WO 55, 1661, Pt I, f. 236

XI

27 July 1643

Received out of his Mats stores for the vse of Collonell Rawdon his Regimt of ffoote

Powder.............................1 cwt)
Match...............................1 cwt) weight
Muskett Shott.................1 cwt)

Thomas Langley

WO 55, 458, Pt 66, f. 19

XII

27° July

dd out of his Mats Stores to Capt Emerye
Col: Rawdon for the use of Colonell Rawdons Regimt

drumbe.............1 broken

WO 55, 1661, Pt I, f. 237

XII

28° July dd out of his Mats Stores to Capt Henn of
Col Rawdon Colonell Rawdons Regimt beinge formerly brought into the said stores to be fixed

Muskets......................7

Col Rawdon dd out of his Mats Stores to Capt Emory of Col Rawdons regiment for which he prom- isseth to gett A warrante.

Swordes......................2

WO 55, 1661, Pt I, f. 237

XIII

The first day of August 1643
Received out of his Mats Magazine by virture of
his warrant for the vse of the Regiment of ffoote
of Colonel Rawden

Powder Baggs wth girdles } and hangers for Musketteers }	75
Badndoleers	25

By me Thomas Johnson

WO 55, 458, Pt 65, f. 49

XIV

2nd August 1643

According to a warrt: from ye: Lord Generall to me directed you are forthwith to issue out of his Mats: Magazine three barrells of powder with match proporconable, And ye same to deliver to this bearor Collonell Roydon, [and] with which you are to appoint one Conductor to bee sent hither with ye: said three barrells of powder where ye said Collonells directs And for your soe doing this shallbe your warrt: Oxford ye 2: of August 1643

To Sr: John Heydon knt: Lieutent:
Generall of ye: Ordnance And to ye
Officers of ye: same H Percy

WO 55, 459, Pt II, f. 371

XV

Oxford The second day of August 1643

Received out of his Mats: stores upon this warrant (it being for the defence of the Lord Marquis of Winchester his house at Basinge)

Powder..............3 barrels being 3cwt
Match...............3c weight

Marmaduke Rawdon

WO 55, 459, Pt II, f. 370

XVI

You are forthwith to issue out of his Mats Magazine One barrill of powder with match and ball propoconable And ye same to deliver to such as Sr William Penyman Knt shall appont to receaue ye same

Oxford the 13th of August 1643

To Sr John Heydon Knt Linttet Genall of the ordnance and to ye officers of ye same

H Percy

I doe dipute & authorise this Gentleman Capt Rosewell to recieue the proertion oboue mentioned

W Pennyman

WO 55, 459, Pt II, f. 395

XVII

Oxford The xiiith day of August 1643

Received out of his Mats Magazine by virtue of the warrant within written

Powder........................1 cwt

Match.........................1 cwt

Muskett shott.................1 cwt

By Mee W Rosewell

WO 55, 458, Pt 65, f. 54

XVIII

14th of August 1643

Col Rawdon Received from Capt Emery of Col Rawdon's Regiment to be repaired

Musketts............7 (inde 4 barrells)

WO 55, 1661, Pt I, f. 124

XIX

ffor Baseinge You are to issue out of his Mast Magazine 3 drakes to be sente to Baseinge with 30 rownd and powder proportionable with such gunners and officers as shall be necessary Where of you may not faile as you will answer the contrary Given at the campe the 22th August 1643

H Percy

To Sr John Heydon knt.

The Kinge hath sent A command to the Comissioners to delivre all the powder
and Match they have by them.

Oxon A Proporcon of Powder Match Shott &c to attend 3 Peece of Brass. Ordnance assigned for Bazing by warrt: from the right honble Henry Lord Percy dated the 22th of August 1643. vizt

Brass ordnnce wth	(6lb Peeces	2	ye Queens
their equipage vitz	(3lb Peeces	1	
Round shott of iron	(6lb Peeces	50	
for	(3lb Peeces	25	
Cases of tyne filled	(6lb Peeces	10	
with muskett shott for.	(3lb Peeces	5	
Powder	2 barrells		
Match	3c.dj one Carte		
Budge	barrells one) 1	5	
Browne Bills	20)		

Gonners.............3

John Lasby	each gonner
John Gilbert	had a poleaxe
James Browne	

I doe acknnowledge yt I have received ye proporcon of powder, match, shotte &c above mentioned this 25th August 1643

Winchester

W.O.55.459, ff. 410-11, 415
R.O.P. p.277

XX

26o August 1643

Baseinge: You are to take charge of the 3 drakes with 50 pound of powder shott and Match proporconable and havinge made delivery thereof to the Lord Marquesse of Winchester at Baseinge you are to defire and bringe with you the acknowledgmt of his Lopps receipte thereof as well for yor owne as for the discharge of his Mats Magazine

Jo: Heydon

To John Ball principall conductor of the Matrozes &c belonginge to his Mats Trainie of Artillerie

For all this above mencioned
this 26th day of August 1643

Winchester

WO 55, 458, ff. 31-32 - also Hants Record Office 11M49/F/02

[Noted on reverse of original warrant]
Mrs Davis Bookseller behinde Allhallowshu

Sergt Maior Johnson

WO 55, 459, f. 114

XXI

18 Septem

dd out of his Mats stores for the vse of Colonell Rawdon Regimt of foote

Bandelears....................20
swords........................ 2

Bibliography

Black, W.H., (ed.), Docquets of Letters Patent 1642-6, Xerox Copy, unpublished

Carlton, C., *Going To The Wars, The Experience of the English Civil Wars 1642–1651*, (1992, Routledge)

Childs, J., *The Siege of Loyalty House*, (Penguin, 2022)

Dale, T.C., (ed.) *The Inhabitants of London in 1638 Vols 1&2*, (1931) Society of Genealogists

Dale, T.C., (ed.) *Returns made by Parishes in the City in 1641*, (1934) Society of Genealogists

Davies, R., (ed.) *The Life of Marmaduke Rawdon of York*, (1863) Camden Society, Vol. 85, London

Emberton, W., *Love Loyalty. The Close and Perilous Siege of Basing House 1643–1645*, (1972)

Godwin, Rev G.N., *The Civil War in Hampshire (1642-45)*, (1882 and 1904) London

Goold Walker, G., (ed.), *The Honourable Artillery Company 1537–1926*, (1926) Bodley Head, London

Killick, H.F., (ed.) *Memoirs of Sir Marmaduke Rawden, Kt.1582–1646* (1920), Yorkshire Archaeological Journal, Vol. 25, Leeds

Long, C.E., (ed.), *Diary of the Marches of the Royal Army During the Great Civil War kept by Richard Symonds*, (1859), Camden Society

Nagel's L., *Prince Rupert's Blue Coats* (1975), London

Newman, P., *Royalist Officers in England and Wales, 1642–1660* (1981), Garland, New York and London

Philip, I.G., (ed.), *Journal of Sir Samuel Luke, 1642–1644*, (1947) Oxfordshire Record Society

Raikes, G.A., (ed.), *The Ancient Vellum Book of the Honourable Artillery Company*, (1890), Richard Bentley, London

Reid, S., *All The King's Armies*, (1998), Spellmount

Reid, S., *Officers and Regiments of the Royalist Army*, 5 Vols, (1985–1988), (Partizan Press, ND)

Roberts, K., London and Liberty: Ensigns of the Trained Bands, Partizan Press 1987

Ross, Lt. Col. W.G., (ed.), 'A Description of the Siege of Basing Castle' in 'Military Engineering During The Great Civil War 1642–1649' *Royal Engineers Institute Occasional Papers. Vol. XIII*, (1887)

Roy, I., (ed.), *The Royalist Ordnance Papers 1642–1646, Part 1 and 2*, (1964 and 1975) Oxfordshire Record Society

Tibbutt, H.G., (ed.) *The Letter Books 1644–1645 of Sir Samuel Luke*, (1963), HMC JP4, HMSO

Toynbee, T., (ed.), *The Papers of Captain Henry Stevens*, (1962), Oxfordshire Record Society

York, Minster Library, *Rawdon Family, Commonplace Book,* Add MS 122
Young, P., *Edgehill 1642,* (Kineton: 1967)
Young, P., *Marston Moor 1644*, (Kineton: 1970)
Young, P., *Naseby 1645* (London: 1985)

SP 29/159,45_*List of Several Colonels*, (1666)
Brit Lib AC 8113/80 and Add.MS 34206
Hertfordshire Record Office, Manuscript Deed, Ref. D107
Hertfordshire Record Office, Manuscript Memoirs of the Rawdon Family 1667, Ref. 79959X
Hampshire Record Office, Undated Ms. , 40M93/1

4

Dragoon Warfare in the Welsh Borders during the British Civil Wars

Andrew Abram

The aims of the following article are two-fold: firstly, to briefly establish the purpose, nature, and operational role of dragoons during the British Civil Wars, including the wider context of military innovation and development of mounted forces; and secondly, to explore the complexion of dragoon formations and activities in terms of border conflicts and 'regional warfare'. In 1616 the German soldier-writer, Johann Jacobi von Wallhausen, divided cavalry into four kinds: lancers, cuirassiers, carabineers, and dragoons. He stated that although the latter rode on horseback, they fought on foot.[1] Though not deemed to be true cavalry, the dragoon was another form of mounted soldier. According to John Cruso, writing in 1632, 'The dragoon was invented for special services to assist the cavalry as infantry; considering there be many exploits which cannot be effected by the cavalry alone'[2]. This assessment was shared by Sir John Turner, who served as a mercenary under King Gustav II Adolf of Sweden during the 1630s; he wrote, 'seldom there is any occasion of service against an enemy, but wherein it is both fit and necessary to join some foot with the horse, dragoons then go consider not only before to guard passes (as some imagine) but to fight in open field'[3].

With the disappearance of the light horseman or lancer in early seventeenth-century Britain, it became commonly accepted that there were three types of mounted soldiers: the cuirassier, the harquebusier, and the dragoon. Dragoons,

1 Johann Jacobi von Wallhausen, *Kriegskunst zu Pferd* (Frankfurt: 1616), pp. 16–17.
2 John Cruso, *Militarie Instructions for the Cavallrie* (Cambridge: 1632), p. 44.
3 Sir James Turner, *Pallas Armata: Military Essays of the Ancient Grecian, Roman, and modern art of war written in the years 1670 and 1671* (London: 1683), p. 236.

then, were an essential component of seventeenth-century armies; their development, during what some historians have referred to as the 'military revolution' in tactics and warfare in Europe during the first half of the seventeenth century, appears to have been gradual, however. Though effectively mounted, infantry who rode rather than marched to the battlefield, the role of these troops in supporting the cavalry by providing fire support (mainly via dismounting to fire, then remounting) and extra mobility, came to be regarded as a distinct characteristic. Thus, the dragoons became invaluable for raiding expeditions where musketry provided the horse with a distinct advantage, either as support for cavalry combat or for assaults on enemy garrisons. Such was the usefulness of this arm that in July 1644 the Parliamentarian commander Sir William Waller proposed to convert his entire army to dragoons but was prevented by a lack of suitable horses.[4] Similarly, in April 1645, during the blockade of Oxford, Oliver Cromwell, a soldier highly practiced in mounted warfare, lamented, 'It is a great pity we want of dragoons, I believe most of their [Royalists'] petty garrisons might have been taken in and other services done, for the enemy is in huge fear'.[5]

Regiments of dragoons and individual companies (also referred to as troops in some documents) were recruited by both sides, although some came and went, and several units remain obscure, both in their origins and history. Dragoons in the Earl of Newcastle's forces in the north were few, whilst evidence for their existence is slight and often dependent on oblique references to officers' names. Sir Edmund Duncombe's regiment, for instance, was recruited hurriedly in August–September 1642, before fighting at Edgehill with the Oxford Army, where it was described being '500 strong'.[6] However, as there are suggestions that various individual troop formations were combined into one specific regiment, which later participated in the Royalist assault on Cirencester before returning to its native Yorkshire. The mounted role of dragoons also allowed for some reorganisation into and redeployment as cavalry formations. Often this was indicative of battlefield attrition and operational requirements, but losses (particularly amongst officers and non-commissioned officers) and the hazardous nature of their duties, were also responsible for a level of interchangeability among regiments and minor units. units. Captain Hercules Hannay commanded a company of dragoons in Sir

4 *CSPD 1644*, p. 460.

5 Andrew Barclay, Tim Wales, and John Morrill (eds), *The Letters, Writings, and Speeches of Oliver Cromwell* (Oxford: Oxford University Press, 2022), I, pp. 267–268.

6 *A Most True Relation of the Present State of His Majesties Army: Wherein Also the Truth of that Declaration Published by the Parliament, of Their Happy Victory in the Battaile at Keynton, is Both Justly Asserted and Abundantly Proved, Humbly Presented by the Author who was Personally Present, to the Honourable the Lords and Commons in Parliament Assembled* (London: 3 December 1642). TT, E244[2].

Thomas Myddelton's forces from June 1644, but six months later this converted to harquebusiers. During its existence as dragoons, this had served alongside Sir Thomas' regiment of horse in Wales and the Welsh borders.[7]

Even so, during 1642 and early 1643 considerable numbers of dragoon regiments were raised and maintained by the Royalist and Parliamentarian armies, although the effectiveness of some units – sometimes raised quickly and disbanded after campaigns, was reduced by the lack of available horses and suitable equipment. Although in autumn 1642 the King probably had plenty of cavalry, there is some evidence that he was short of such troops. In terms of organisation, in most cases dragoon units were organised along the same lines as infantry regiments, with their officers and non-commissioned officers holding similar ranks, except the cornet, who carried the guidon or colour of each company. But although they were formed into companies, some –°mostly those attached to cavalry regiments – in their operational roles were akin to troops. It was more usual for regiments to consist of five or six companies or troops. Although some managed to come close to this, especially during the early months of the fighting, other regiments never reached that number and were often no more than large companies. The Establishment for civil-war dragoon regiments was 500 soldiers in ten companies of 100 dragoons each, besides officers, but this was rarely achieved in practice. The Establishment for the New Model Army's only regiment of dragoons was revised by the Commons in January 1645 to 1,000 dragoons – besides commissioned and non-commissioned officers – in ten companies.[8] However, throughout 1645 and 1646 Okey's possessed a strength of no more that 650 to 700 men.[9]

The involvement of dragoons during the British Civil Wars in combined arms or all-arms combat – modern concepts involving the mutual deployment of the fighting components of an army on the battlefield – was an increasingly important aspect of their role. Some contemporary military writers implied that the conflicts in Britain encouraged a rethinking of cavalry tactics. Although Cruso's manuals, which embraced both infantry and cavalry drill based on the Dutch model, made no direct mention of combining the two arms on the battlefield, he mentioned, 'The occasions for the combat of the cavalry are many and frequent. Sometime by

7 TNA, SP28/41/4, ff. 472r.-73v., 476v., 480r., 482r.

8 *CJ*, IV, pp. 16–17.

9 Stephen Ede-Borrett, 'Some Notes on the Raising and Origins of Colonel John Okey's Regiment of Dragoons, March to June, 1645', *Journal of the Society of Army Historical Research* (henceforth *JSAHR*), 87 (2009), pp. 206–213; Andrew Abram, *Dragoons and Dragoon Operations in the British Civil Wars, 1638–1653* (Solihull: Helion & Co., 2023), pp. 275-6.

a sole company, sometime by more troops, otherwhile by all the horse together'.[10] Similarly, the Englishman, Henry Hexham included a key section on the presence of cavalry squadrons in supporting the first line foot in which he portrays engaging, 'Battalions of horse, interlaced, and placed betwixt the intervals, and distances of the foot, as the ground necessity may require. For, if an enemy's horse should be ranged between his battalions of foot, it is needed then, that the other side should observe the same form likewise, and have horse to encounter horse, lest they should break in upon the foot divisions'[11]. Hence, the dragoons played an increasingly vital part in the conflict.

Various examples of combined operations involving the deployment of dragoons with the horse, in which they dismounted to provide firepower can be found in some campaign accounts. At Edgehill in 1642 and the First Battle of Newbury in 1643 two brigades of Royalist dragoons cleared the hedges in advance of the King's cavalry forces, even though they suffered significantly high casualties.[12] Experienced exponents of this kind of soldiering on the Continent included professionals such as Sir Arthur Aston and Colonel James Wardlaw, in addition to junior officers in various armies. Likewise, the retreat of Essex's horse from Lostwithiel in August 1644 was covered by a fighting retreat by Captain Jeremiah Abercrombie's dragoons. As the fugitives neared the safety of Saltash, the dragoons, left behind as part of the rearguard, covered them by making a fighting retreat[13].

Dragoons during the British Civil Wars were supplied with inferior horses, and equipment akin to infantrymen. Hence, they were cheaper to recruit and maintain than the expensive regiments of cavalry. According to Cruso, a dragoon's horse was to be the 'least price, the use thereof being but to expedite his march, alighting to do his service'[14]. Cavalry or troop mounts could sell for £10 or £12, although the cost of £4 was typical for dragoon horses. In October 1642 Colonel Richard Browne of the Earl of Essex's army was paid £3,000 to mount the 600 dragoons in his regiment. This equates to £5[15]. By comparison, purchases made for the New Model Army in 1645 included various quantities of dragoon horses at £4 apiece.[16] Moreover, compared with cavalry saddles (priced around 16s. each) those for

10 Cruso, *Military Instructions*, p. 38.

11 Henry Hexham, *The First Part of the Principles of the Art Military practiced in the Warres of the United Netherlands* (Delft: 1642), p. 58.

12 C.E. Long (ed.), *Diary of the Marches of the Royal Army during the Great Civil War; kept by Richard Symonds*, Chetham Society, Old Series, 74 (1859), pp. 64–66.

13 John Rushworth, *Historical Collections of Private Passages of State* (London: D. Browne, 1721), II, p. 702; Sir Edward Walker, *Historical Discourses upon Several Occasions* (London: W.B., 1705), pp. 67–68.

14 Cruso, *Militarie Instructions*, p. 31.

15 TNA, SP28/1A, f. 164v.; SP16/503/62, f. 62r.

16 TNA, SP28/29/1, ff. 166r.-v., 204r.; SP28/29/2, f. 258r.

dragoons were far cheaper. Saddles purchased in Hertfordshire for the Eastern Association forces in 1644 cost 6s. 6d. each, whilst in June 1645 one contract agreed for the New Model with Elizabeth Betts – a major producer of troop and dragoon saddles, and saddle furniture in London was for 140 'new dragoon saddles with furniture at 7s. 6d. per saddle', although the earliest saddles to be issued to Sir Thomas Fairfax's dragoons were reconditioned.[17]

As increasingly specialist troops, some dragoons were supplied with matchlock muskets, bandoliers and/or power bags, whereas others, such as Brereton's Cheshire companies received snaphaunces from the beginning and the soldiers were habitually referred to as 'firelocks'. Similarly, from its establishment in April 1645 Okey's New Model regiment was issued with full-bore 'dragoon muskets with snaphaunce locks' and 'snaphaunce dragoons' – possibly lighter and shorter versions of the standard weapon – at 15s. 6d. each.[18] Additionally, '500 cartridge boxes for dragoon muskets at 10d. apiece' were delivered by the contractor Nathaniel Humpries on 11 April, and he was paid £20 16s. 8d. 'in full for his contract'. A further 500 more cartridge boxes (*cartouches*) for the dragoons were received from Richard Bradley on the 23 April 1645.[19] Moreover, during the relief of Taunton on 14 July Captain John Farmer, took receipt of 200 snaphaunce muskets, 200 dragoon saddles and 200 cartridge boxes, 'being for the recruiting [supplying] of Colonel Okey's regiment'.[20]

Some authors have suggested that civil-war dragoons were a fighting elite – versatile and highly specialised troops accustomed to hazardous service – who were often commanded by professional soldiers and recruited from veterans of other conflicts. There is some truth in this, yet there are various examples of inexperienced, and poorly equipped and officered dragoon units during the early stages of the wars. Nevertheless, some military experience is evident from the beginning, when some Royalist dragoons seemed better trained and disciplined than others of Charles I's armies. For the Parliamentarians, many recruits were obtained in London from returning veterans and foreign professionals. Among Brereton's dragoons, some of his captains were commissioned in the capital, and in autumn 1642 some soldiers enlisted there, possibly in part from Dutchmen or from British soldiers returning from abroad.[21]

17 TNA, SP28/31/5, f. 539r.; SP30/37, ff. 21v., 45r., 51r.

18 TNA, SP28/29/1, ff. 198r., 218r.-219r.

19 TNA, WO47/1, f. 235r.; SP28/29/1, ff. 233r.; SP28/29/2, 249r.; Bodleian Library (henceforth Bodl. Lib), Ms Eng. C14, ff. 8v., 15v.

20 TNA, WO55/1646, f. 146r.; William Salt Library, Ms Salt 463, unf.

21 TNA, SP28/252/1, f. 184v.; SP28/265/1, ff. 68r.-v., 70r.; BL, Ms Harley 2128, ff. 20v.-21r., 31v.; Andrew Abram, 'The Influence of Military Professionals and Trained Band Officers in

It is also suggested that given the nature of many dragoon operations, dragoons were highly suited to regional warfare. Part of the reason may be that such 'contested' areas contained relatively high numbers of opposing garrisons, while the fighting was often fluid and varied in nature. In the Welsh Borders this appears to have been the case, although many Royalist recruits and units were drawn into the Oxford Army during the early stages of the wars. In the region, where the conflict had begun by September 1642, the raising and equipping of dragoons was distinctly variable. Even so, they were employed widely by the King's forces operating along the Welsh borders in 1643, though with differing levels of success. One company was raised in and around Shrewsbury by its governor, Sir Francis Ottley. He was authorised to, 'to take the said company of volunteers into [his] charge, and them to command, train, discipline, and exercise, as their captain and leader, willing and commanding the said soldiers to be obedient, and ready to receive and accomplish the directions, commandments and summons, of you, their captain, and of the officers you shall appoint under you in all things which shall concern, and be for the preservation of Our said town, and Our good subjects inhabiting there. was "to be employed in his Majesty's special service for the defence of this town"'.[22]

Another Royalist unit was raised by the Flintshire gentleman Sir Thomas Hanmer. Duly commissioned on 7 September 1642 to raise a dragoon regiment from North Wales, he already commanded a troop of horse.[23] In late December 1643 Hanmer acted as governor of Chirk Castle, and his dragoons were probably part of the garrison. Likewise, in 1642 Sir Robert Howard of Clun was appointed one of the Commissioners of Array for Shropshire. By January 1643 most of his locally raised regiment of dragoons joined the King's Oxford Army and participated in various operations until mid-1644 when it returned to Shropshire.[24] Howard's men later participated in the defence of Bridgnorth, of which town he had been appointed governor. In June 1643 the commander of the King's artillery had been requested to, 'deliver to the bearer hereof, Edward Jones, lieutenant in the regiment of Sir Robert Howard's Dragoons, for the use of their regiment, 200

Lancashire and Cheshire during the British Civil Wars', *Transactions of the Lancashire and Cheshire Antiquarian Society*, 112 (2020), pp. 113–134.

22 Shropshire Archives (henceforth SA), 6000/13294; W. Phillips (ed.), 'The Ottley Papers Relating to the Civil War', *Transactions of the Shropshire Archaeological and Natural History Society* (henceforth *TSANHS*), 2nd Sers, VII (1895), pp. 241–360 (p. 266).

23 National Library of Wales, Ms Bettisfield 111; John Lord Hanmer, *Memorial of the Parish and Family of Hanmer in Flintshire* (London: Chiswick Press, 1877), pp. 64–65.

24 SA, 6000/13288, 13291; 'Ottley Papers', *TSANHS*, 2nd Sers, VII (1895), pp. 286–287; Eliot Warburton, *Memoirs of Prince Rupert and the Cavaliers* (London: S. & J. Bentley and Henry Fley, 1849), II, pp. 237, 314.

cwt of powder, with match and shot proportional', thus indicating that they were armed with matchlocks.[25]

On 16 January 1643 the Royalist commander Sir Thomas Aston was commissioned to raise 500 dragoons in Cheshire.[26] Four companies were recruited from his tenants and volunteers in Cheshire and Lancashire, although some of the officers were Chester men. Captain Thomas Newland, for instance, 'brought in 60 foot ready raised' to form one unit. Aston's dragoon formation seems to have operated largely with his horse in a larger, combined 'regiment', even though this often caused it to be obscured among its listings.[27] These dragoons, though, were not formed in time to take part in operations against Brereton's forces in Cheshire in early 1643, but it is possible that after Sir Thomas' defeat at Middlewich on 13 March, and the problems encountered by him in securing pay and provisions from the Commissioners of Array at Chester, and the ensuing return of his cavalry to the Oxford Army, there was a scaling down of dragoon recruitment. Either way, though Sir Thomas initially enrolled 220 dragoons, the unit was mauled at Newbury in September 1643, losing about 100 men. In February 1643, while back at Chester, a number Aston's troopers received new clothing, while his new dragoon were equipped and clothed as they were recruited.

Such problems encountered by commanders such as Sir Thomas in raising dragoons were not uncommon in the King's armies, especially in Cheshire and the Welsh borders, which after the surge of 1642 were repeatedly beset by recruiting problems occasioned by lack of resources and potential recruits. One contemporary observed how the Royalist Colonel Samuel Sandys of Ombersley in Worcestershire, commanded a cavalry troop during the Edgehill campaign, and 'raised three regiments: one of horse, one of foot, one of dragoons all at his own charge'.[28] The county persistently encountered problems in raising the basic Assessment, the monthly distribution of which was the source of the disagreement between Sandys and the governor of Worcester, Sir William Russell. This created disorder among Sandys' troops, who were left to furnish themselves from the civilian population as best they could, appropriating rations, clothing, and even bedding. A later statement of expenses made to the King's Commissioners of Array recounted that in August 1643 James Hill of Doddingtree was robbed by Sandys' dragoons, who took, 'certain clothes, woollen and linen to the value of £5'[29]. Thus,

25 Bodl. Lib, Ms Rawlinson Misc. 395; William Macray (ed.), *Ruthven Correspondence: Letters and Papers of Patrick Ruthven, Earl of Forth and Brentford* (London: JB Nichols, 1868), p. 78.

26 BL, Ms Harley 6852, f. 98r.

27 BL, Ms Add. 36913, ff. 88r.-94v., 101v., 105r., 107r. –108v.; Ms Harley 6853, ff. 149r. –151v.

28 Symonds, *Diary*, p. 12.

29 Birmingham City Archives, Ms 3312/18/29.

the recruitment of Sandys' dragoon unit was never completed, and in late 1644 it was reformed as a troop of horse in his own regiment under Captain Thomas Symonds. Some commissions for the raising of troops, including dragoons, were either too ambitious in their expectations, and thus yielded few recruits or for various reasons the units themselves failed to materialise.

Throughout the period 1643 to 1646 dragoon formations in the Welsh borders were employed in various roles, including flexible mounted operations, raiding, reconnaissance, special assaults and proving firepower in support of cavalry troops. However, by August 1643 the situation had become more difficult for the Royalists. On 10 August, the Parliamentarian garrison at Nantwich was reinforced by Sir Thomas Myddelton, who had returned from London, where he had been increasing his forces. Notwithstanding the vigilance of Lord Capel, the recently installed Royalist military commander in the Welsh borders, he arrived safely with seven pieces of large ordnance, four cases of drakes, and about 40 carts of ammunition. Additionally, Sir Thomas and the Cheshire commander, Sir William Brereton, dispatched a force to besiege Eccleshall Castle, which was occupied by the Royalists, and Capel's intention was to muster sufficient forces to raise the siege. On 17 August, Sir Arthur wrote to Ottley from Shrewsbury, requesting dragoons:

> I am solicited by the gentlemen of Staffordshire for those dragoons which are at Shrewsbury commanded by Captain Allen; I suppose them to be raised by the town and liberties, and formerly commanded by Captain Owen, I desire from you to be informed of their number, and condition for arms and horses, and as I shall receive information from you, I shall give further order … I desire further to be informed by you how the mounting of Colonel Crowe's dragoons is proceeded in, and what I expect to be done therein, and by what time.[30]

Following a lengthy blockade of the castle by Parliamentarian forces its garrison deserted on 29 August. The Cheshire dragoon companies led by Captains John Bramhall, John Lea and John Cheswis had participated in the siege, and with other Cheshire and Staffordshire soldiers received a bounty from the sale of the goods of Eccleshall Castle, amounting overall to £5,000.[31] A small number of defenders who had fled the skirmish in the town rode hastily to beckon the assistance of Colonel Hastings at Tutbury Castle. Not recognising that Eccleshall had been taken, he came to its aid, but was spotted by Brereton's scouts. According to one source,

30 'Ottley Papers', *TSANHS*, 2nd Sers, VII (1895), pp. 244–245.
31 Cheshire Archives (henceforth CA), ZCR63/2/702, f. 24r.

'Sir William understanding the whole design, made as speedy preparations to meet [Hastings], and upon notice of his near approach, placed his abuscades very secretly behind hedges, and afterwards faced the colonel with a small party of horse, skirmished a little with him, and then made a seeming retreat'.[32] The Royalist horse continued its pursuit, only to encounter the Cheshire dragoons, who were waiting in ambush. Opening fire, they overwhelmed Hastings and his soldiers, who were, 'put to an absolute rout, about 100 of his horse slain in the place, and about as many were taken prisoners; himself wounded, and with a few of his ragged troops escaped, and fled to Tutbury Castle'.[33] The loss of Eccleshall seriously curtailed the Royalist grip on Staffordshire in late summer 1643 and in turn exposed much of neighbouring Shropshire to Parliamentarian activity.

As already mentioned, the Parliamentarian army in Cheshire commanded by Sir William Brereton contained various dragoon units. These served at the forefront of operations as both specialist mounted soldiers and assault troops. Brereton himself received commissions as colonel and captain of foot, captain of a troop of harquebusiers, and colonel of a regiment of horse.[34] Nevertheless, in November 1645 he informed the Committee of Accounts, 'I raised and took down with me [to Cheshire] in December [1642] these companies of dragoons: Captain Bramhall, Captain Goldegay and Captain Lea which, together with my horse and all the force with me, were put upon service by the way and the first night after we came into Cheshire'[35]. In his accounts he added that he received no pay for commanding the 'good regiment of dragoons' from 'his first coming down into Cheshire until the time I returned to the Parliament on 24 June 1645', due to lack of a commission.[36]

Brereton subsequently wrote to a friend, 'there is accounted for a regiment of horse from 16 April 1644, whereof I commanded a good regiment of horse from 1 March 1643 and another regiment of dragoons, both of which there hath been perfect lists given to the Committee of Accounts, the truth thereof I do attest upon oath'[37]. Similarly, when he compiled a list of his forces for the Committee of Both Kingdoms on 30 April 1645 the dragoons were unquestionably part of them and therefore had to be included, but as the regiment did not officially exist the companies were included in the strength of his infantry own regiment. When in October he produced another schedule, this time of his own regiments, the

32 *A Perfect Diurnall of Some Passages in Parliament*, 4–11 September 1643. TT, E250[8].
33 John Vickers, *God's Ark overtopping the World's Waves* (London: 1646), p. 63.
34 John Rylands Research Institute and Library, TW/262; TNA, SP28/35, fols 164r. –5v., 168r.; SP28/152/7, f. 20r.; SP28/300, f. 558v.; BL, Ms Add. 11332, f. 43r.
35 BL, Ms Add. 11332, f. 43v.
36 TNA, SP28/152/7, f. 20r.
37 CA, ZCR/63/2/691, f. 13r.

dragoons were left out.[38] Evidently, this was aimed to support Brereton's accounts, in which he claimed no pay for leading them due to the lack of a commission.

Originally raised in London and Cheshire, Brereton's dragoons served in the defence of London in November 1642. Upon their arrival in Cheshire two months later, they saw action against Sir Thomas Aston's troops at Nantwich and the First Battle of Middlewich, before participating in Parliamentarian operations in Staffordshire and the engagement at Hopton Heath in March 1643. Three companies of Cheshire dragoons participated in the capture of Eccleshall Castle on 30 August, and despite some initial battlefield inexperience, the Cheshire dragoons developed into versatile and highly specialized troops who were accustomed to hazardous service. Furthermore, they were commanded by resourceful and experienced officers, who for the most part were professional soldiers (some of whom had previously served in the Irish wars).

Like some of their Royalist counterparts, in terms of equipment, tactics and leadership Brereton's dragoons or firelocks seem to have been 'sufficiently different' to the rest of the army and towards at forefront of what has been considered an evolution in the role of mounted operations in seventeenth-century warfare. Owing to battlefield attrition, the capture, reassignment and promotion of officers, and the influx of recruits from the Protestant army from Ireland, in 1644 Brereton's dragoons were reorganised into three companies, led by Captains Finch, Gilbert and Holt, although other commands and detachments are known from later in the war under different officers. Thus, Sir William spoke more than once of 'three to four' companies of dragoons under his command. Like other parliamentarian forces in Shropshire and the borderlands of Wales, those of Cheshire were bolstered by soldiers from the English army in Ireland who had changed sides after the Battle of Nantwich and the siege of Liverpool in 1644.

Perhaps 600 of the 1,500 soldiers captured at Nantwich took service with Brereton's army. Some of these might have served previously in the firelock companies of Captains Sandford and Langley. Nothing is known of the latter's fate, but Sandford played a leading role in the capture of Hawarden Castle and with eight of his men took Beeston in a surprise operation. He was killed leading an attack on Nantwich on 17 January 1644. According to the Parliamentarian chronicler Thomas Malbon, papers outlining plans for the assault were found in his pockets.[39] The range of operations undertaken by the dragoons belonging to the Cheshire Army of Parliament – including direct and costly assaults on the

38 BL, MS Add. 11332, f. 43v.; MS Add. 11332, f. 3r.

39 Historical Manuscripts Commission, *14th Report*, App. VII, pp. 124, 131, 143; Andrew Hopper, *Turncoats and Renegadoes: Changing Sides during the English Civil Wars* (Oxford University Press, 2012), pp. 89–90.

defences of Chester in 1645 – was extremely wide and varied, from small-scale raids, intelligence gathering, skirmishes and foraging operations (often in enclosed country) to full-scale assaults and combined arms warfare.

When in May 1645 the King's army moved northwards from its base at Oxford, Brereton was ordered to rendezvous with the forces of Lords Fairfax and Leven at Barlow Moor, an open heath on the north bank of the Mersey, south of Manchester. It was decided by the Committee of Both Kingdoms that the Scots, the northern Parliamentarians, and troops from some Midland counties could deal with the Royalist threat, and that Fairfax should remain, for now, besieging the Royalist capital. In a letter to Leven on 22 May Brereton described his dragoons, 'which were soldiers in Ireland' as 'very serviceable' and 'well-accommodated'. He added, 'I can bring no more foot than one regiment and some choice dragoons – firelocks which were soldiers in Ireland lately mounted'.[40] The following day the Cheshire commander informed the Committee from Manchester, 'The Cheshire foot which I expect are not above 500–600. There are 8–9 troops of Cheshire Horse and 3–4 very serviceable companies of dragoons, well-accommodated'. Moreover, on 27 May, after waiting at Barlow Moor for the agreed meeting to materialise, Brereton reported to his Lancashire ally William Ashurst, 'I have brought up the Cheshire horse and dragoons, and what foot could possibly be spared'[41]. These troops, under the overall command of Lieutenant Colonel Michael Jones, Brereton's cavalry commander, subsequently assisted the Parliamentarian follow-up operations following the New Model Army's victory at Naseby and march to Leicestershire.

40 BL, Ms Add. 11331, f. 142v.

41 BL, Ms Add. 11331, ff. 148v., 151r., 164r., 169r.

5

Locating the Battle of Stow-on-the Wold 1646

Simon Marsh & Sam Wilson

The traditional site of the battle of Stow-on-the-Wold is located around 2.6 kilometres north of the town square, on Horsington Hill north-west of the village of Donnington. This is the area that was registered by Historic England[1] in 1995, though an unpublished 1999 English Heritage (as Historic England was before 2015) report suggested an amendment to the registration, moving the battle southwards to 1.2 kilometres north of the town.[2] This paper looks at the documentary, map and archaeological evidence for the location of the battlefield and questions the current Historic England registration.

Prelude and battle

By early 1646, with royalist fortunes waning badly in the Civil War, the King ordered Jacob, Lord Astley, his General for Worcestershire, Staffordshire, Herefordshire and Shropshire, to gather troops from garrisons in his command and proceed to Chipping Norton via Stow-on-the-Wold where he would be met by 1,500 soldiers from Oxford to form a royalist field army for the 1646 campaign. Astley gathered 2,000–3,000 men and probably departed Worcester on 17 March. He headed north to Droitwich as a feint, ostensibly to threaten the parliamentarian besiegers around Lichfield, before turning south through Alcester and crossing the river Avon at Bidford. The parliamentarian authorities had early warning

1 See <https://historicengland.org.uk/listing/the-list/list-entry/1000037?section=official-list-entry>

2 English Heritage Battlefield Panel 2/99, *Annex 5 – Possible revision Stow on the Wold* (unpublished).

of royalist plans and responded by ordering the parliamentarian governors of Gloucester, Hereford, and Evesham to withdraw troops from their garrisons and join a detachment under Sir William Brereton, then besieging Lichfield, to prevent the conjunction of royalist forces.[3]

Brereton marched from Lichfield to Coleshill on the day Astley left Worcester with 800 horse and 200 firelocks (essentially dragoons), but delayed any further advance until he received intelligence on the whereabouts of the royalists. Meanwhile Parliament's Gloucester, Hereford, and Evesham forces had rendezvoused near Evesham on 16 March with Colonel Thomas Morgan, the governor of Gloucester, in command. Struggling to defend all the crossings on the Avon with a force of 1,600 men, Morgan decided to move across the river to Chipping Campden on 19 March as the routes from the crossing points on the Avon would take any royalist march on Stow toward Chipping Campden.[4]

After crossing the Avon at Bidford using a bridge of boats on 20 March, Astley then marched down the old Roman road, Buckle Street, toward Chipping Campden. Morgan ordered 500 cavalry and some infantry to intercept the royalists to slow their march in the hope that Brereton's force would soon come up; Morgan appears to have judged that he did not have sufficient men to be certain of victory as he sent away one of his cornets to seek cavalry reinforcements from the parliamentarian commander at Woodstock in Oxfordshire when the fighting near Campden commenced. The skirmishing there lasted around four hours until the royalists reached the top of the 'Camden hills' and the parliamentarians broke contact, by which time it was 8–9 p.m. in the evening and dark.[5]

3 Sir Edward Walker, *Historical Discourses*, (London:1705), p.152; British Library Thomason Tracts (BL TT) E.329[7], Thomas Morgan, *Colonel Morgan's Letter*, (London: 1645[6]), pp.3–4; The National Archives (TNA), SP16/513, f.77; House of Lords Journal (LJ) Vol 8, (London, 1767–1830) pp.189–190. W.D. Hamilton, (ed.) *Calendar of State Papers Domestic 1645–1647*, (London: HMSO, 1891), p.368.

4 Wing S139, R.S, *A True and fuller relation of the Battell fought at Stowe on the Would*, (London: 1646), unpag.; E.329[7], pp.3–5; Bodleian Library, MS Tanner 60 ff.560r-560v; Rev T.W. Webb (ed.), *Military memoir of Colonel John Birch*, (Hereford: Golden Valley Publications, 2004), p.34. Birch's account from late on 16 March 1646 indicates the forces rendezvousing at Evesham numbered 1,600 men. The later memoir written by his secretary (who may have been serving in a military capacity with Birch at the time of the battle) suggests there were 2,700 men in Morgan's command, but we have used the lower figure as likely being more accurate given it was written in the days leading up to the battle rather than some time afterwards. The lower figure would also better explain Morgan's decision not to seek battle with Astley near Campden given this disparity in the strength of the opposing forces.

5 *Birch memoir*, p.34; Wing S139, unpag.; E.329[7], p.4; Mary Anne Everett Green, *The Proceedings of the Committee for the Advance of Money*, Vol II (London: HMSO, 1888), p.713.

Brereton had marched from Coleshill to Stratford on 19 March before receiving incorrect intelligence late in the day that the royalists had turned back and 'bended [their] march toward Lichfield'. He therefore withdrew toward Birmingham and quartered around four miles from Stratford that night. Late at night he received further intelligence that the royalists were 'within three miles' of his force, so he ordered his men to mount up immediately and marched to Knowle, around 13¾ miles north of Stratford, unsure whether his enemy were intent on relieving Lichfield. New intelligence on the morning of 20 March revealed the royalists had crossed the river Avon and that Morgan would face them, so Brereton reversed his march, arriving at Stratford by sunset where he learned of the fighting around Chipping Campden. After a slow crossing of the Avon at Stratford – the bridge was broken down and the horses could only cross on planks one at a time – Brereton reached the Camden hills by midnight and then continued toward Stow.[6]

Morgan had earlier resolved to continue the pursuit of the royalists, marching off at around 11 p.m. after giving his opponents a two-to-three-hour head start. At around 3 a.m. Brereton caught up with Morgan's infantry and cavalry. The combined force then marched another mile before scouts reported that the royalists were just ahead of the parliamentarian army. Morgan ordered out 400 cavalry and 200 firelocks, 'to charge home his [Astley's] rear-guard, to put him to a stand before he should pass through Stow upon the Wold'. This forced the royalists to deploy into battle array and the parliamentarian force did likewise before advancing to confront their enemy.[7]

Colonel John Birch, commanding the Hereford detachment, said battle commenced at break of day and Brereton noted the parliamentarians attacked between 4–5 a.m. Dawn on 31 March (allowing for the ten days adjustment between the Julian and Gregorian calendars for when the battle was fought) is normally 5:08 a.m. GMT at Stow on the Wold, though first light occurs at 4:27 a.m. GMT.[8] On this basis the parliamentarian attack is likely to have occurred nearer 5 a.m. then 4 a.m. and certainly after 4:30 a.m. GMT.[9]

The battle commenced with a general attack by the parliamentarians across the whole front. Their left wing of cavalry, apparently commanded by Birch, and infantry deployed in the centre, commanded by Morgan, were repulsed, but the right wing of horse and firelocks, under Brereton, had more success with their superior numbers and forced the royalist cavalry on that side of the battlefield to

6 Wing S139, unpag.

7 *Birch memoir*, pp.34–35; E.329[7], 5; BL TT E.348[1], John Vicars, *England's parliamentary chronicle*, (London: 1646), p.398

8 See <Sunrise and Sunset times for Stow-on-the-Wold, Gloucestershire on Thursday 31 March 2022 (thetimeandplace.info)> for these calculations; LJ Vol 8, 231.

9 LJ, Vol 8, 231.

flee. The disintegration of the royalist left wing of cavalry seems to have occasioned a rout of at least some of the army, which then fled back to Stow, where further parliamentarian attacks were made before the royalists eventually surrendered. Birch said the battle had lasted one hour and he, Brereton and Morgan sent a joint letter about the victory and the gathering of prisoners in the church to the Speaker of the House of Commons at 6 a.m. on 21 March, indicating the battle was over by this time.[10]

Location of the battle

Landscape

In determining the likely location of the battle, it is important to first consider the approach to the battlefield. The royalists were observed by Morgan's force advancing toward Chipping Campden after crossing the river Avon at Bidford. The route they took was undoubtedly along the old Roman road, Buckle Street. Around Weston-Sub-Edge the royalists had the option of continuing on Buckle street to climb up to the modern A44 running across Fish Hill or to bear east and follow an ancient salt way that skirted the edge of Chipping Campden before turning south toward Stow.[11]

It is clear from Ogilby's 1675 map that the A44 existed at the time of the battle. Ogilby's Plate 2 (London to Aberystwyth strip map) shows this road passing over Broadway Hill with a route toward Chipping Camden to the east between the 88- and 89-miles markers and another turning to Stow between the 87- and 86-mile markers. Part of this route is shown on Ogilby's Plate 85 (Sailsbury to Campden strip map) from around the 'turning' to Worcester at mile point 74, which is the road down Broadway Hill, to the turning around mile point 72 to Bourton on the Hill, which is shown on Plate 2 running toward Bourton on the Hill after the turn-off toward Stow. Beyond mile point 72 on Plate 85, the road runs into Stow, following the line of the modern A424 with Longborough to the east and Upper Swell to the west. A possible variation on this route for an advance into Stow was for the royalists to follow the Roman road network westward from Fish Hill and then south which would eventually bring them out on the Tewkesbury to Stow road west of Stow.[12]

10 Wing S139, unpag.; *Birch memoir*, p.35; E.329[7], 5; Walker, p.152; LJ Vol 8, 231; Bodleian Library, MS Tanner 60, ff.586r-587r.

11 *Birch memoir*, p.34; the authors are grateful to Tony Spicer for advice on the route of the Salt Way.

12 John Ogilby, *Britannia*, (London: 1675), plates 2, 85

The salt way route, after skirting Chipping Campden, ran roughly parallel to the A44/A424, passing through or nearby Broad Campden, Blockley, Bourton on the Hill and Donnington, before turning toward Broadwell. At the time of the battle, a trackway, now a public footpath running from Donnington to the Fosse Way, would have been the direct route from the latter village into Stow.

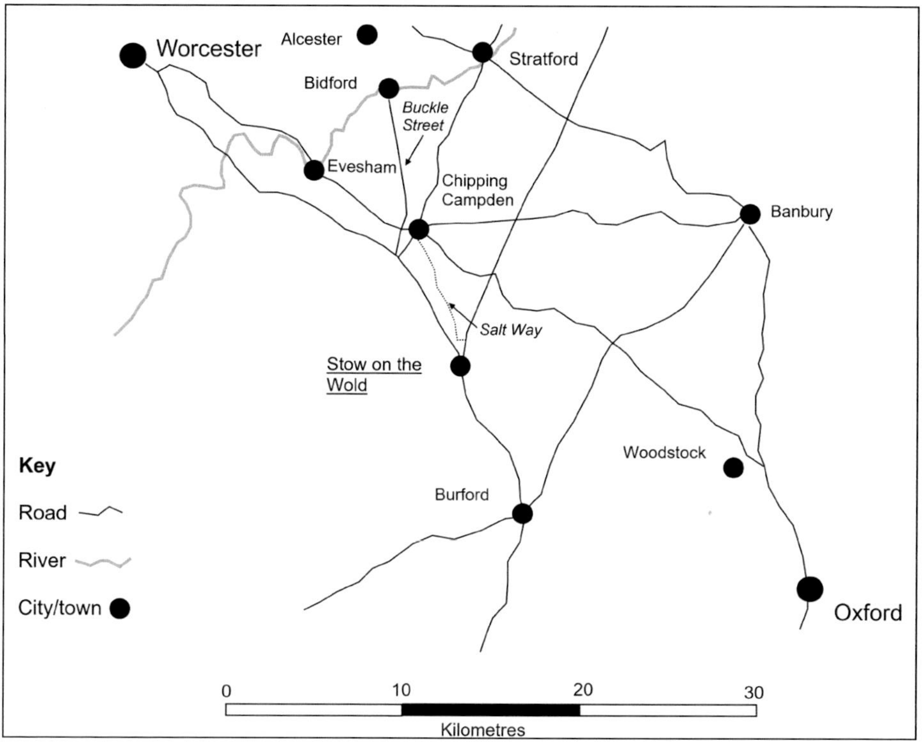

Figure 1. Stow area of operations March 1646

Both routes allowed a running fight to take place as the royalists ascended a hill near to Chipping Campden. For the A44/A424 route this involved climbing up what is now Fish Hill and on the salt way route at the climb out of Broad Campden toward Blockley. It is unlikely that the royalists would wish to march along the salt way, which would have taken them closer to the main parliamentarian force at Chipping Campden, and probably toward the detachment that was harrying their rear, as the evidence from the primary accounts indicated they were attempting to get away from the parliamentarians, who were trying to hold them up.

As Morgan's letter makes clear, nearer to Stow the royalists were 'put to a stand' by his attack with 400 cavalry and 200 firelocks. This indicates the royalists were in line of march when this happened and, as they had baggage waggons with them, were almost certainly on a roadway. It follows from this that the battle must have taken place close to a route into Stow. The roads into the town from the Chipping Campden area run roughly from north to south and any manoeuvring over distance off a road to the east or west would have exposed the flank of the royalist army to further attack by the parliamentarians. The battle is therefore likely to have taken place across or close by a road.[13]

There is only one specific landscape clue about where the battle was fought. This comes from the *Moderate Intelligencer* which says the parliamentarians, 'charged them [the royalists] in a plain or common neer Stow'.[14] A landscape study commissioned by the Battlefields Trust indicates that most, if not all, of the land north of Stow was probably open at the time of the battle (see figure 2). In Broadwell parish, which abutted Stow on its north side to the east of the Fosse Way, the land appears to have been unenclosed pasture fields near the town, becoming unenclosed arable fields further north. On the western side of the Fosse Way was the parish of Upper Swell. Here unenclosed arable fields ran to what is now the A424 with other, open arable fields and meadow to the west of the latter road. It is possible that the area to the west of the A424 contained the 'common grounds or commons called the Sheephill and the Cowpasture' described in the 1724 enclosure act covering Upper Swell. If so, this might be the reference to 'a plain or common neer Stow' which was reported as the location of the battle by the *Moderate Intelligencer.* Even if these fields were situated elsewhere in Upper Swell parish, the appearance of open pasture and arable land adjacent to the A424 is consistent with the description of the area as a plain or common, particularly if whoever reported this to the *Moderate Intelligencer* did so on the basis of seeing the ground rather than knowing about its status. Nevertheless, as noted above, the area north of Stow appears to have been almost entirely open fields, so the reference to a plain or common cannot be located precisely. It is unclear whether there was a hedge or fence that marked the boundary between Upper Swell and Broadwell parishes, though the Fosse Way itself may have been a sufficiently clear marker. Nearer to Stow, what is now the Abbotswood Estate, bounded by the roads to Tewkesbury and Lower Swell, had been emparked in the thirteenth century. It is likely a substantial barrier was constructed to keep animals such as deer inside the park and poachers out. That the park was used to hold deer is possibly evidenced

13 E.329[7], p.5.

14 BL TT E.329[14], Anonymous, *The moderate intelligencer*, Issue 55, (London; 1645[6]), p.359.

by an etching by Johannes Kip of Sir Robert Atkyn's estate at Swell in around 1710, showing deer in the southern part of the park.[15]

Around Donnington, the fields to the south-west and south-east of the settlement appear to have also been open and in cultivation as suggested by the remnant ridge and furrow earthworks shown in 1940s RAF vertical air photographs. A 1777 map of the area shows a mature tree plantation on Horsington Hill, on the north side of the traditional battlefield, but whether it was established before the Civil War is unclear.[16]

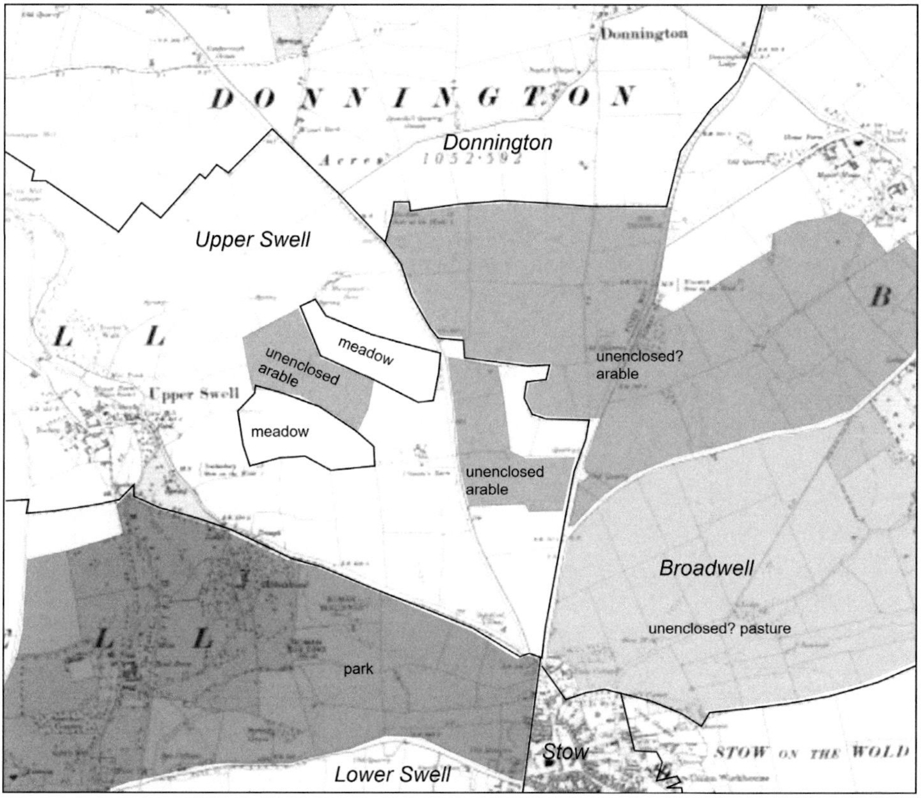

Figure 2. Stow-on-the-Wold battlefield landscape (Reproduced with the permission of the National Library of Scotland under a CC-BY licence)

15 Tracey Partida, Stow-on-the-Wold Battlefield Landscape (Battlefields Trust, 2023). The 1724 enclosure act is from Gloucester Records Office P323 SD 1/1; <https://www.parksandgardens.org/places/lower-swell-park>.

16 Isaac Taylor, 'Map of the County of Gloucester 1777' in Bristol and Gloucestershire Archaeological Society, *A Gloucestershire and Bristol Atlas*, (London and Bradford: Percy Lund, Humphries and Co. Ltd., 1961), p.9.

Documentary accounts
The primary accounts of the battle indicate that the battlefield was close to Stow (author's emphasis in all):[17]

> *I commanded 400 horse and 200 firelocks to charge home his rear-guard, to put him to a stand* ***before he should pass through Stow upon the Wold*** (Thomas Morgan letter to the Speaker of the House of Commons, published 24 March 1646).[18]

> *About three in the morneing we gott close up to the enimy then* ***drawne up in a ffield neer Stowe****, it being very darke.*
> (John Birch account written by his Secretary Roe, sometime between June 1646 and 1691).[19]

> *we marched about a mile, and by that time the Scouts brought word* ***Enemy were drawn into a body neer Stow in the Ould****.*
> (RS account, written at Stratford upon Avon 23 March 1646).[20]

> *but he [Astley] makes his passage good and marches all Night, imagining they had not followed him any further,* ***and so early begins to draw into quarters****, when they appeared and fell upon him.*
> (Sir Edward Walker's account, written around 1664).[21]

> *and the last Day the Enemy came over the River Avon very strong (as it was reported Three Thousand), and* ***so came before us to Stow this Morning****.*
> (John Birch letter to the Speaker of the House of Lords, written at 5 p.m. 21 March 1646).[22]

> *I came up to Colonel Morgan and Colonel Birch about Three of the Clock this Morning (****near Stowe, on Cotscole Hills****).*

17 These references exclude a series of letters written in the months after the battle by Sir William Brereton where he describes the battle as being 'at Stow' see Ivor Carr & Ian Atherton, Sir William Brereton's Letter Book 1646, (Bristol: Staffordshire Record Society), 2007, pp.99, 109, 115, 121.
18 E.329[7], p.5.
19 *Birch memoir*, p.35.
20 Wing S139, unpag.
21 *Historical Discourses*, p.152.
22 LJ Vol 8, p.231.

(Sir William Brereton letter to the Speaker of the House of Lords, written at 7 a.m. 21 March 1646).[23]

But he [Morgan] ***got to Stow*** *before Sir William came in to him with his horse. Yet the aforesaid Colonel* ***at his entrance into that place*** *clapt a party of Horse and Dragoons at the breech of him, which much disturbed him... Early in the morning, and, say the letters, an houre before day, we* ***charged them in a plain or common neer Stow.***
(*Moderate Intelligencer*, 19–26 March 1646).[24]

The Kinges forces intending to fighte, had taken theire ground, a place of advantage, for theire musketeers ***neere the Towne*** [of Stow on the Wold]. (Thomas Malbon account 1651).[25]

Letters brought by M. Temple, informed that Col. Morgan Governor of Glocester with his Forces, and those of Sir William Brereton joyned together; fell upon Sir Jacob Ashley, and all his Forces intending for Oxford, ***at Stow in the Woald****, on the edg of Glocester-shire, and after a sore conflict on both sides, Sir Jacob Ashley was totally routed.* (Bulstrode Whitelock, *Memorials of the English Affair*, 1682, written from his contemporaneous journal).[26]

Morgan's account says that the royalists were about to pass through Stow when he stopped them whilst the *Moderate Intelligencer* suggested this was 'at the entrance' to the town. The latter source probably drew on Morgan's account to produce its narrative, so was not independent. Nonetheless, it is indicative of how contemporaries interpreted Morgan's version of events. Most of the remaining accounts reference the battle being near Stow or at Stow. Walker's full account of events leading up to the battle indicates that Astley had been ordered to march to Stow with his army. The section of his account above indicates that the royalists were about to go into quarters and therefore probably near a place with buildings, but he does not directly name the location. However, given the other primary sources place the royalists at or near Stow it seems likely that the quarters were to be in the town and therefore that the army was about to enter Stow when the battle was fought.

23 *Op cit.*
24 E.329[14], p.359.
25 James Hall (ed.), *Memorials of the Civil War in Cheshire*, Lancashire and Cheshire Records Society Vol XIX (Lancashire and Cheshire Records Society, 1889), p.202.
26 Bulstrode Whitelock, *Memorials of the English Affair*, (London, 1682), p.204.

No settlement other than Stow is mentioned within the primary accounts of the battle. Moreover, the fact that the royalists were able to flee into the town and some fighting continued there suggests that the distance, for an army in rout, was not far. In addition, the time between the battle starting after 4:30 a.m. and prisoners being collected in the church by 6 a.m., suggests Birch's estimate of fighting lasting about one hour is correct and that the time taken to reach the town by the royalists after being routed was short. This further supports a battle site close to Stow.[27]

Accounts of the location of the battle from secondary sources from 1658–1712 are also worth examination. Of the 15 identified (see Appendix I), eleven name Stow or near Stow as the location of the battlefield. Four of them, detailed below, identify Donnington (sometimes with 'near Stow' added) as the place of the battle. These are listed below (author emphasis in all):

> *Lord Astleys being vanquish›d* ***at a place called*** **Donnington** ***neer Stow*** *on the Wold, on the 21 of March.* ***In which fight himself was taken prisoner,*** *and with him all* ***the Kings hopes lost of preserving*** **Oxford**, *till he could better his condition.*
> (Peter Heylyn, *A Short View of the Life and Reign of King Charles ... from his Birth to his Burial,* 1658).[28]
>
> *In the twenty first of March, Sir Iacob Astley* ***was beaten at Donnington neer unto Stow in the Wold, in the which fight himself was taken prisoner, and the kings hopes quite lost.***
> (Anonymous, *The Faithful Analist ... or, The epitome of the English history,* 1660).[29]
>
> *And that which compleated the* ***Ruin of all the King's Affairs*** *in England, was the Surprize and Defeat of my* ***Lord Astley at Donnington near Stow on the Wold,*** *where he* ***was taken Prisoner*** *the 21st of March.*
> (Roger Coke, *A detection of the court and state of England during the four last reigns and the inter-regnum consisting of private memoirs, &c.,* 1696).[30]

27 LJ Vol 8, 231; Bodleian Library, MS Tanner 60, ff.586r-587r.

28 Wing H1375B, Peter Heylyn, *A Short View of the Life and Reign of King Charles ... from his Birth to his Burial,* (London, 1658), p.127–128

29 Anonymous, *The Faithful Analist:, or, The epitome of the English history,* (London, 1660), pp.286–287.

30 Wing C4973, Roger Coke, *A detection of the court and state of England during the four last reigns and the inter-regnum consisting of private memoirs, &c.,* (London, 1696), p.315.

> ***Donington;*** *The Lord Aston receiv'd a total Defeat by Collonel Morgan in this place March 21 1645* ***upon which all Hopes of preserving the King's Garrison in Oxford were lost****.*
> (Sir Robert Atkyns, *The Ancient and Present state of Gloucestershire,* 1712).[31]

Atkyns' account is included as his father (also Robert) lived at Lower Swell and Atkyns junior may have had the opportunity to discuss the battle on his visits to his father or afterwards when he inherited the house in 1710, before his own death in 1711. Whether he did so or not is unclear, but the formulation of his entry about Astley's defeat, particularly the reference to 'all Hopes of preserving the King's garrison in Oxford were lost', was very similar to Peter Heylyn's account which also identified Donnington as the place of the battle saying, 'and with him all the Kings hopes lost of preserving Oxford'. Given the similarity in the formulation of these statements about the battle, it seems likely that Atkyns followed Heylyn's account.[32]

The anonymous author of the *Faithful Analist* in 1660 also appears to have followed Heylyn as he talked about 'the King's hopes quite lost' because of the battle and his narrative continues in the same way as Heylyn's after the battle. Roger Coke, writing in 1696 and distantly related to Sir Jacob Astley, also puts the battle at Donnington with language that is different from Heylyn, though covering the same points, perhaps suggesting he may also have relied upon him as a source.[33]

Heylyn's history was published four years before his death in 1662 when he was around 62 years old. His account of the battle was written some years after it occurred and in late March 1646 he was either at or had just escaped from Winchester. He then moved from place to place until he settled at Minister Lovell in Oxfordshire in 1648. Whilst he had served as an editor of the Oxford royalist newssheet *Mercurius Aulicus* in the early years of the war, Heylyn was not able to hear immediately first-hand where the battle had occurred from any of those fleeing the fight, and it seems likely his information about its location was obtained, perhaps third hand, sometime after 1648. One possibility (and it is no more than that) is that Heylyn, in compiling the notes for his history, managed to conflate the site of the battle with the siege of Donnington castle in Berkshire which ended in late March 1646 and was therefore the next significant defeat to befall the royalists

31 Sir Robert Atkyns, *The Ancient and Present state of Gloucestershire,* London, 1712, p.694.
32 'Parishes: Lower Swell', in *A History of the County of Gloucester: Volume* 6, ed. C R Elrington (London, 1965), pp.165–172. *British History Online* <http://www.british-history.ac.uk/vch/glos/vol6/pp165-172> [accessed 15 November 2022].
33 Roger Coke, p.311.

during the first Civil War. Heylyn did not mention this siege in his history and in an era without copy editors it is conceivable that he might have misread notes or misunderstood testimony referring to the siege of Donnington and linked this to the battle (and village) near Stow, with subsequent authors following his account. In the broader scheme of Heylyn's history, such a mistake would be a minor one and easily made.[34]

Problems with the traditional site of the battle

Notwithstanding the primary accounts that locate the battle near to Stow, English Heritage, when it first registered the battlefield in 1995 designated the site as being on and around Horsington Hill in Donnington parish. English Heritage was guided in its decision by a report produced on the battle by the National Army Museum (NAM). The NAM produced over sixty reports for English Heritage on English battlefields of which 43 were taken forward to registration, with Stow being one of these.[35]

The Stow report was one of the weaker ones produced by the NAM. In a paragraph explaining the sources for the battle, the NAM said '[t]he sources for the Battle are fragmentary and it has not been possible to consult any original contemporary record. Secondary sources only have been used in the compilation of this report'. The report went on to conclude, '[t]he sources of the Battle are few and fragmentary and it is doubtful whether further research would produce anything of substance'. In listing the sources used, the NAM identified Ron Field's unreferenced twenty-four-page 1992 monograph on the battle, which placed its location on Horsington Hill, and the Calendar of State Papers Domestic 1645–47. The former was used specifically by the NAM to provide a quote describing the fighting from RS, a trooper serving with Brereton during the battle, and the latter for the Committee of Both Kingdoms letter of congratulation to Colonel Morgan after the battle.[36]

The RS account did not state where the battle was fought, but Field's 1992 monograph locating the battlefield at Horsington Hill appears to have encouraged the NAM to identify this as the battle site. This lies to the north and west of Donnington, close to the salt way which runs along the hill's eastern side. It is, however, a problematic battlefield. If Horsington tree plantation, first shown on mapping in 1777, was there at the time of the battle then it could not have been

34 Mandell Creighton, 'Peter Heylyn' in Leslie Stephen & Sydney Lee (ed.), *Dictionary of National Biography*, Vol 26 (London: 1891), p.321.

35 National Army Museum Templer Study Centre, *The Battlefield of Stow on the Wold (21 March 1646)*, 2000/07/88/59.

36 NAM report, *The Battlefield of Stow on the Wold*, pp.3, 5; Ron Field, *Stow on the Wold, 1646*, (Design Folio: 1992), p.13; Wing S139; *CSPD 1645–1647*, pp.387–388.

fought on the hill as the action would have not developed in the way described by the primary sources, nor could the battlefield be described as a 'plain or common'.[37]

If the plantation was not there, it is conceivable that the royalists could have deployed upon the hill if they had been 'put to a stand' by the parliamentarians as they came upon the hill from the north via the salt way or were about to pass by it. If instead they had travelled down what is now the A424 and attempted to move onto Horsington Hill after being stopped by the parliamentarians they would have had to make a circa 900 m march with their left flank exposed to the enemy which they knew to be in close proximity. This seems an unlikely course of action for an experienced commander such as Astley.

If the royalists had deployed on the hill, the length of which could only allow some of their army to occupy the higher ground and would have disrupted sight-lines for commanders across its front, it is unclear why the parliamentarians would attack the position. The northern slope, which military logic suggests would be defended by the royalists, is very steep (see Figure 3) and it would be a foolhardy commander that attempted an assault there. From 375 m north of the crest of the hill the ground rises by 45 m, a little less than a one in eight gradient, but for the final 100 m of this climb it becomes a one in six and a half gradient. None of the primary accounts mention the parliamentarians being faced with an attack uphill and, if this is what had happened, it is likely they would have said so given the providential style of battle accounts, which emphasised the challenges faced in the fighting which were overcome through God's support, that were written at this time. By way of comparison the battle of Lansdown in July 1643 involved a royalist assault led by infantry and supported by cavalry up a one in six and a half gradient initially turning to a one in five and a half gradient to reach the hill top where the parliamentarians were deployed. Most of the royalist cavalry were driven off the hill by parliamentarian attacks and it was only the doggedness of the royalist infantry that saved the day. Whilst the circumstances were not identical, for Stow this perhaps suggests a successful assault on a royalist position on Horsington Hill would have required the parliamentarian infantry to have taken ground, which the primary accounts make clear they did not. In any case, if faced by this position, the parliamentarian commander could simply have marched around the royalist deployment, cutting off any further movement toward the King whilst waiting for them either to surrender or come-off the hill to fight.[38]

The accounts of the battle separately indicate that once the royalists were defeated they fled back to Stow. As noted above, the hill is approximately 2.6

37 Taylor's map, 1777; E.329[14], p.359.

38 Charles Chadwyck Healey (ed), *Bellum Civille*, (London: Somerset Record Society, 1902), p.54 .

kilometres from the market square in Stow and it seems inconceivable that any army that had been 'put to a total rout', particularly when 'all the[ir] horse had turned about and fled', could, in the short time available, have made a coherent withdrawal back into Stow over the distance involved whilst being harried by over 1,000 parliamentarian cavalry troopers and have still been able to put up some sort of fight in the town.[39]

Figure 3. Looking south toward the northern slope of Horsington hill. Note the steepness of the climb, particularly through the trees in the distance to the top of the hill (author's photograph)

These problems, in part, caused English Heritage to revisit the registration at Stow in 1999 when its independent Battlefield Panel took a paper prepared by English Heritage recommending that the battlefield registration should be changed. This suggested that the battle 'took place approximately 1,200 metres north of the village (sic) [of Stow] on a north-facing slope between the Evesham [A424] and former Donnington roads'. No further action seems to have been taken on this recommendation and the original registration has remained unchanged.

39 E329[7], p.5; *Historical Discourses*, p.152.

Since then, only John Barratt's book covering the end of the war in the Welsh marches, which contained a chapter on the battle of Stow, has attempted to address the site of the battle, with him favouring a location nearer to the town than the traditional one.[40]

Archaeology

It was these problems with the traditional site of the battle that encouraged the Battlefields Trust to look again at where it was fought. In 2015, a battlefield survey project was initiated with the aim of finding battlefield archaeology which would locate the site.

A series of metal detector surveys were undertaken between October 2015 and November 2022 (Figure 4) testing the traditional battlefield site on Horsington Hill as registered by Historic England, revised locations to the south and south-west of the traditional site, proposed by the Battlefields Trust, and a site much closer to Stow.

Initial survey work was conducted in October 2015 across ten different areas, including fields to the south of the traditional site as well as the revised site proposed by the Battlefields Trust. High specification metal detectors were used along with sub-metre GPS for recording the location of all finds and the transects along which metal detecting had taken place. Metal detecting was undertaken by experienced detectorists who had worked on other battlefield sites and used 10 m transects which were deemed to be of sufficient intensity to locate Civil War artefacts had the detected area been in a location where fighting had taken place.[41]

Detecting was also undertaken for non-ferrous metals only. By far the most prevalent find on a Civil War battlefield is lead shot, and the recovery of these artefacts in sufficient quantity would confirm that the battlefield had indeed been located. It was therefore not appropriate to survey for all metals as the abundance of ferrous objects across most land would have incurred a severe time delay and therefore had a significantly detrimental impact on the amount of ground that could be covered during the survey.

Most of the fields surveyed in 2015 had been ploughed within the previous ten years and many had been ploughed that year. Ploughed fields provide good detecting conditions as artefacts in the topsoil are brought toward the surface through the ploughing action. Fewer finds are likely to be made on long term/permanent pasture than on arable or pasture land which has been cultivated in

40 English Heritage, 'Annex 5: Possible Revision – Stow on the Wold' in unpublished minutes from *English Heritage Battlefield Panel 99/2 – Agenda item 5* (English Heritage: 1999); John Barratt, *The Last Battle,* (Warwick: Helion and Co Ltd, 2017).

41 Glenn Foard & Richard Morris, *The archaeology of English battlefields*, (York: Council for British Archaeology, 2012), p.28.

recent decades. In part, this is due to objects having passed down toward the bottom of the soil column due to weight and bioturbation, making detection more difficult. In extreme cases this can place objects out of the range of modern metal detectors.[42]

A total of 69 artefacts of potential archaeological interest were recovered from the surveyed areas in 2015, a remarkably low number. Finds identified as 'junk' were collected by transect, later assessed, and then discarded. No finds were recovered that could be identified as being of probable Civil War date.

The lack of any Civil War dated finds in 2015 indicated that fighting had not occurred in any of the areas surveyed, casting doubt on both the traditional and revised battle sites hypotheses. By 2022, further permission had been obtained to metal detect on the Horsington Hill (traditional) battlefield site and in November a single day of metal detecting was organised there using the same method as in 2015, though with navigation grade GPS to geolocate search areas and finds and five metre transects used to try and find evidence of the battle. None was found and the oldest object recovered was a very worn George III half penny, probably dating from 1770–1775. The field detected had last been ploughed in the early 1980s[43] and it is unlikely that all lead shot, had they been present on the site, would have sunk in the soil column beyond the range of modern metal detectors. This detecting covered a little under half of the core area of the traditional battlefield site, with gaps between survey areas varying from 45–110 m – insufficiently wide for the royalist deployment to have occurred, and therefore the fighting not to be identified through metal detecting. This work confirmed the conclusion reached in 2015 that the battle of Stow was not fought on Horsington Hill. Furthermore, the lack of evidence to the immediate south of the registered battlefield suggested that no rout had occurred through that area either.

In 2018, in light of the failure to find evidence of fighting in the 2015 survey and after a careful re-reading of the primary accounts, a new hypothesis – that the battle was fought much closer to Stow across what is now the A424 – was developed. Between 2018–2022 permission was obtained to investigate a series of fields on the east and west sides of the A424 around Greenfield farm. Survey methodology similar to that used in 2015 was employed, but this time using a mixture of 5 m and 2.5 m transects.

The survey conducted in April 2018 recovered 18 lead shot of various forms with an additional four probable fragmented bullets. The bullets were a variety of calibres and most showed evidence of having been fired. Additionally, several

42 Battlefields Trust, *Battlefield Investigation Policy and Guidance*, (2022), p.17 (see <https://www.battlefieldstrust.com/cms/viewdoc.asp?a=23&b=400&c=619&d=11591571>).

43 Information provided by the landowner.

distinctly 17th century military forms of shot were present within the assemblage including two slugs, a quartered bullet, and a bullet showing clear evidence of having been double or triple-loaded. An assessment of some of the 2018 bullet finds by Dr Glenn Foard found that 'the assemblage shows an exceptional frequency of high impact damage … [which is] probably the result of the shallow soils over the limestone geology which, especially if ploughed in 1646 or earlier in the century, may have brought limestone brash into the topsoil'. Dr Foard also noted that, 'the

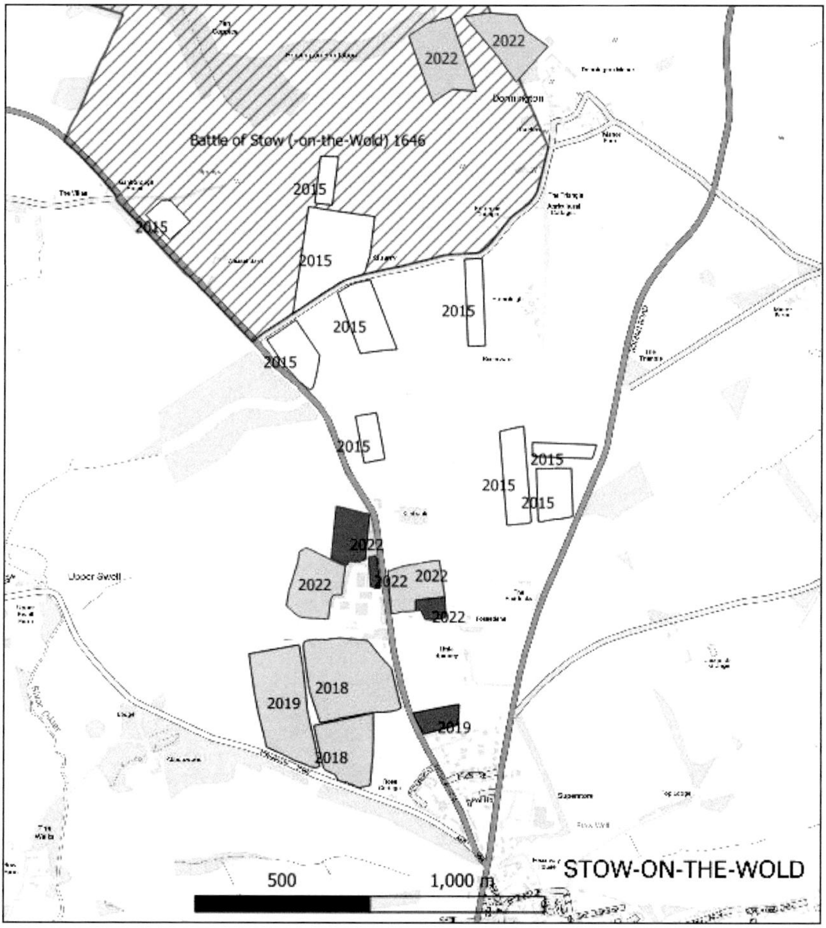

Figure 4. Survey areas at Stow on the Wold
Fields investigated during the survey labelled by year of investigation. Dark grey indicates use of 2.5m spaced transects, mid- grey 5m spaced transects and white, 10m spaced transects.. Registered battlefield is hatched.
(Registered Battlefield information © Historic England 2018 used under an Open Government Licence v3.0. Base map Ordnance Surevy Open Data 2022 containing public sector information licensed under the Open Government Licence v3.0).

degree of impact distortion was so massive on some bullets that it is likely that some of the other irregular pieces of lead recovered from the site are bullets but lacking recognisable characteristics'.[44]

Further work in January 2019 demonstrated that the spread of finds did not extend further to the west of the area investigated in 2018, discounting the hypotheses that the royalists advanced along the Tewkesbury road to Stow, but supporting the view that it was fought across the A424 as, in a field to the east, three bullets from infantry and cavalry weapons were found. In January 2022, surveying of areas north of the land investigated in the two previous phases found further evidence of fighting on both sides of the road, including two bandolier powder caps, five bullets from infantry and cavalry weapons, and three probable fragmented bullets.

Six other bullets (two probably from muskets, and four weighing 6.7–9 grams) were also notified to the detecting team as being found by a detectorist on fields west of the A424 around Greenfield farm. The two musket balls appear to be related to the others found in this area, though the four lighter weight balls may be

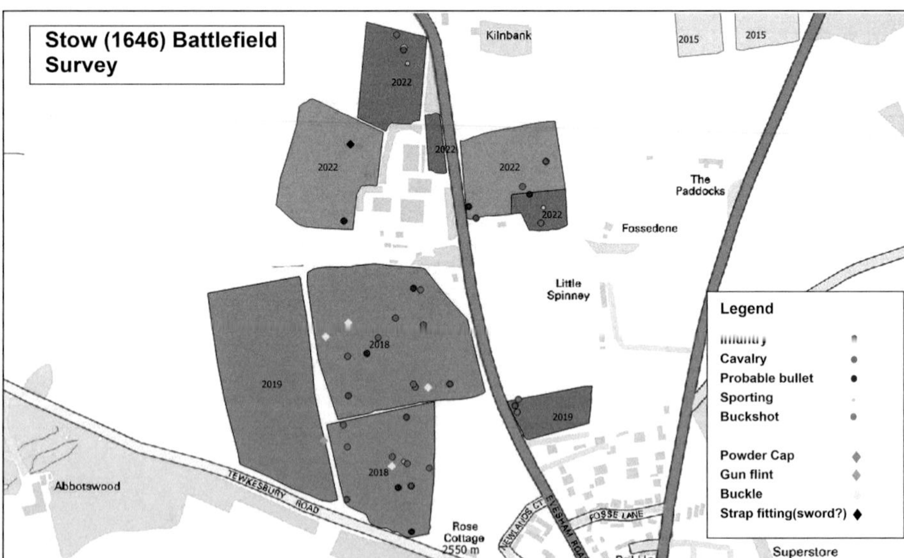

Figure 5. Lead shot and other finds distribution at Stow on the Wold (Fields shaded mid grey were surveyed using 5 m transects, those in dark grey 2.5 m transects.) (Base map Ordnance Survey Open Data 2022 containing public sector information licensed under the Open Government Licence v3.0)

44 Dr. Glenn Foard, *Report on bullets from the 2018–2022 survey Battlefields Trust on the 1646 Stow on the Wold battlefield,* unpublished, 2023), p.1.

from later sporting activity as they appear too small to be from Civil War pistols. Moreover, at least one other hobby detectorist is known to have made bullet finds in the fields on the eastern side of the A424 and it therefore appears that some battle related archaeology has been lost from there as a consequence.

Assessment

Whilst the finds around Greenfield farm confirm that fighting occurred there in the Civil War, it is important to assess whether they could have been deposited during actions other than the battle fought on 21 March 1646. Separately, if the finds do come from the battle of Stow, what do they tell us about the engagement?

Other Civil War actions around Stow

Five engagements, other than the battle fought in March 1646, have been identified around Stow during the Civil Wars. The first was in in mid-September 1642 when Anthony Wood, in Oxford, reported that Sir John Byron, travelling from Oxford with cavalry troopers, was set upon by the 'country' at Stow-in-the-Wold. Wood's account was second hand and not completely accurate as he incorrectly reported Byron had been killed. Sir Robert Cooke, writing to his cousin Sir Robert Harley on 13 September 1642 also seems to reference this incident when he described the rescue of an Oxford delinquent from Mr Stephen's house in Worcestershire by, 'some troopers that were thought to come from Oxford' and who were subsequently pursued by 'Colonel Fynes' from Broadway to Pershore and then toward Bridgenorth. Byron had left Leicester in late August 1642 with three troops of horse and had lost 46 men in a skirmish at Brackley before continuing to Oxford where he recruited from amongst the scholars before heading toward the rest of the royal army, which was marching toward Shrewsbury. 'Colonel Fynes' is probably a reference to one of Lord Say and Sele's sons who was presumably commanding local forces at that time. If this was the force that pursued (and attacked?) Byron then it must also have been made up of cavalry and possibly dragoons in order to pursue the royalists in the way described. Wood's account is vague and inaccurate, and Cooke's letter suggests Fiennes did not follow the troopers, who were thought to come from Oxford, until they were in Worcestershire. It is therefore far from certain that this incident occurred close to Stow and, in any case, the area in which finds have been made, which covers 300 m by 700 m, appears too large for the numbers involved in the type of action Wood and Cooke describe.[45]

45 Andrew Clark (ed.), *The Life and Times of Anthony Wood*, (Oxford: Clarendon Press, 1891), p.60; Historical Manuscripts Commission 14th Report Part II, *The manuscripts of his Grace the Duke of Portland*, Vol III (London: HMSO, 1894), p.98; BL TT, E.117[11],

A second action in the vicinity of Stow occurred in, probably, June 1643, when the parliamentarian governor of Gloucester, Edward Massey, attacked the village of Slaughter with 120 horse and dragoons, surprising a royalist horse quarter before continuing to Oddington to attack another cavalry quarter. Massey was subsequently engaged by royalist cavalry near Slaughter whilst returning to Gloucester. Upper and Lower Slaughter are located around four kilometres south-west of Stow and the route from there to Oddington (around three kilometres east of Stow) would most likely have made use of the Fosse Way and then the road to Maugersbury (one kilometre south-east of Stow), which Ogilby shows on his 1675 map. None of the action described in the primary accounts appears to have taken place in the immediate vicinity of Stow and the route used by Massey would not have taken him close to where the archaeological finds have been made.[46]

Separately, in early September 1643, the Earl of Essex's army, which was advancing to relieve Gloucester, was engaged by a royalist cavalry force east of Stow around the villages of Upper and Lower Oddington. The account of this action from Sergeant Henry Foster of the Red regiment of the London trained bands makes clear that royalist cavalry was forced by artillery fire to withdraw up to the slope that leads into Stow from the east. They were then driven from that slope by more parliamentarian artillery fire and pursued by Essex's men for three miles before turning to engage again. The pursuit was toward Naunton (probably along a side road identified on plate 85 of Ogilby's *Britannia*) as, according to the official parliamentarian account of the campaign, the army quartered at Naunton that night. Neither Foster's account nor the official parliamentarian one indicated any fighting in the three-mile pursuit of the royalists from Stow. This is unsurprising given the royalist force was made up entirely of mounted troops with the parliamentarians having to advance at the march pace of the infantry and train of artillery. A pursuit following the road to Naunton and the likely lack of any fighting for three miles beyond the eastern side of Stow mean the archaeological finds from around Greenfield farm cannot come from this action.[47]

On 7 May 1645, according to George Purefoy, the parliamentarian garrison commander at Compton Wynyates, there was an attack by a party of 30 of his

Anonymous, *A true and perfect relation of the manner of the apprehension and taking of 46. rebellious cavalliers at Brackly*, (London: 1642), p.1; BL TT, E.122[13], Anonymous, *A Perfect diurnall of the passages of the souldiers, that are under the command of the Lord Say in Oxford, (London: 1642), p.1.*

46 John Corbet, *A Historical relation of the military government of Gloucester*, (London: 1645), p.37; Ogilby, Plate 85.

47 BL TT, E.69[15], Henry Foster, *A True and exact relation of the marchings of the two regiments of the trained bands of the city of London*, (London: 1643), unpag.; BL TT, E.70[10], Anonymous, *A true relation of the late expedition of his excellency, Robert, earl of Essex*, (London: 1643), pp.7–8.

troopers on the rear of the royalist army 'within a mile of Stow'. Richard Symonds, who was serving as a cavalryman with the King's army at this time, said that the army had advanced from Oxford on 7 May and quartered at Woodstock before marching to Stow on 8 May. Notwithstanding the discrepancy in dates between the two accounts, an attack on the royalists as they advanced to Stow from Woodstock would have taken place on the eastern side of the town rather than the northern side and cannot therefore account for the archaeological finds that have been made. Purefoy's letter also says he sent out a party on 9 May, 'to bang them [the royalists] up in the rear'. Here Purefoy is describing why he sent out his troopers, but he says they 'marched straight to [Chipping] Camden' indicating that between sending them out and reaching Chipping Campden there was no fighting with the royalists and therefore no action near Stow.[48]

Interpretation of archaeological results

Overall, the numbers of Civil War military finds from the archaeological survey were limited. Nevertheless, the fields surveyed using 5 m transects in 2018 had a density of lead shot finds of around 1.3 bullets per kilometre surveyed (1.5 bullets per kilometre if probable bullets are included). From the 2022 survey, field four (see figure 5 below) produced 0.74 bullets per kilometre surveyed (1.3 bullets per kilometre if probable bullets are included). This compares to 0.3–7.8 bullets per kilometre for various fields surveyed at Edgehill.[49] Detecting conditions as well as duration and intensity of combat (ie the amount of lead shot deposited in the ground over time) are obvious variables in comparing the battles of Edgehill and Stow. The latter was in all respects a much smaller affair than Edgehill and did not involve artillery firing case shot; at Edgehill case shot may have increased the concentration of finds in certain areas of the battlefield. Moreover, the fields surveyed at Stow seem to be mainly on the western flank of the armies, where predominantly a cavalry action took place. Bullet finds would be expected to be less per kilometre in this area than in the main infantry action as use of firearms generally gave way quickly to a melee in Civil War cavalry actions, particularly this late in the war. October 2023 work at the battle of Langport (1645) by the Battlefields Trust also indicated low density of lead shot per kilometre surveyed (0.66–1.27) and it is possible that Civil War battles of relatively short duration with

48 BL TT, E.260[36], Anonymous, *Perfect passages of each days proceedings in Parliament*, (London: 1645), p.232; C.E. Long & Ian Roy (eds.), *Richard Symond's diary of the marches of the royal army*, (Cambridge: Cambridge University Press, 1997), pp.164–165.

49 For detail on fields surveyed at Edgehill see Glenn Foard, *Battlefield Archaeology of the English Civil War*, (Oxford: BAR British Series 570, Archaeopress, 2012), p.149.

limited numbers engaged generate this type of relatively limited archaeological signature.[50] Further work is required to test this hypothesis.

One possibility is the bulk of the finds represent the initial engagement that put the royalists to a stand. If this is correct, then the eventual royalist deployment would have been even closer to Stow, with the parliamentarians perhaps deployed on the southern edge of where archaeological finds have been made. But the nature of the initial engagement, which is likely to have been short and sharp given the dark conditions and, according to the primary accounts, focused only on the royalist rear-guard in line of march, seems unlikely to have generated the scatter of finds that have been made.[51]

A more likely interpretation is that the royalists were caught in line of march on what is now the A424 at a point north of the most northerly field shown as surveyed in 2022 in Figures 4–7, perhaps just within the Donnington part of Stow parish, which conceivably provides another explanation for the battle being said to have taken place at Donnington. Finds in this northern field may be from this initial engagement, either as over-shots or because the action involved the royalists continuing to move south to escape the attack. With the parliamentarians close by, the royalists were forced to deploy their army. Astley may have identified or been told about the gully (see figure 7), which seems to have been meadow land at the time of the battle, to the west of what is now Greenfield farm which would have provided good protection for his left wing of horse. He may have deployed to leave a gap of 100 m or so between the gully and his troopers further south. This would also have given his cavalry on that side of the battlefield an opportunity to charge any advancing parliamentarians as they reached the top of the gully slope, no-doubt disorganised, and may reflect Colonel Birch's comment to his secretary that the parliamentarians had disadvantage of ground. The lack of finds to the west of the fields surveyed in 2010 indicates that the action did not spill into this area, probably because the parliamentarians avoided crossing the gully during the battle. One other possibility is that some form of enclosure did exist between the fields surveyed in 2018 and 2019 Field 1 (see Figure 7) which allowed Astley to anchor his flank and channelled the parliamentarian attack. The landscape study was unable to rule-out or confirm this. The preponderance of lead shot associated with horse arms in this area also suggests it formed a cavalry flank for both armies with the smaller number of musket shot and powder caps recovered perhaps representing parliamentarian firelocks and royalist commanded musketeers (see below).[52]

50 Wilson and Marsh (forthcoming).
51 E.329[14], p.359.
52 *Birch memoirs*, p.35.

The rest of the royalist army would have deployed eastwards reaching as far at the Fosse Way. Astley appears to have led the infantry in the centre and acted as commanding general. Sir Charles Lucas, the senior royalist cavalry commander at the battle, probably led the right wing and Sir William Vaughan the left wing. On the parliamentarian left (east), Birch and 32 of his regiment had their horses shot when they attacked. This appears a significant number of horse casualties if it was the result of a cavalry action alone and it seems likely that it was commanded musketeers withdrawn from the royalist infantry battalions and interlined with their cavalry squadrons to strengthen the flanks on that side of the battlefield which caused these losses. This was a tactic used by the royalists in other battles.[53] Given that most of the parliamentarian cavalry seems to have been on the western side of the battlefield, it would have made sense for the royalists to strengthen their cavalry with commanded musketeers on that wing as well. A conjectured deployment for the royalists would place 450 cavalry and 120 commanded musketeers on each wing with about 1,160 infantry in the centre.

The parliamentarians, after their initial contact with the royalists also formed up in battle array and marched forward until they found the enemy deployment. They then waited for daylight. Brereton commanded the parliamentarian right wing of cavalry consisting of 800 troopers and 200 firelocks. The firelocks would probably have been deployed as commanded shot between the cavalry squadrons. Birch seems to have led the parliamentarian left of perhaps 500 cavalry. Morgan is said to have commanded the 'van', which, according to one account was not the left or right wing of cavalry, indicating, by a process of elimination, that this referred to the circa 1,100 infantry in the centre.

Survey (2022) field 4 (figure 7) may have been part of the initial parliamentarian position. Bullet finds might be expected to be lower here because the primary accounts indicate the parliamentarians advance to attack the royalists and most royalist fire would therefore have taken place at a range much closer than the initial deployment distances. Nonetheless this would have resulted in some over-shots back into the initial parliamentarian position, and these may be represented by some of the finds made in field 4.

In this interpretation, the archaeological finds indicate that the battle was fought across the A424. A conjectured deployment of the armies based on the archaeology and the key terrain features suggests the royalist (~2,300 men) were positioned across a front[54] of perhaps around 607 m aligned east-west at a point between

53 See, for example de Gomme's depiction of royalist deployments at Marston Moor, Naseby and the so called third battle of Newbury, British Library MS Additional 16,370 ff.60, 63, 65.

54 This assumes the royalist and parliamentarian cavalry were deployed three deep, the royalist infantry three deep and the parliamentarian infantry six deep. It allows four feet

Greenfield Farm and the modern outskirts of Stow and the parliamentarians (~2,600 men) also aligned east-west on a front of about 705m around 275m north of the royalist position (figure 5). As noted above, the gully which runs westward from Greenfield farm (figure 6) possibly shaped the action, given the absence of finds in the main field (2019 Field 1) investigated in 2019.

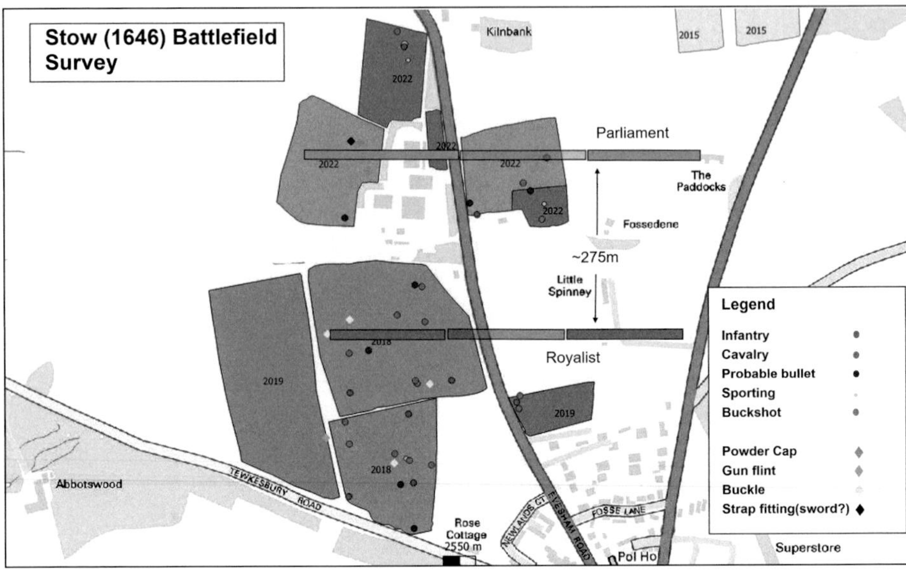

Figure 6. Battle of Stow finds distribution with conjectured army deployments. (Base map Ordnance Survey Open Data 2022 containing public sector information licensed under the Open Government Licence v3.0).

frontage per man as suggested by Sir James Turner (see Sir James Turner, *Pallas Armata,* (London, 1683), pp.271–272) except for the royalist infantry, which would have been deployed in order at around three feet frontage per man. This deployment also assumes the royalists are using 120 commanded musketeers between the cavalry squadrons on each wing (240 in total) and the parliamentarian right wing has its firelock companies similarly deployed.

Figure 7. Lidar view of survey areas showing the location of the gully on the western side of the proposed battlefield. The lines each represent a detected transect.

Conclusion

Despite a small number of accounts from the second half of the 17th century and early 18th century placing the 1646 Stow battlefield at Donnington, the traditional site of the battle at Horsington Hill is problematic. Its location in relation to the most likely route of royalist advance, distance from Stow and implications of its steep northern side, makes it an unlikely battlefield. The lack of battlefield archaeology from recent metal detecting appears to confirm this.

Why later 17th and early 18th century accounts placed the battle at Donnington is unclear, though most, if not all, appear to repeat initial claims by Peter Heylyn, who may simply have been confused or misinformed. Alternatively, the initial engagement before the battle commenced may have occurred within the Donnington part of Stow parish and led to suggestions of the battle being fought there, though this seems an overly technical explanation. The accounts of the battle from those who participated or were written in the days following suggest it was fought close to the town rather than where the traditional site is located.

The battlefield archaeology is limited. This is, in part, due to the time that has been available for survey work, because some fields under pasture are likely to have produced less finds than if they had been ploughed, and because permission to survey some fields was not forthcoming. Recording of bullets has also been complicated due to the stoney nature of the ground, which appears to have caused shot to disintegrate or deform to such an extent that it is impossible to be sure that all of them have been identified. Hobby detectorists may also have caused some of the archaeology in the fields around Greenfield farm to have been lost. Nevertheless, sufficient finds have been found to make a good case that the location of the battle is around Greenfield farm. Other Civil War actions around Stow have been considered as possible explanations for the archaeology discovered, but none fit the location of the finds or their distribution. The balance of probability therefore suggests that the Stow battlefield has been located.

The battlefield archaeology found could form part of the initial attack by the parliamentarians that put the royalists moving in line of march to a stand, though the wide extent of the scatter makes this unlikely. A more convincing explanation is that the archaeology represents the western side of the battlefield and a conjectural deployment based on the finds suggests it is located around 800 m from the centre of Stow, a more realistic distance than the traditional site on Horsington Hill for the royalists to flee back into the town in sufficient order for groups to continue fighting. Metal detecting on fields that have so far been inaccessible would be necessary to confirm this interpretation and it is likely that fighting stretched into what are now built-up areas of the town.

Appendix I

Contemporary or near contemporary secondary accounts describing the battle's location at or near Stow

---

and ***neer Stow on the old****, where old Ashly was taken*
(G.W., *Respublica Anglicana*, (London: 1650), p.10)

Lord Astleys being vanquish'd ***at a place called*** **Donnington** ***neer Stow*** *on the Wold, on the 21 of March. In which fight himself was taken prisoner, and with him all* ***the Kings hopes lost*** *of preserving Oxford, till he could better his condition.*
(Peter Heylyn, A Short View of the Life and Reign of King Charles.. from his Birth to his Burial, (London: 1658), pp.127–128)

In the twenty first of March, Sir Iacob Astley ***was beaten at Donnington neer unto Stow in the Wold****, in the which fight himself was taken prisoner,* ***and the kings hopes quite lost****.*
(Anonymous, *The faithful analist:, or, The epitome of the English history*, (London: 1660), pp.286–287)

Morgan and Brearton follow in our Rear, Whom for to fight, ***at*** **Stow** ***inforc'd wee were***
(Andrew Cooper, *Stratologia*, (London: 1662), p.154)

and the ***Lord Astley defeated at Stow in the Would****, two thousand kill'd, and taken prisoners; and so ended this year, the next beginning with the same face of affairs, several surrenders being made to the Parliament.* (Anonymous, *Royall and loyall blood shed by Cromwell and his party, &c*, (London: 1662), p.25)

and ***the Lord Astley defeated at Stow in the Would****, two thousand kill'd, and taken prisoners; and so ended this year.*
(James Heath, *A brief chronicle of all the chief actions so fatally falling out in these three kingdoms*, (London:1662), pp.24–25)

he got a considerable Army, which for want of the Horse promised him from Oxford, a streight wherein he could not avoid fighting, ***he lost at Stow in the Old March 21. 1645/6***. (David Lloyd, *Memoires of the lives, actions, sufferings & deaths of those noble, reverend and excellent personages that suffered by death, sequestration, decimation, or otherwise, for the Protestant religion and the great principle thereof, allegiance to their soveraigne, in our late intestine wars,* (London: 1667), p.644)

March. ***Lord Ashly defeated near Stow.***
(George Meriton, *Anglorum gesta, or, A brief history of England being an exact account of the most remarkable revolutions and most memorable occurrences and transactions in peace and war,* (London: 1675), p.350)
The King, Duke of York, Prince Rupert, and Prince Maurice, were all this while at Oxford, surrounded with the Enemies Forces, expecting only the relief of the Lord Astley's Foot to join with the Kings Horse at Farrington; but these ***by the way at Stow*** **in the** *Woulds, are encountred by Brereton and Morgan, and totally routed.*
(Francis Sanford, *A genealogical history of the kings of England, and monarchs of Great Britain, &c.,* (London: 1677), p.555)

HereuponSirIacobAstley.. ***beingsetuponnearStowonthewouldsinGloucestershire.***
(William Dugdale, *A short view of the late troubles in England,* (London: 1681), pp.202–203)

March [1646] **L. Asley defeated near Stow.**
(R.B, *The Wars of England, Scotland, And Ireland,* (London: 1681), p.135)

[date 21 March 1646] Sir Jacob Astley, who was the last hopes of the King›s Army, ***defeated near Stow.***
(Samuel Clarke, *The historian's guide, or, Britain's remembrancer being a summary of all the actions, exploits, sieges, battels, designs, attempts, preferments, honours, changes &c.,* (London: 1690), p.29)

so that the Royalists hopes were very low, only they had some expectations from a party still remaining under Sir Jacob Astley, but Coll. Morgan **encountring him** ***near Stow in the holds****, utterly Routed him.*
(R.B., *The history of Oliver Cromwel being an impartial account of all the battles, sieges, and other military atchievements wherein he was engaged,* (London: 1692), p.18)

And that which compleated the Ruin of all the King's Affairs in England, was the Surprize and Defeat of my ***Lord Astley at Donnington near Stow on the Wold****, where he was taken Prisoner the 21st of March.*
(Roger Coke, *A detection of the court and state of England during the four last reigns and the inter-regnum consisting of private memoirs, &c.*, (London: 1696), p.315

Donington; The Lord Aston receiv'd a total Defeat by Collonel Morgan in this place March 21 1645 upon which all Hopes of preserving the King's Garrison in Oxford were lost. (Sir Robert Atkyns, *The Ancient and Present state of Gloucestershire*, (London: 1712), p.694)

Appendix II

Military related finds from the Stow battlefield survey

Bullets

MD No.	Date	Type	Mass (g)	Diameter (mm)	Fired/ unfired	Military Type
9	27/04/2018	bullet	27.43		fired	Infantry
13	27/04/2018	bullet	23.41	16.37	fired	Cavalry
14	27/04/2018	probable bullet	8.703		fired	Probable
15	27/04/2018	bullet	20.12	15.46	fired	Cavalry
19	27/04/2018	bullet	13.46	12.58	fired	Cavalry
79	27/04/2018	bullet – slug	55.9	13.35	fired	Cavalry
20	28/04/2018	bullet	20.04	21.2	fired	Cavalry
23	28/04/2018	bullet	15.57	13.51	unfired	Cavalry
28	28/04/2018	probable bullet	14.17		fired	Probable
46	28/04/2018	bullet	13.89	13.64	fired	Cavalry
50	28/04/2018	bullet – double shot	31.18	17.72	fired	Infantry
51	29/04/2018	bullet	13.04	13.36	fired	Cavalry
53	29/04/2018	bullet – cut	12.75	17.68	unfired	Infantry
56	29/04/2018	bullet – slug	33.45	15.07	fired	Cavalry
58	29/04/2018	bullet	22.19	15.67	fired	Cavalry
59	29/04/2018	bullet	9.15	11.78	fired	Sporting
62	29/04/2018	bullet	22.11	15.36	unfired	Cavalry

63	29/04/2018	bullet	15.87	16.65	fired	Cavalry
65	29/04/2018	bullet	37.33		fired	Infantry
66	29/04/2018	probable bullet	15.06		fired	Probable
71	29/04/2018	bullet	30.61	17.07	fired	Infantry
78	29/04/2018	probable bullet	14.66		fired	Probable
SF1034	18/01/2019	bullet	27.12	16.48	fired	Cavalry
SF1035	18/01/2019	bullet	34.77	17.84	fired?	Infantry
SF1039	18/01/2019	bullet	26.53	16.61		Cavalry
SF001	14/01/2022	probable bullet	7.89		fired	Probable
SF040	15/01/2022	bullet	31.25	18.09	fired	Infantry
SF041	15/01/2022	buck shot?	4.95	10.15	NK	Buck shot
SF043	15/01/2022	bullet	10.39	12.92	fired	Sporting
SF044	15/01/2022	bullet	16.39	14.68	fired	Cavalry
SF062	16/01/2022	bullet	29.52	20.4	fired	Infantry
SF064	16/01/2022	probable bullet	12.64		fired	Probable
SF087	16/01/2022	probable bullet	13.19		fired	Probable
SF088	16/01/2022	bullet	21.65	15.71	NK	Cavalry
SF096	16/01/2022	bullet	21.94	15.79	NK	Cavalry
SF098	16/01/2022	bullet	9.05	11.64	fired	Sporting
SF102	16/01/2022	bullet	25.48	17.52	NK	Infantry

Other military related finds

MD No.	Date	Type	Diameter (mm)	Military Type
67	29/04/2018	Gun furniture (18th century)		Gun Furniture
SF1004	16/01/2019	flint – possible gunflint		Gun flint
SF012	14/01/2022	powder cap	~20	Powder cap
SF013	14/01/2022	strap fitting (probable sword/ baldric)		Strap fitting
SF028	14/01/2022	powder cap	~21.6	Powder cap

6

Countermarch, Caracole and Charge, 1642

Dr Pádraig Lenihan

The seventeenth century evolution of tactics and weapons to optimise firepower was just that, an evolutionary process of gradual and incremental change. Except when it wasn't.

Infantry Tactics

An example of accelerated tactical change that is relevant for present purposes is the sudden switch from Dutch to so-called Swedish infantry tactics in the English Civil Wars. Firing by two ranks advanced, the 'countermarch', was probably the 'preferred way of firing' at the start of the wars. In this manoeuvre the front two ranks of musketeers marched forward ten or twenty paces. The front rank then presented and fired, faced to the left or right and marched in single file to the rear of the body, each man falling in behind five or seven men at the rear of his file. As soon as the first rank was out of the way the second rank fired and then marched to the rear to reload. Once the second rank had fired the third and fourth ranks began to march forward to where the first two had halted to fire (or beyond it if they were advancing), and then fired in their turn. A second method of firing was when single files marched forward, wheeled across the face of the unit and then, by halting and facing the enemy, the file became a rank. After firing, each file marched back to its original place to reload. At Edgehill (23 October 1642) the contending armies found that this so-called Dutch system of firing was not capable of breaking an enemy formation. Afterwards the royalists and then the parliamentarians made a 'fairly immediate and dramatic change to how they fired. They now held their fire until they were within a pike's length of the enemy, whereupon three ranks discharged massed volleys.[1] This salvo, followed by a massed charge 'increasingly became a royalist trademark'.[2] The caracole was the cavalry equivalent of the counter march and if we believe the memoirs of Richard Bulstrode, at Edgehill Prince Rupert ordered his cavalry:

> … to march as close as was possible, keeping their ranks with Sword in Hand, to receive the Enemy's Shot, without firing either Carbine or Pistol, till we broke in amongst the Enemy. [3]

In the twelve months before Edgehill, English armies in Ireland using the counter march and caracole in combat faced different challenges than those that would emerge in England, and a huge opportunity. English armies in Ireland retained Dutch practice while English armies in England quickly switched to Swedish tactics, which involved greater emphasis on salvos rather than volleys, combined with a readiness to close fast with blade weapons. Different evolution: different evolutionary imperatives.

As part of his counter-insurgency strategy, Lord Deputy Wentworth had strictly controlled the quantity of gunpowder in private hands and amassed a large store of munitions and firearms in Dublin Castle. These weapons and munitions were available to arm the regiments raised from settlers and resupply the units that began to disembark from England by the beginning of 1642. The English reinforcements were mustered in the ideal ratio of two musketeers for every pikeman and were supplemented by a company of firelocks.[4] In contrast, the insurgents were 'without arms, ammunition, storehouse, king or prince to assist or second them'.[5] Specifically, they possessed very little gunpowder which was, admitted the Lords Justices, the 'only advantage' Dublin Castle enjoyed in their counterinsurgency. [6] The severity of that shortage is plain from the prices. Powder could be bought in the Low Countries for a shilling per pound weight but cost anything from five to twenty-five times that in Catholic-held Ireland.

To evaluate the tactics of such asymmetric warfare, the counter march versus the charge, let's begin with two English columns that set out from Dublin on 27

1 Blackmore, David J, 'Destructive and Formidable': 'British infantry firepower, 1642–1765 Ph D. Nottingham Trent University, August 2012, p. 37. Barriffe, William, *Military Discipline* (London: Thomas Harper, 1635), pp.45, 48.
2 Reid, Stuart, *All the King's Armies*, (Staplehurst: Spellmount,1998), p.9.
3 Cited in Reid, *All the King's Armies*, p. 24.
4 Reid, *All the King's Armies*, p.5.
5 *Contemp. Hist.*, I, p.15.
6 Lord Justices to Commissioners for Affairs of Ireland 1 September 1642 in *Irish Confed.*, ii, pp.57–59, 62.

November, one marching north to resupply and reinforce Drogheda, the other marching south to relieve the Black Castle of Wicklow town.

Sir Patrick Wemyss, lieutenant of the cavalry troop nominally commanded by James Butler Earl of Ormond (commander-in-chief of the army) escorted a column of 600 foot soldiers under Major Christopher Roper on a leisurely march from Dublin to reinforce and resupply Drogheda and had reached Julianstown bridge on the Nanny by the morning of 29 November. Hugh O'Byrne, commander of the troops who loosely ringed the capital had been shadowing Wemyss and sent his groom ahead to rouse the regiment of Philip MacHugh O'Reilly at Slane, on the Boyne. O'Reilly's 'ragged regiment' of some 1,500 men formed the sharp end of a pincers tentatively closing on the lifeline from Drogheda to Dublin.[7] O'Byrne was a long service veteran of Spanish service and O'Reilly had served time in Flanders as a young man, before resuming his duties as a landowner and most recently member of parliament for County Cavan. [8]

Wemyss had proceeded for a quarter of a mile north of Julianstown Bridge along the 'dirty lane' cut through the bocage. Visibility was poor because the lane was bordered by a high 'ditch' (meaning the fosse, the embankment created by the excavated spoil and the hedge planted on top of the bank) when a hostile force loomed out of a 'mighty fog' in a large field of corn stubble. [9] Already they were within musket shot. Wemyss 'advised' Roper (evidently no one was in overall command) to have his men clamber over the ditch into the stubble field.[10]

> The Captains presently began to draw up their men into a Battalia, and entered the field, The Soldiers seemed at first to be overjoyed to meet them, The Rebels making a stand, they did so also, But it so fell out as they were ready to give fire, one of the Officers (who dying in the place prevented the like punishment for it) commanded a Countermarch, in which they being compelled to take a Ditch were disordered, and the Enemy judging it a flight gave such a shout that frighted them into a further confusion, and so presently charging them were routed, most were slain,... [11]

7 Deposition of Arthur Culme, fol. 131v; Deposition of Francis Greham fol. 153v; *TCD MS 833 (County Cavan).*

8 O'Lochlainn, Colm (ed.) *Irish Chiefs and Leaders: Studies by Father Paul Walsh.* (Dublin: Sign of the Three candles,1960), p.369.

9 Patrick Wemys to Ormond, Drogheda, 29 November, *Irish Confed.* iii, p. 336.

10 *Ormonde*, p.240.

11 Bernard, Nicholas, *The whole proceedings of the siege of Drogheda in Ireland*...(William Bladen: London, 1642), p. 16.

Ormond's report to the king blamed the hapless infantrymen, most of whom were slaughtered, rather than his client Wemyss or his troopers who escaped to Drogheda unscathed. [12]

> The foot were for the most part of those English that had been pillaged by them [the Irish] and had, I doubt, with their goods lost their courage. They betook themselves to their heels upon sight of the enemy, not once shooting one shot or striking one stroke. The men had as many arms as all the rebels in the kingdom, and were as well trained as they … The foot, when I saw them in the field, I thought they had not soldiers faces; and now it appears they had not soldiers' hearts.

It is hard to believe that a battle cry could prove so unnerving but there are other examples of comparable panic. Old-timer James Hamilton Viscount Clandeboy held on to his coastal stronghold of Killyleagh County Down and on Christmas Day 1641 he felt confident enough to send out one Major Barclay and Captain Inglis with 240 men, 140 of them musketeers and the rest pikemen. [13]

> They met with a party of the rebels, whose custom is to fall one with a great shout or cry, whereupon the most part of the soldiers that were with Barclay and Inglis fled before ever the rebels charged them; so as these two or three gentlemen, with the most part of all the men, together with their arms were lost.

The crown soldiers were hastily embodied refugees captained by raw officers. For example, one of the six captains was Edward Aldridge who owned a plantation estate south of Clones County Monaghan and recruited men from the adjacent Fermanagh-Monaghan borderland.[14] The bedrock of the Ulster plantation should

12 *Warr of Ireland*, p.155.

13 Viscount Montgomery, Mount Alexander, 31 December 1641 to Alexander Montgomerie, 6th Earl of Eglinton Hill, George, *The Montgomery Manuscripts: (1603–1706).* (Cleeland & Dargan: Belfast, 1869), pp. 309–310.

14 Deposition of Avis Braishawe, fol 81r; Deposition of Agnes Machem, fol 135r; Deposition of Barbary Morton, fol.145r; Deposition of Elizabeth Parker, fol.153r; Deposition of Margaret Riddington, fol. 157r; Deposition of Elizabeth Dickison, fol.101r; Deposition of Ann Booth, fol.78r; Deposition of Margaret Blower, fol.77r; Deposition of Eleanor Barton, fol. 72r; Deposition of Elizabeth Dewsberry, fol. 100r; Deposition of Dorothy Talbot, fol. 175r; Deposition of Ann Band, fol. 190r; Deposition of Daniel Morris, fol. 245r: *TCD MS 835, (County Fermanagh).* Deposition of William Aldrich, fol. 173r; Deposition of Jane Bordman, 191r; Deposition of Mary Ward, fol. 80r; Deposition of Mary Beddell, fol. 219r; Deposition of George Creighton, fol. 230r; Examination of Shane Brady, fol. 290r; Examination of Conor Maguire, fol 291r: *TCD MS 832, (County Cavan).* Deposition of

have been armed, trained and regularly mustered settlers: the muster of Aldridge's tenants in 1629 recorded 45 men with 32 swords, 21 pikes, a caliver and a musket between them.[15] But Aldridge's men and their comrades had at least as much training as O'Reilly's followers.

What had gone so wrong at Julianstown? 'countermarch' probably signified 'firing by two ranks advanced' a manoeuvre that would have been too complex for inexperienced troops to execute in a timely fashion after scrambling over a ditch.[16] And the first rank would necessarily have turned their backs to the enemy, if they got off a volley at all. [17] O'Byrne or O'Reilly noticed the confusion and the soldiers set up a 'shout'. This battle cry should be distinguished from the 'word' that was designed for mutual recognition in the heat of battle: the usual word would be 'Sancta Maria', in imitation of the Habsburg armies of the Thirty Years' War'. This battle cry may have sounded like that 'hubbub' which Spenser's *View* describes as an onomatopoeia for the 'terrible yell … which their kern use at their first encounter' and which ended in the words or '*a bua*'/aboo [to victory].[18] Or the cry may have sounded something like the 'Rebel yell', a falsetto whoop repeated over and over. The Irish were agreeably surprised that the yell paralysed the English who did not fire their muskets even once. [19]

Aldridge and Thomas Moyne of Lisreagh (south of Cavan town) were killed and their companies wiped out. [20] Major Roper together with captains William Cadogan and Charles Townley made it to Drogheda, though with the tally of their companies 'very defective'.[21] The difference in outcome between complete and partial disaster probably depended on where the companies stood in the battle line and if they fled back towards the Nanny or forward to the safety of Drogheda. An unknown number of camp followers were also slaughtered: Cúconnacht O'Gowan

Ann Haughton, fol. 122r; Deposition of Mary Marriott, fol. 125r: *TCD MS 834 (County Monaghan)*.

15 Johnston, John, 'An Irish County in 1630: the Muster Roll of County Monaghan', *Clogher Record*, vol. 20, No. 2 (2010), pp. 239–40.

16 Anon., *The Military discipline wherein is martially showne the order for driling the musket and pike*, (London, 1642), p.4. Barriffe, *Military Discipline* p.184; Elton, Richard, *The Compleat Body of the Art Military*, (Robert Leybourne: London, 1650), pp. 192–193.

17 Roberts, Keith, *Pike and Shot Tactics 1590–1660*, (Osprey: Oxford, 2010), pp.39–40; Blackmore, 'British Infantry Firepower, 1642–1765', p.34.

18 Dryden, John, *The Works of that Famous English Poet, Mr. Edmond Spenser*, (Henry Hills: London, 1679),
p. 219.

19 Deposition of George Creighton, *TCD MS 833 (County Cavan)*, fol. 232r.

20 Davies O. 'The Castles of Co. Cavan: Part II', *Ulster Journal of Archaeology*, Third Series, Vol. 11 (1948), pp.114-5.

21 Royal Commission on Historical Manuscripts, *The Manuscripts of the Marquis of Ormonde, Fourteenth Report* (London: Eyre and Spottiswoode, 1895) I, pp. 120–123.

sergeant in the company of Hugh MacPhilip – the colonel's son – bragged of skewering a 'Calliagh' [hag] who was wife of one of the soldiers, with his long skeane.[22]

Charles Coote who led the expedition to Wicklow was an altogether more formidable character than Wemyss or Roper. He had served as a captain during the closing years of Tyrone's Rebellion (1596–1603), been rewarded with plantation lands across the Gaelic midlands and recalled to the colours as a brigadier in Wentworth's army.[23] On the seaward side of the Wicklow massif Fiach O'Toole of Castlekevin had hung on as a lessee on part of the confiscated O'Toole patrimony and was now beleaguering the Black Castle of Wicklow town.[24] Coote reached Wicklow on 29 November (the same day that Wemyss had his 'unfortunate rancounter'), scattered the besiegers and set about terrorizing the natives: [25]

> Three women whereof, one Gentlewoman big with Child, and a boy were hanged on the Bridge of Neuragh, [Newrath] by command of old Sir Charles Coote in his first march to that County, and caused his guide to blow into his Pistol and so shot him dead, he also hang'd a poor Butcher on the same march, called Thomas McWilliam.

Coote returned between mountain and sea by way of Newcastle, where he passed the night. The manuscript 'Breviary of the Services done around Dublin', takes up the story: [26]

> … we marched from Newcastle loaded with the pillage of the enemies, who showed themselves to our fronts making ready to fight, and when we had marched about two miles they came down towards Sir Charles Coote and his men as they were in a narrow lane, a bog being on one side of them and a little wood on the other. Thinking there to have got the advantage of that place which is called Kilcoole, Sir Charles and his men being in some little disorder at the first, the enemy came on boldly

22 Deposition of Symon Wesnam, fol. 205; Examination of Shane Brady, fol. 290r; Examination of Conor Maguire, fol.291r: *TCD MS 833 (County Cavan).*

23 Wanklyn, Malcolm, *The Army of Occupation in Ireland 1603–42: Defending the Protestant Hegemony* (Warwick: Helion, 2022), pp. 147, 148, 150. Armstrong, Robert, 'Coote, Sir Charles', DIB.

24 O'Byrne, Emmet, O'Toole, Fiach (Luke) and O'Byrne, Aodh *DIB*. Deposition of Richard Carpenter, fol. 34r; Deposition of Edward Deane, fol. 40r; Deposition of Richard Bretner fol. 29r: *TCD MS 811 (County Wicklow).*

25 R.S. *A collection of some of the murthers and massacres committed on the Irish in Ireland since the 23d of October 1641* (London: 1662) p.15.

26 'A Breviary of the Services Done about Dublin', Bodleian Library, MS. Clarendon 21 fol. 14.

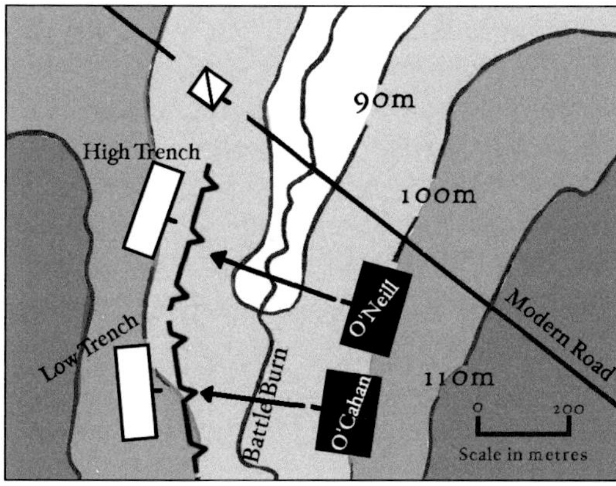

Glenmaquin

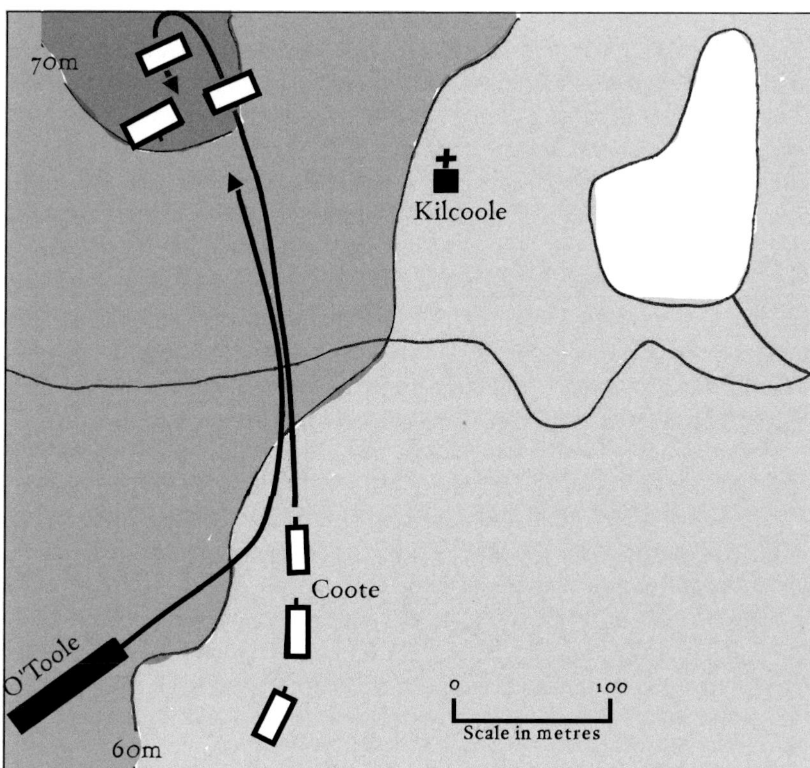

Kilcoole

> and swiftly with a great shout after their barbarous manner; but by the time that two or three volleys of shot were given on both sides Sir Charles and his men recovered the hill where they found good ground both for horse and foot, from which place our musketeers played on them very fiercely and both slew some and hurt a great many so that they suddenly dispersed themselves and fled towards the bogs and into the Woods …[27]

The operation described here would grow common. The English had regular standing troops and so they could choose the when and where of any thrust into Irish held territory. The Irish on the other hand assembled men in response to incursions and could never mobilise in time to contest the outward march. Usually, they tangled with the enemy at a pass or 'bealach' though bogs or at a ford or bridge on his return march when he was encumbered by evacuees, booty, and worn-out horses.

Terrain analysis and a close reading of the 'Breviary' suggests that O'Toole's thousand marched west of Coote on a converging course to reach a point where the road sloughed through a stream at Kilcoole, just as Coote's column was crossing. Wemyss had worried about getting caught at just such a defile – Julianstown Bridge – and relaxed his guard fatally after he negotiated the bridge.

All sorts of things could happen at a defile that could be captured in that phrase 'some little disorder'. Those wading a ford might wet their powder bags and bandoliers like the hundred reivers from the garrisons of Jamestown and Carrick-on-Shannon in County Roscommon. Seizing the moment, their pursuers charged, killing sixteen men and wounding four while the survivors scrambled to a nearby castle.[28] The column might thin out or bunch up, men might stumble, cart wheels bog down, or at the very least the front or rear might be isolated. O'Toole probably fell on Coote's rear but the old soldier improvised a rearguard action. O'Toole's mistake was to press the attack once Coote's men had reached the nearby hill and could turnabout, deploy and loose volleys. The third volley supposedly cut down the officer leading the attack, an ensign and a drummer. This claim is not true (Fiach O'Toole would be alive and well twelve years later) but it suggests aimed fire at high value targets. We see other examples of musketeers picking out officers who no doubt would have been identifiable as the men clad in bright cloth and lace waving their swords. On 13 April 1642 a Catholic detachment launched 'a bold but disorderly charge' near the suburbs of Cork city on, 'English foot who, having the advantage of a ditch where they had planted themselves, wounded so many of the

27 Fissel, Mark Charles, *English Warfare, 1511–1642*, (London: Routledge, 2001), p.247. *Irish Confed.*, i, xxxiii.

28 Deposition of Walter Fraser, *TCD MS 831,* (County Leitrim), fol. 35r.

Irish officers, as there were hardly any left to lead on the men, which occasioned their sudden retreat'.[29]

Back to Kilcoole. O'Toole's men pulled back and Coote's cavalry pursued and bagged another eight dead Irishmen (or twenty-seven, the account is confusing) and an assortment of discarded weapons, 'many fowling pieces, pikes, [pitch] forks, halberds and darts with three bags of powder [and] two bags of bullets'. The Lords Justices, spooked by the Julianstown disaster, beseeched Coote to 'come with all speed' to the capital where they appointed him military governor. [30]

The natives of County Wicklow were more cautious in future and confined themselves to hit-and-run guerrilla actions. Colonel Crawford returned to his garrison at Bullock from a foray into County Wicklow in July 1642: [31]

> … wherein he hath done good service by burning of above two hundred Towns wherein the Rebels did harbour themselves, and taking cattle and sheep from them, but the Rebels never stood to fight, although they showed themselves in great multitudes but as our Army came near them, they run all away, our men beat them out of the woods, bogs, and mountains, wheresoever our men came, and yet these wicked Traitors upon all advantages, if they meet with a few of our men, and they many, would set upon them, by which we have lost three men, and in one night as our Troop horses were feeding, stole many of them away, which loss is not small …

Glenmaquin (16 June 1642) was unambiguously a battle, not a skirmish, with four times as many men fighting as at Julianstown or Kilcoole. On one side stood an army raised from protestant settlers in the fertile Laggan lowlands of north-east County Donegal and built around a core of regular soldiers. It comprised two regiments, Sir William Stewart's and Sir Robert Stewart's, 700 more infantrymen in detached companies, and 300 horsemen: over two thousand altogether. [32] Sir Robert Stewart the effective commander-in-chief was William Stewart's younger brother and like so many Scots younger sons, he had fought for the Swedes in the Thirty Years' War. Coming back to Ireland, he was appointed governor of Culmore Fort on Lough Foyle guarding the entrance to the plantation city of Derry.

29 *Irish Confed.* i, p.76. Deposition of Symon Bridges, *TCD MS 823 (County Cork)*, fols., 171r–172v.
30 *Ormonde*, i, p.242.
31 Anon., *True relation of such passages and proceedings of the army of Dublin, in the Kingdome of Ireland as hath happened from the seventh of July to this present.* (London: William Bladen, 1642), p.4.
32 *Letters and Papers*, p.46.

Driven from east Ulster by Monro's Scots Covenanters and from north Leinster by the English, the Irish rebounded towards the north-west. Phelim O'Neill led about twice as many men as Stewart. Half of them were refugees from east and north Ulster led by Manus Rua [Red] O'Cahan seconded by the redoubtable Alasdair Mac Colla Mac Donald: their roles would be reversed when fighting with Montrose in Scotland 1644–45. The other half comprised O'Neill's and Rory Maguire's own followers from mid-Ulster. Phelim waded across the Finn, sacked the town of Raphoe (the bishop's fortified house held out) in the heart of the Laggan and marched north-west across the shoulder of Mongorry along the line of the perfectly straight modern road connecting Raphoe and Letterkenny. Taken by surprise, Stewart put the best gloss he could on this by claiming that he had deliberately lured O'Neill into the Laggan the better to crush him.[33] A London pamphlet even conjured up an entirely fictitious victory for Stewart on the 'Ford of the Finn'.[34] On Wednesday the 15th Stewart took up a blocking position on a hill descending steeply to a stream that later came to be called the 'Battle Burn' by its Scots planter inhabitants.[35] On this hill his men threw up earthworks (the sub townland placenames 'High Trench' and 'Low Trench' doubtless recall that frantic digging and shovelling in the darkness) but when dawn broke the next morning the works were still short of breast height. Facing them they could see the Irish on the opposite slope standing in two 'brigades' (by which Stewart meant any composite body larger than a battalion) corresponding to the O'Neill and O'Cahan/Mac Donald contingents, opposite William and Robert's 'brigades' respectively. Friar O'Mellan is terse, as always:

> Early in the day they were up and at each other. They advanced to the combat [na himghona], shots were fired and men felled. The Scots [na hAlbonaigh] broke and returned to the shelter of the sconce [sgonnsa]. They gave fire [Tugsat na Piléir uatha] and the pikemen at the rear of the Irish broke ...[36]

Sir Robert Stewart gives more details, though he makes no mention of digging sconces or breastworks on the crest.[37] The first exchange of fire happened when

33 *Letters and Papers*, p.45.

34 Anon. *A most true relation of a wonderfull victory* (London: R. Oulton and G. Dexter, 1642), p.6.

35 O'Donnell, Terence [ed.], *Father John Colgan, OFM, 1592–1658: essays in commemoration of the third centenary of his death,* (Dublin: Assisi, 1959), pp.98–100. The Schools' Collection, Volume 1102, pp. 38, 74; National Folklore Collection, UCD.

36 *Cín Lae*, p.12.

37 Sir Robert Stuart to Sir John Borlase, 21 June 1642, *Letters and Papers*, p.49.

Stewart sent out some horsemen and commanded musketeers to probe O'Neill's position with orders to pull back to the main body if attacked. O'Neill's men, 'came on with a furious and swift march, making a terrible outcry in their march according to their manner'. The scouts backed up the steep hill in an orderly fashion, giving fire as they did so. The Irish, 'apprehending that retire to be a flight marched close together in two brigades towards ours, which after we had perceived, having obtained our end in drawing them towards that little hill where we were situate, we began to march slowly, they still advancing.' O'Cahan's brigade attacked William Stewart's, 'so fiercely in so much that they were not far from coming to push of pike, but seeing the resolution and constancy of our men advancing still and not losing ground galled them with continual shot, finding their rear to shrink back first and then to fly …'

Stewart's claim that his troops advanced, firing as they did, makes no sense. Why would they clamber over their own breastworks and scramble down a steep slope? The reality is that the two Laggan army brigades very sensibly stood behind cover, at the top of a slope, and delivered successive volleys. The outcome hung in the balance on the scarp for fifteen minutes, which is a long time to endure close range volley fire. Perhaps the scarp was so steep that the attackers were hard put to close the final few yards and strike with sword or pike but equally, most of Stewart's shots must have flown over their heads. But one ball felled Mac Colla who was 'alone' out in front, and the O'Cahan formation began to unravel as pikemen at the rear 'broke': the rearmost soldiers were usually the first to slip away because they could melt away more easily than the men standing in the front ranks.[38] Seeing what happened, the second square under Phelim O'Neill, 'did bear their countrymen company'.

PS. the author of the *Aphorismical Discovery* was no friend of Phelim O'Neill's and he sneered that his men no 'sooner showed their face onto the enemy than their heels'.[39]

The Irish outran any foot soldiers who ventured to pursue: 'broken upon they are sure not to be killed, they run so well,' said O'Neill in a barbed compliment to his followers.[40] Stewart's cavalry were almost certainly posted along what would later be the road to Letterkenny and they pursued the runaways. To judge from the names of the three captains who were killed – an O'Donnelly, O'Hagan and an O'Neill – Phelim's brigade must have stood to the right or north of O'Cahan's brigade in the path of the cavalry and so bore the brunt of the subsequent 'chase and execution' over six miles. O'Mellan admits the Irish lost 180 men, which he

38 *Warr of Ireland*, p.23.
39 *Contemp. Hist*, i, p. 42.
40 Contemp. Hist., i, p.42.

considered a 'lot' [*iomad*].[41] Mac Colla was the doughtiest warrior on the Irish side [*do bfhearr lámh and sin*] and he had already launched the first of what would come to be known as the 'Highland Charge' – at Bendooragh – delivering a salvo at close range and closing with blade weapons.[42] No doubt, Glenmaquin was a learning experience for him.

The Laggan men won because they fired from behind cover and there were enough of them to lay down heavy fire. Had they been fewer and had they been caught in the open they might have been overrun as happened elsewhere. For example, the 'Adventurers', as subscribers to Irish war loans were called, funded an expedition under Alexander Baron Forbes which made landfall at Kinsale in County Cork in July 1642. In concert with the Bandon town companies, Forbes marched to relieve an isolated castle and, on his way, swept up an enormous prey of livestock. He next left three of his own companies together with a Bandon company behind at Clonakilty to guard the livestock. Cormac Mac Carthy Reagh's soldiers had been lurking nearby and attacked whereupon most of the English fled for safety to a nearby 'fort' (probably an old earthen rath) except for one of Forbes's companies and some Bandonmen who stood and opened fire but, 'after the first discharge the enemy fell in upon them & routed them'.[43] The survivors who fled to the fort were 'beleaguered' by Mac Carthy's 'varlets' drawn up 'in a square Battle': evidently Mac Carthy Reagh did not care to press an attack against musketeers firing from behind cover but lingered ineffectually until Forbes turned back and rescued the survivors.[44]

Volley fire, cumbersome as it was, usually worked even when the Irish were the ones sheltering behind embankments. The 'Breviary' describes how in February the Irish tried to defend their main camp at Kilsallaghan Castle, north of Dublin which was girdled by 'many high ditches and strong enclosures'.[45] They posted musketeers behind the ditches and, '… at first they did fire very fast but the shot coming too hot and very sure upon them from our side they forsook the field and leaving two bags of bullets and a large leather wallet full of powder behind them they got behind huge high ditches for their refuge.'[46]

41 *Cín Lae*, p.12. *Letters and Papers*, p.50. McCarthy, Patrick, 'Preserving Donegal: the battle of Glenmaquin, 16 June 1642', *The Irish Sword*, Volume XXIII. Number 94. Winter 2003, pp. 361–383.

42 Smith [Mac Gabhann], P. P. (2017). 'An Historical Tract in Irish Relating to the Confederate Wars in Ireland', Studia Hibernica, 43, p.15.

43 Cleland, James, 'Account of the rising in Munster', *TCD MS 840* , fols. 47v, 48r.

44 Peters, Hugh, *A true relation of the passages of Gods providence in a voyage for Ireland*, (London: John White, 1642), p.7. Deposition of Edmond Mc Carty, *TCD MS 823* (County Cork), fol. 143v.

45 Ormonde, p.283.

46 Breviarie, fol .17

Until Kilsallaghan, Dublin Castle's writ ran no further than two miles inland, the semi-circle described by today's M50. From this narrow beachhead the Lords Justices would reconquer the plain of the old Pale over the spring and summer of 1642. 'The Rebels want powder' warned one pamphlet, but if they contrive to run blockades and import 'great store' then 'it will be a long and miserable war'. That's what happened. In September 1642 twenty ships carried a 'vast quantity' of arms and ammunition from Dunkirk, Saint Malo, Nantes and La Rochelle to be disgorged at Wexford. Afterwards gunpowder could be bought for a 50 percent markup on continental prices: pricey, but not ruinously so and Catholic armies switched to conventional pike and shot tactics.

Cavalry Tactics

The modern take on the caracole is that it was a close order fire by ranks manoeuvre rather like the counter march on horseback. On the face of it, cavalry sacrificed their unique assets of momentum, mobility and shock but it could work against a pike square if the *reiters* halted just beyond the reach of the pikes, fired their pistols or carbines, turned aside or about to reload, and did the same again, and again.

> The first rank, having given fire, is to wheel off to the left (unless the ground will not permit it, but that it must be to the right) making ready and falling into the rear; the second rank immediately gives fire upon the wheeling away of the first, and so the rest successively.[47]

It would be like shooting fish in a barrel but if the pike square was screened by ranks of musketeers, then the contest between muskets fired from the ground and lighter firearms fired from an unstable horseback platform would be a one-sided one. Fortunately for English cavalry, where the Irish did not charge, they deployed big pike squares, without a screen of shot. At Ballintober (July 1642) Sir Robert King's troop of cavalry fired their carbines 'within two Pikes lengths' (or about twelve yards) of the Irish while a nearby 'forlorn hope' or advanced detachment of English musketeers also gave fire. King noticed that the pikes of the fallen had become entangled with the pikes of their comrades and seized on the disorder to fall on a corner (always a weak point) of the *tercio* while the foot soldiers fired at the massed formation's flank. The *tercio* broke.[48] It was unusual for pike squares

47 Cruso, John, *Militarie Instructions for the Cavallrie* (Cambridge: Printers to the Universitie of Cambridge, 1632), p.98.

48 Lenihan, Padraig, *Raw Generals and Green Soldiers: Catholic Armies in Ireland 1641–43*: (Warwick: Helion, 2023), pp. 66–67.Borlase, Edmund, *The history of the execrable Irish*

to stand alone, and the practice can be seen as another response to the gunpowder famine.

Swedish king Gustavus Adolphus (1594–1632) realised that mounted pistoleers could not compete with well-trained musketeers in a firefight, so he inserted musketeer 'platoons' of fifty men in amongst them and discarded the caracole in favour of more aggressive cavalry tactics. Gustavus's cavalry was deployed in three ranks and trained to charge right up to the enemy. The first and second ranks would then fire one of their pistols before advancing with drawn swords, keeping the other pistol in reserve for the melee. The third rank attacked with drawn swords, keeping both pistols charged for the melee. Prince Rupert's preference for 'Swedish' (by 1640 all sides in the Thirty Years' War were following the Swedish lead) cavalry shock over firepower, explains why the Royalist horse carried the day so often during the early part of the English Civil War.

Whatever about the relative merits of caracoling or charging against foot soldiers, cavalry should never try caracoling against cavalry. The clash of French *reiters* (in Muscovite pay) against Polish lancers at Klushino (1610) made that plain to see.[49] Yet English armies in Ireland were as slow to follow so-called 'Swedish' on horseback as they were on foot.

The Battle of Liscarroll (3 September 1642) was a potential point of articulation where history failed to turn. Had the Munster Protestants lost, they would have been done for. They won and hung on, just. Dragging 'Bess', their giant cannon, around in a hollowed tree trunk, the Catholic forces (contingents came and went so there was no army, as such) had mopped up every protestant hold in County Limerick in July and August and after passing through the Ballyhoura Gap into north County Cork they quickly took Liscarroll Castle. Murrough O'Brien, Baron Inchiquin, commander of the English forces in Munster chose to gather all his available troops and force a battle rather than wait to be defeated piecemeal. Fought just before munition imports picked up, Liscarroll belongs to those nine months when – in effect – one side had the use of firearms and the other hadn't. The scale was comparable to Glenmaquin, with the Irish having twice as many foot soldiers as had the English. Not that this mattered. The Irish had 400 horsemen, Inchiquin marginally more, and the win-lose outcome would hinge on the opening cavalry action.

Garret Barry the Irish general, a veteran of Spanish Flanders, drew up his infantry in three squares, a big one comprising pike, flanked by two smaller squares of shot. The westernmost square stood 'upon a little rising ground' in rolling open-field

rebellion (London: Henry Brome et.al., 1680) pp.76–81.

49 Radoslaw Sikora, Battle of Kłuszyn (Kluszino) <http://www.radoslawsikora.republika.pl/materialy/Kluszyn.pdf>

grassland so 'the whole body of cavalry' was posted here to offer flank protection.[50] Inchiquin's formation was a mirror image of Barry's. [51] At nine o'clock in the morning the encounter began and, one might very well say, ended with cavalry combat. Inchiquin sent a troop forward to lure the Irish into attacking. Barry's cavalry duly advanced, carefully co-ordinating their movements with those of the detached shot scurrying alongside. The English troop, and assorted gentlemen riders, pulled back, facing about from time to time in a show of bravado. The Irish came on relentlessly, 'resolved to put the whole stake on the game' with 'their musketeers running before them to bushes and ditches from whence with security they played on us, their body of Horse following to second their muskets.'[52] Lewis Viscount Kinalmeaky, son of the Great Earl of Cork, wore full armour but a fowling piece fired from behind a hedge shot him in the neck. The dying man grasped the reins of his brother's horse but the latter was too harried to recover his body which was quickly stripped. By now Inchiquin's men had been pushed back almost back to their starting position, at which point Barry's men retreated.[53] Next, Inchiquin's whole army advanced in a line but his cavalry broke alignment and made for the Irish cavalry who charged, in their turn:

> they [the Irish] did suppose that the English were better experienced and armed with guns (most of them being a furnished with a carabine and a case of pistols) than themselves. They put on a resolution Pell Mell … to fall in amongst them, that they should have little time to discharge, none to recharge, and by that means to make their swords and numbers to be decisive. The first, second, and third ranks of the English squadron gave fire as they were directed and wheeled off to the rear. This the hindmost rank interpreted as retreat, and they began to rout. [54]

Ormond's cavalry perpetrated the same potentially fatal mistake at the Battle of Ballinvegga (17 March 1643).[55] The main body on Ormond's right wing was led by

50 O'Brien, Barry, 'Battle of Liscarroll' in Irish Sword no. 90, (2001), p.399. Broket, William, *Good newes from Ireland* ... (London: L. Thomas, 1642), p.4.

51 Anon., *A Journal of the most memorable passages in Ireland* (London: T. S, 1642), pp.4, 6.

52 Buckley, James 'The battle of Liscarroll, 1642', Journal of the Cork Archaeological and Historical Society Ser. 2, Vol. 4, No. 38 (1898), p.94.

53 Johnson, Thomas, *A true relation of Gods providence in the province of Munster…* (London: William Ley, 1642), p. 3.

54 Anon. 'A Discourse of the Battle of Liscarroll', TCD MS 840, No. 20.

55 Anon., *A full and true relation of the late great victory, obtained by the Protestants against the rebells in Ireland* (London: Henry Overton, 1643), p.2. Miller, Amos, 'The Battle of Ross; a controversial military event', *Irish Sword* no.39 (1971), pp.141–158. Creichtoun, George, 'A Faithful Account ... by G. Creichtoun chaplain to his Lordship's Regiment' in

Philip Sidney Viscount Lisle, the callow lieutenant-general of the Horse, along with Sir Richard Grenville and Sir Thomas Lucas, veterans of the Swedish and Dutch service respectively. Lisle cantered towards a scattering of enemy horsemen who had just escaped murderous artillery fire in a hedged-in boreen, their comrades, 'goodly men and horses lay there all torn, and their guts lying on the ground'.[56] When Lisle's front rank fired: [57]

> the word was they should wheel about, which they did in good order, when suddenly some of the enemy horse fell in amongst the English horse, and fell to work with their swords, cut Sir Thomas Lucas in the head and struck him from his horse, as likewise Alexander Burrows, the Marshall.

Another account claims that Lucas was struck with a poll axe, a sort of long-handled hammer whose head had a flat bludgeoning face, called a 'poll' on one side, and a spike on the other. Lucas survived the blow but it 'shortened his life'.[58] Lisle galloped back to the baggage train and cried out '£10 for a guide' to lead him to safety: or so we are told by partisans of Ormond, his factional rival. Witnesses at the subsequent court of inquiry agreed that the cavalrymen followed Lisle back in the state of panic and disorder shouting, 'We are betrayed. We are all lost'. One major Morris who lay wounded on a litter in the baggage train testified that Grenville rode among the wagons. The clear implication was that Grenville was hiding but very likely he was trying to chivvy his men who were lurking there out of sight.[59] Grenville was like Coote, cruel but cool in a crisis. He clapped Lisle on the shoulder and turned him around: 'Come my Lord, we may yet recover it'. Soon 'the two bodies of horse were mingled together, slashing one another for a time, till at last rode away together'.[60] Like Grenville at Ballinvegga, Inchiquin saved the day at Liscarroll After hacking his way to safety, he set to pulling his cavalry back into rank and file while the Irish horsemen, 'scattered all the field' in pursuit of fugitives and stragglers, 'so as hardly could twenty be seen in a body'.[61]

P.H. Hore, *History of the Town and County of Wexford: Old and New Ross* (London, 1900), p.297. *Contemp. Hist.* i, p.58.

56 Ormonde, i, p.405.

57 Gilbert, *Irish Confed.* ii, pp .256–57.

58 Firth, Charles Harding (ed.) Newcastle, Margaret Cavendish Duchess of, *The Life of William Cavendish, Duke of Newcastle, to which is Added the True Relation of My Birth, Breeding and Life* (London, J.C. Nimmo, 1886), p. 285.

59 Miller, Amos, 'The Battle of Ross; a controversial military event', *Irish Sword* no.39 (1971), pp. 151, 152.

60 *Contemp Hist*, I, p.62.*Ormonde*, p.405.

61 *Irish Confed.*, i, pp.93–94.

Conclusion

The Irish charge was comparable to the Swedish Gå–På or the French á prest attack and can best be seen as a response to a critical shortage of gunpowder. The trick was to shadow the enemy, keep out of range of his shot until he fell into disorder and then race across the musket killing zone to close with the blade: firing a single salvo at close range came later. Easier to describe than to do. So much depended on the leader's 'eye', that ability to recognise the stirrings of disorder or hesitancy in enemy ranks and pounce. Dutch style fire by ranks was least effective as a counter measure when practiced by smaller formations (typically companies) of raw troops in open country but otherwise worked very well against an enemy short on firepower. Once gunpowder prices fell, the Irish quickly adopted conventional pike and shot tactics, with mixed results. They beat the Scots by 'push of pike' at Benburb (1646) but were annihilated by English armies at Dungan's Hill (August 1647) and Knocknanuss (November 1647). The only bright spot in those twin disasters was the performance of Irish and Scots veterans of Montrose's campaigns. Using clouds of gun smoke and 'some enclosures and ditches' to good effect, Mac Colla came 'thundering downhill' in a Highland Charge and routed Inchiquin's left wing even as the latter's right carried all before them. [62] Perhaps the Irish should not have been quite so wholehearted and quick to abandon the charge. But that is another story.

62 An officer of the Parliaments army, *A perfect narrative of the battell of Knocknones*, (London: Robert Bostock, 1647), p.8.

Abbreviations

Breviarie	'A Breviarie of the Services Done about Dublin', Bodleian Library, MS. Clarendon 21 fols.14-19.
Cín Lae	Tadhg Ó Donnchadha ed. 'Cín Lae Uí Mhealláin' *Analecta Hibernica* iii, (1931).
Contemp. Hist.	Gilbert, J.T., ed. *A Contemporary History of Affairs in Ireland from 1641 to 1652* (3 vols., Dublin, 1880).
DIB	James McGuire and James Quinn (eds), Dictionary of Irish Biography. (Cambridge, 2009). http://dib.cambridge.org.
Irish Confed.	Gilbert, J.T., ed. *History of the Irish Confederation and the War in Ireland 1641–1649* (7 vols., Dublin, 1879–80).
IHS	*Irish Historical Studies*
Letter and Papers	Hogan, James, (ed.) *Letters and Papers relating to The Irish Rebellion between 1642–46.* (Dublin: IMC, 1936).
ODNB	*Oxford Dictionary of National Biography* https://www.oxforddnb.com/
Ormonde	Carte, Thomas, *An History of the Life of James Duke of Ormonde* (3 vols, London, 1736), i.
Impartial Relation	Gilbert, John T., Colonel Henry O'Neill's relation of transactions of General Owen Neill and his party in *A Contemporary History of Affairs in Ireland from 1641 to 1652.*, Dublin, Irish Archaeological and Celtic Society (1880) volume 3, pp. 196–214.
Warr of Ireland	Hogan, Edmund, ed. *The History Of The Warr Of Ireland From 1641 To 1653 by a British Officer of the Regiment of Sir John Clothworthy* (McGlashan and Gill: Dublin, 1873).

7

Montrose's Armies, 1644–1646

Dr Edward M. Furgol

The paper deals with armies the marquis of Montrose led from April 1644 until 30 July 1646. The first topic is Royalist military organisation and practices. It then examines the marquis' first two armies (April-July 1644), which were overwhelming English. From August 1644 until February 1645, it would be fairer to call the marquis's army: Montrose's and Alasdair MacColla MacDonald's. From February until early September 1645, it is more accurate to call it Montrose's, Alasdair's and Lord Gordon's or Viscount Aboyne's army. All will be examined in greater depth.

I. A Command structure – military

From the perspectives of 17th century military organisation in continental Europe and Great Britain and Ireland, perhaps Charles I set Montrose an impossible task. In January 1644 Montrose presented the king with a plan to regain Scotland. It required Randal MacDonnell, 2nd earl of Antrim (soon to be 1st marquis of Antrim) to raise Irish troops, landing them in western Scotland; the king of Denmark (Charles' uncle) to send German mercenaries (an idea entirely overlooking Christian IV's antipathy to Charles due to the British king's failure to aid him in 1625–1629, which had led to Christian's loss of power abroad and at home, and his willingness to mediate between Charles I and the Covenanters in 1640); shipments of arms and ammunition to arm Scottish Royalists; and Montrose's invasion of Scotland with cavalry provided by William Cavendish, 1st marquis of Newcastle (who faced a Covenanter army of over 20,000 men). On 20 January 1644, the king commanded Antrim to persuade the Irish Confederate council to levy 10,000 men to serve in England, and 2,000 to invade the Covenanter Archibald Campbell, 1st marquis of Argyll's lands. The king appointed Antrim General of the Highlands and Isles, and joint justiciary of the Isles with George Mackenzie, 2nd earl of Seaforth. Montrose received appointments as Lieutenant-General of Scotland (January-February 1644) and (from May 1645 but to his knowledge only from August 1645) Lieutenant-Governor and Captain-General of Scotland. In February, the king also commissioned his nephew Prince Maurice as Lieutenant-Governor and Captain-General, and the northeastern magnate George Gordon, 1st marquis of Huntly, as Lieutenant-General of Royalist forces raised from Aberdeenshire to Caithness and any entering that area. In Maurice's absence Montrose had overall command.

On 28 January Antrim and Montrose signed an agreement pledging the former to invade Argyll's lands from Ireland and to raise men in the Isles, while Montrose gathered troops in northeastern England and from the Borders to invade Scotland – all to occur on 1 April. Huntly was to take the field in the northeast. For centuries writers have stated that Huntly's unwillingness to cooperate with Montrose arose from the latter's role in his 1639 arrest and imprisonment by the Covenanters.[1] Other factors existed. First, Huntly had consistently supported Charles I – unlike Montrose. Second, the House of Huntly had great regional significance as an extensive landholder in Aberdeenshire and Banffshire, as a feudal superior over lands stretching across Scotland from the North Sea through Badenoch to Lochaber, as head of the large Gordon kin group and its allies, and constable of Inverness Castle. Furthermore, the marquis had decades more military experience than Montrose with service both in Scotland and the French army.[2] To complicate the situation further Antrim resented the appearance of subordination to Montrose, while Antrim's zone of authority conflicted with Huntly's feudal superiority, and many Scottish Royalist nobles disliked Montrose's appointment.[3] The king had created a military command structure that enshrined strategic dissonance.

I. B Command structure – civil

The lack of a civil government apparatus further complicated Montrose's situation. Why is this important? Montrose planned, executing to the best of his ability, a conventional war. He also intended to recruit a large regular army to aid the king in defeating the Parliamentarians. Only Huntly briefly considered waging a

1 Gordon, *Abridgement*, 49; Cowan, Montrose, 73–4, who condemns the idea.
2 Gordon, *Abridgement*, 89–90, 183.
3 Gordon, *Distemper*, 90–91; Cowan, *Montrose*, 144–145, 231; B. Robertson, *Lordship and Power in the North of Scotland: The Noble House of Huntly 1603–1690* (Edinburgh, 2011), 127–128; D. Stevenson, *Alasdair MacColla and the Highland Problem in the Seventeenth Century* (Edinburgh, 1980), 103.

guerrilla war. Examples existed of governing councils in all three kingdoms (for example, Prince of Wales Council for the West [of England], Irish Confederate Council, Scottish Committee of Estates, and the Committee of Both Kingdoms), and shire committees (Covenanter, English Parliamentarian and Royalist[4]) Montrose would choose to establish neither. Committees are value-added. If one lives by committees, one flourishes, because no one person can do everything. For instance, the English and Welsh Royalist ones maintained armies for nearly four years. The Irish Confederates kept their armies in the field for nearly a decade. The Covenanters' committees allowed them to sustain armies for twelve years.[5] Most impressively, the English Parliamentarian committee system conquered three kingdoms. After Kilsyth, when Montrose finally contemplated creating a civilian government, he proposed a parliament (to be held in Glasgow starting on 20 October 1645) and not a constantly sitting governmental body. Between 15 August and 4 September, he made no effort to revive the Scottish Privy Council despite the presence of the Marquis of Douglas, the Earls of Airlie, Airth, Annandale, Hartfell, and Mar, and peers' heirs Lords Carnegie, Drummond, Erskine, Fleming and Seton, and the Master of Madderty at the Bothwell army camp. The marquis focused on military operations to the exclusion of civilian government.

What roles did civil government have in military organisation and operations? Regardless of the place or ideology it initiated the levying of units, their equipage, training and pay. Despite his experience as a Covenanter officer in 1639–1641, Montrose ignored those examples, preferring a strictly military regime. The lack of a funding system, even one as fraught as the Covenanters'[6], meant that most units in the army were not under arms permanently or even for an entire campaigning season.

Added to that was the lack of a central authority to pursue a single strategic goal. Montrose was lieutenant general for Scotland, while Huntly had command for Aberdeenshire to Caithness. While Scotsman Major General Alasdair MacColla MacDonald answered to the Irish Confederate Supreme Council and to Antrim – the leading MacDonald/MacDonnell in Ireland. The three men had different strategic objectives. Montrose wanted to conquer Scotland then lead an army to help the king. Huntly wanted to ensure his regional power, then aid the king.

4 R. Hutton, *The Royalist War Effort 1642–1646* (New York, 1982), 87–90, for English and Welsh Royalist shire committees.

5 The Covenanters followed the Dutch example, which fielded more powerful armies and fleets than the French and Spanish, J. Glete, 'The Dutch Republic as a Great Power: Political Interaction and Armed Forces', 77–95, in *De Ruyter: Dutch Admiral*, eds. J.R. Bruijn, R. Prud'homme van Reine, R. yan Hövell tot Westerflier (Rotterdam, 2011).

6 See D. Stevenson, 'The Financing of the Cause of the Covenanters, 1638–1651, *SHR* (vol. 51, no. 152, pt. 2, October 1972), 89–123.

Alasdair and Antrim wanted to destroy the power of Clan Campbell and restore the pre-eminence of Clan Donald in Antrim and the southwest Highlands. (Alasdair also sought land to compensate for his father's loss of Colonsay.) Antrim might appear to favour the king, but his personal aggrandisement came first. For instance, in 1646 he used an Irish Confederate regimental commission, whose purpose was to reinforce Alasdair, to send nearly 300 men or a third of the unit to the Spanish Army of Flanders. One can see from that why the Irish Royalist leader and Lord Lieutenant of Ireland, James Butler, 12th Earl of Ormonde, distrusted him. Had the king sent his nephew Prince Maurice to Scotland as its Lieutenant Governor and Captain General as planned in February 1644, a constant army and a single strategy might have arisen from the divergent ones.

The data for the following discussion is insufficient to provide solid information for detailed charts. What roles did religious fervour and cultural loyalties have in motivating men to join Montrose's army? Looking at denominational dedication first, an affinity existed among four MacDonald clans (Clanranald, Glencoe, Glengarry and Keppoch) – they were Roman Catholics. Alasdair, the Stewarts of Appin, and Maclean of Lochbuie shared their faith.[7] These units fielded well over 2,000 men. The war as a religious crusade meant more to them than battling for Charles I. The presence of a priest in the first three regiments of the Irish Brigade enhanced their devotion.[8] The cultural enmity between Montrose's Gaelic troops and Scots speaking Covenanters supplied an additional motivation for the former during the campaigns.[9] All of Alasdair's units were Gaelic speakers, while they fought for the Gordons they accounted for a third of the elements, and for Montrose occasionally two-thirds. For example, at Kilsyth over 3,000 Gaels in the Royalists would have despised the Scots speaking Covenanters as culturally inferior. Certainly, the men of Montrose's army could easily identify the enemy as the other'. However, in 1651 many of the clans who had fought for Montrose and Alasdair raised forces to fight the English New Model Army.

While Montrose achieved success in under twelve months' campaigning his methods were hardly conducive to gaining support from his former Covenanter associates or the Hamiltonian Royalists or neutrals. Alasdair's Irish Brigade, which from the start killed every Campbell male of military age it encountered, earned a blood thirsty reputation.[10] The slaughter following the Covenanter defeats, including the cold-blooded killing of Aberdeen men after they had taken off their

7 *Memoirs of Scottish Catholics*, i. 317, 319; Stevenson, *Alasdair*, 53-5, 151, 158.

8 *Memoirs of Scottish Catholics*, i. 281, 303–308, 310, 320, 343, 348; Stevenson, *Alasdair*, 121–122, 146, 224.

9 Stevenson, *Alasdair*, 6, 8, 17–18, 23, 29, 54, 202–203, 212 n. 16, 267–268.

10 D. Stevenson, *Alasdair MacColla and the Highland problem in the seventeenth century* (Edinburgh, 1990), 215.

clothes so their blood would not spoil them[11], gave many non-Royalist Scots the desire for revenge and certainly none for accommodation.

Montrose followed the method of 'Let war pay for war', because he lacked a revenue stream based on land and excise taxes, fines of Covenanters, the sale of forfeited lands or customs duties, due to his refusal to establish a territorial base. He chiefly rewarded his soldiers with plunder.[12] Plunder satisfied his men at the

11 Tippermuir perhaps 1,000 routed Covenanters killed, Baillie, *Letters*, ii. 225, 233, 262; *Commentarius Rinuccinianus*, 6 vols., eds. D. O'Connell and B. O'Ferrall (Irish Manuscripts Commission, 1932–1949), i. 168, 462, iii. 295, iv. 357, v. 50; Gordon, *Abridgement*, 73–75; Napier, *Memorials*, ii. 149–151; *A true relation of the happy success*, 7–8; T. Carte, ed., Collection of original letters and papers, 2 vols. (London, 1739), i. 73-74; Wishart, *Memoirs*, 56–62; Stevenson, *Alasdair*, 128. For Aberdeen, *Extracts from the council register of the burgh of Aberdeen, 1643–1747*, ed. J. Stuart (Edinburgh, Scottish Burgh Records Society, 1872), 29; Gordon, *Abridgement*, 161; R. Gordon, *Genealogical History of the Earldom of Sutherland* (Edinburgh, 1813), 521; J. Spalding, *Memorials of the Trubles in Scotland and England, A.D. 1624–A.D.1645*, ed. J. Stuart (Aberdeen, Spalding Club, 1850), ii. 407–413. Argyll campaign 895 Campbell males killed – some in fighting, Carte, *Original Letters*, i. 75; Gordon, *Abridgement*, 98; *Reliquiae Celticae*, ii. 183; Spalding, *Memorials*, ii. 442–443; Wishart, *Memoirs*, 81; Stevenson, *Alasdair*, 147. Inverlochy 1,500 Covenanter dead – not all in rout, Carte, *Original Letters*, i. 75–76; Gordon, *Abridgement*, 100–102; Guthry, *Memoirs*, 179; Napier, *Memorials*, ii. 176–177; *Reliquiae Celticae*, 2 vols., eds. A. MacBain and J. Kennedy (Inverness, 1892–1894), ii. 183–185; Spalding, *Memorials*, ii. 444–445; Wishart, *Montrose*, 83–85; [J.C. Sinclair], *Historical and genealogical account of the Clan Maclean* ... (London, 1838), 124–125. Auldearn over 2,000, Gordon, *Abridgement*, 125–127; Gordon, Genealogical History, 524–525; J. Fraser, *Chronicles of the Frasers, The Wardlaw Manuscript* (Scottish History Society, 1905), 294–297; *Memoirs of Scottish Catholics*, ii. 336–339; *Reliquiae Celticae*, ii. 184–193; Spalding, *Memorials*, ii. 272–274; Wishart, *Memoirs*, 98–102; Stevenson, *Alasdair*, 188–189. Alford number of Covenanter dead vary: 1,600 Gordon, *Abridgement*, 131; 700 Gordon, *Genealogical History*, 526. Kilsyth 3,000 Covenanters killed, 5,469 Gordon, *Abridgement*, 144–145; 4,500 *Memoirs of Scottish Catholics*, i. 350; over 5,000 *The true relation of the late & happie – at Kilsyth* (n.p. 1645), 7; 6,000 Wishart, *Memoirs*, 124; 3,000 Stevenson, *Alasdair*, 202. A total of more than 9,000 dead.

12 After Tippermuir, Montrose spared Perth by excluding the Irish Brigade from entering, but allowed the plundering of its suburbs, and taking ammunition and cloth from the burgh, Gordon, *Abridgement*, 75; Napier, *Memorials*, ii. 152–161, 165; Stevenson, *Alasdair*, 129. For Aberdeen, Gordon, *Abridgement*, 161 (who states since Montrose could not pay his men, he had to allow plundering); Spalding, *Memorials*, ii. 407–413; Stevenson, *Alasdair*,134–135. Argyll December 1644–January 1645, *APS*, vi, i. 361–362, 790–791, ii. 275, 461; Spalding, *Memorials*, ii. 442–443; Stevenson, *Alasdair*, 148–149. Moray in February-March 1645, Stevenson, *Alasdair*, 166–167. Plundering of Dundee in April 1645, *APS*, vi. i. 519–521; Baillie, *Letters*, ii 264; *An extract of several letters from Scotland ... concerning the defeat given to the rebels ...* (London, 1645), 4–6; Gordon, *Abridgement*, 112–117; Guthry, *Memoirs*, 183; Napier, *Memorials*, ii. 186; Spalding, *Memorials*, ii. 458–463; Wishart, *Memoirs*, 88–95; Stevenson, *Alasdair*, 169–170. After Kilsyth, Montrose spared the occupied burgh of Glasgow from widespread pillaging only by moving his troops to Bothwell, Stevenson, *Alasdair*, 204. After capturing Aberdeen in

cost of alienating potential supporters. His soldiers also accepted cash instead of goods. Montrose eschewed the continental practice of contributions, which resembled taxation. Sometimes he required ransom payments, as with Perth in September 1644, Elgin in February 1645, and Glasgow in August 1645.[13] (There, after the army withdrew, lack of cash prevented Captain Murdoch Maclean of Lochbuie from buying clothing his men.)[14]

Between the demands of the agricultural seasons, the need to bring plunder home, and the desire to protect their families from Covenanter depredations[15], maintaining Scots Royalist units in the field for months was a challenge. Only the Irish Brigade served constantly since it had been raised as a permanent expeditionary force to compel the Covenanters to withdraw troops from Ulster, and it lacked ships preventing a return to Ireland. The brigade formed the foundation of Montrose's army from its inception until early September 1645. Even when the victorious army of Kilsyth divided Montrose's sole infantry in his march to the Borders consisted of 400–500 men from the brigade. (Montrose allowed his cousin Colonel Patrick Graham of Inchbrakie to march his Atholl Foot home to rebuild its burnt houses.[16]) Had the marquis established a territorial and financial base

May 1646 Huntly restricted plunder to the burgh's Covenanters for two hours, Gordon, *Abridgement*, 189. Since his men came from his kin group, vassals, and tenants, he could expect obedience and enforce it through his pit and gallows powers. Given the diversity of Montrose's units, the marquis would have found setting and enforcing such limits nearly impossible.

13 Perth's ransom was £60,000 in coin and £1,200 of clothing, Cowan, *Montrose*, 161. Elgin paid £1,300, which failed to preserve the burgh from Montrose's fickle ally Grant allowing his men to burn parts of the burgh, *Ibid.*, 189. Glasgow's ransom was set at 'a thousand double peeces' Gordon, *Abridgement*, 153. Cameron Maclean at Glasgow University suggested that meant £9,000 per R.W. Cochran-Patrick's *Records of the Coinage of Scotland*, 2 vols. (Edinburgh, 1876), ii. 9. In Ayrshire Alasdair received payments of 8,500 merks from the countess of Loudoun to preserve the parishes of Loudoun, Galston and Mauchline from plundering, 4,000 merks from the earl of Eglinton's factor for the earl's estates (of which 600 were paid instantly with remainder due on 31 August), Sir William Mure of Rowallan's tenants agreed to pay 1,000 merks, and Sir William Cunningham of Cunninghamhead's friends promised 1,200 merks – the latter two estates had already suffered £10,000 losses from plundering and damage, J. Paterson, *History of the County of Ayr*, 2 vols. (Ayr, 1847–1852), i. 116–117, which reproduces Eglinton's factor's letter of 13 September 1645.

14 Stevenson, *Alasdair*, 204. Given Montrose's string of successes it seems probable that using the strategy of the central position he could have maintained his army in Aberdeen or Banff.

15 For a discussion of the reasons units left Montrose, particularly after Kilsyth, see Gordon, *Abridgement*, 153–154; Guthry, *Memoirs*, 199; Wishart, *Montrose*, 137–138; Napier, *Memoirs*, ii. 569, 611; J. Buchan, *Montrose* (London, 1931), 281; Stevenson, *Alasdair*, 206–208.

16 Guthry, Memoirs, 158; Wishart, Memoirs, 190–192, ignores it.

the prospect for raising a similar force in Scotland would have existed. Given his experiences in August 1644–August 1645, one must wonder how in September 1645 he thought he could raise thousands of men and lead them into England for months of campaigning.

II. Montrose's Spring 1644 campaigns

Let us follow Montrose's two English-based campaigns in April–June 1644. Adhering to the timeline established with Antrim, Montrose left Oxford in early March. Ludovic Lindsay, 16th earl of Crawford brought two troops from his horse regiment and three companies from his dragoon regiment. Newcastle, dealing with a large Covenanter army, provided Montrose with a hundred horsemen, (including Captain Frances Dalzell's/Mistress Pierson's troop), two cannon and orders for the Cumberland and Westmorland militia to join the marquis. Heading west Montrose reached Carlisle where he gained two regular English Royalist horse troops and a militia one, which with the militia foot amounted to about 1,000 men to invade Scotland.[17] Reaching the border the foot militia mutinied and half went home. The easy capture of Dumfries failed to persuade any Scots to join Montrose, so he retreated, and his army dissolved.[18] Huntly, prodded by his kinsmen rose, but learning of Montrose's retreat and Antrim only authorising Alasdair to raid the western isles, considered fighting a guerrilla war in the Cairngorms, then disbanded as a Covenanter army mustered. In Northumberland Montrose asked for the loan of troops to capture Scottish Covenanter garrisons there and in Durham. He received two Northumberland foot regiments, and cavalry from there and county Durham. Then he besieged and captured Morpeth Castle and the South Shields fort. Returning the borrowed troops and on receipt of orders from Prince Rupert to head south, he left the area with his horse troop, three from Crawford's Horse and three companies of Crawford's Dragoons. On 3 July at Richmond the marquis met a definitive check from the prince, who refused

17 Dumfries campaign order of battle April 1644: Artillery – 2 guns, 2 petards, Cumberland and Westmoreland forces – 800 foot, 200 horse in 3 troops including Governor of Carlisle Sir Harry Stradling's and Sir Philip Musgrave's horse troops, 3 companies of the Earl of Crawford's Dragoons, and 200 Horse – part of the Earl of Crawford's Horse (including Frances Dalzell's/Mistress Persone's troop and 2–3 others/100 men), and Montrose's troop (100). Mentieth states a total of 2,000 men, but 1,350–1,500 seems more likely. *True Relations*, 3; HMC *Laing MSS*, i. 214–215; R. Menteith, *History of the Troubles of Great Britain*, trans. J. Ogilvie (London, 2nd edn. 1738), 163–164; Napier, *Memorials*, ii. 127, 130–132, 144; Wishart, *Memoirs*, 44-47, 362–363; *True Relations of the Happy Success of the Marquis of Montrose* (Oxford, 1645), 1–3; M. Fraser, *The Rivals, Montrose and Argyll and the Struggle for Scotland* (Edinburgh, 2015), 120.

18 Gordon, *Abridgement*, 49–50; Wishart, *Montrose*, 45; Cowan, *Montrose*, 145–147.

the former's request for 1,000 cavalry and ordered the marquis to relinquish the four horse troops and three dragoon companies. That left him with two officers with whom he entered Scotland.[19]

III. Sources of units – commissioned and other sources

In Scotland, the sources of Montrose's units varied. Individuals or groups of clan leaders raised most of the units on their own initiative. A mere eight units (out of about sixty) came from commissions. The Irish Confederate Supreme Council issued four (three in 1644 and one in 1646) for the Irish Brigade. In August 1645 Montrose gave commissions to three nobles and a Highland chief. Monaltrie's, the Strathbogie, and Aberdeen Burghs Foot units revived regiments established by Huntly in March 1644. Montrose's initial three horse troops (Airlie's, Gordon's and Hay's, and Rollo's) took the field due to their commanders' efforts. Alasdair was responsible for encouraging many west Highland clans to take the field. His success in Badenoch [with Clan Chattan] in August 1644 arose from quartering threats. Six of twenty-seven units associated with him were fellow MacDonalds. The harrowing of Argyll and the victory at Inverlochy brought in five clans. Some units, such as Corryborough's and Grant of Freuchie's, existed so briefly that they saw no combat.[20]

19 Northeastern campaign order of battle 9 May–4 July 1644: Artillery – 6 guns. Baillie, ii. 196; Menteith, 164; Napier, *Memorials*, ii. 133–137, 115; Somerville, *Memorie of the Somervilles*, 2 vols. (Edinburgh, 1815), ii. 288–331; *True Relations of the Happy Success of the Marquis of Montrose*, 3–4; *Thurloe State Papers*, (London, 1742), i. 35-6; Wishart, *Memoirs*, 44–47, 362–363; Foot: 2,000; Horse: 500, Earl of Crawford's Horse (including Frances Dalzell's/Mistres Persone's troop and two others), Marquis of Montrose's troop, Earl of Crawford's Dragoons (three companies), Somerville, ii. 297, or 1,500 H+D from Durham and Northumberland under COL Robert Clavering, *True Relations*, 3; <royalist:foot-regiments:sir-robert-clavering - BCW Project Regimental Wiki (bcw-project.org)>, which states Clavering commanded a foot regiment at Sunderland in May as well as a horse regiment at Morpeth, <royalist:horse-regiments:sir-robert-clavering – BCW Project Regimental Wiki (bcw-project.org)>; <https://wiki.bcw-project.org/scots-Royalist/horse-regiments/marquis-of-montrose>, retrieved 2.8.2021. Wishart, *Montrose*, 46–47; Cowan, *Montrose*, 149–150.

20 For Corryborough, Gordon, *Abridgement*, 110-12; Wishart, *Montrose*, ii. 186-7; *RCGA*, i. 271, 283-4; *Ibid*., ii. 422; Spalding, *Memorials*, ii. 454-5; Cowan, *Montrose*, 193; Stevenson, *Alasdair*, 166-8. For Grant, Guthry, *Memoirs*, 147; Wishart, *Montrose*, ii. 172-4; Spalding, *Memorials*, ii. 365, 428, 447, 449-50; Cowan, *Montrose*, 181, 188-9; Stevenson, *Alasdair*, 166-7.

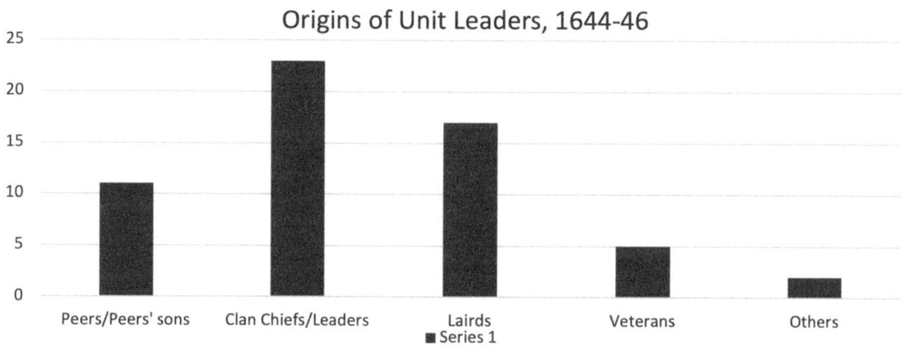

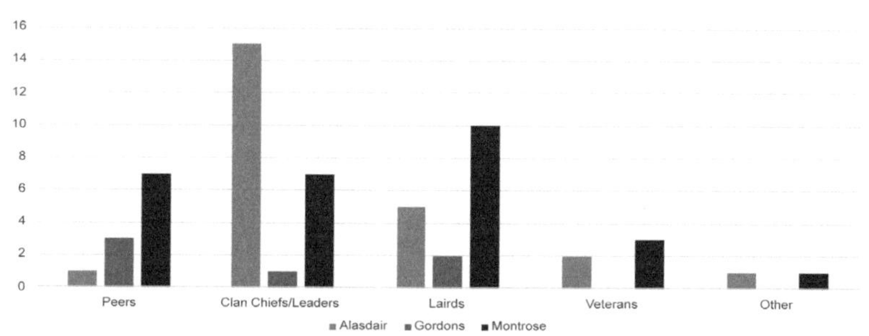

The totals for leaders' origins breaks down as 11 peers, 22 clan chiefs or leaders, 16 lairds, eight veterans, and two others. Three peers – Huntly, Reay, and Seaforth – were also clan leaders; Gordon and Aboyne were the first's sons, making five of the peers with a clan leadership tie. On the graph they only appear as peers. Five of the lairds were clansmen further emphasising the importance of clan support for the Royalists.

IV. Source of units by general

The different leaders – Alasdair MacDonald/Marquis of Antrim, Lord Gordon/ Viscount Aboyne/Marquis of Huntly – for convenience called the Gordons, and Montrose – had different results for the units associated with them. The number of men per unit provides one measure of the leaders' overall effectiveness. Only the first three regiments of the Irish Brigade have anything like a muster. Furthermore, contemporaries failed to give numbers for twenty-four units. The graph over simplifies the situation. Alasdair's weakest units had 100 and 150 men each, while the Gordons had units of 30, 100, and 160. Montrose's came at the bottom of the scale with 20, 50, 60 and three of 125. For those in the 400–600 range Alasdair had seven, with the Gordons having only one and Montrose's three at 400. The marquis's seeming superiority in the 700–1,200 category disappears when one realises that two of the three regiments (with a total strength of 1,500 men) proved to be two of the worst units raised for any leader – rivalling the Covenanter Fife militia at Kilsyth for combat ineffectiveness. For the forces between 400 and 1,200 men – the size of a regular regiment – ten served Alasdair, with ten others under Gordon or Montrose's command – including the two large and worthless forces.

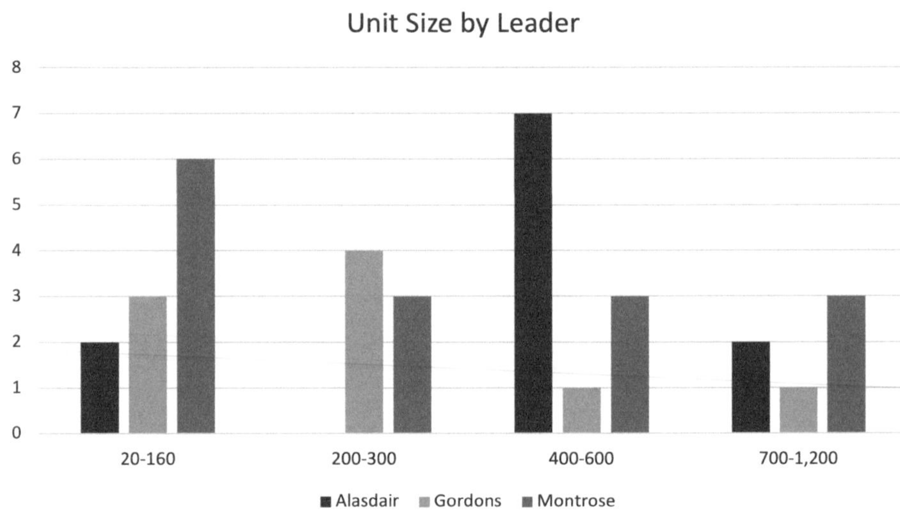

The length of service under a leader offers a better estimate of a unit's quality. Before comparing the commander's achievement, details are necessary. The Irish Brigade's first three regiments were on foot in March 1644, but for fairness they are only reckoned from August. Furthermore, some of its soldiers remained under the command of Alasdair or Antrim in Ireland into October 1648. Only their service in Scotland, which ended in June 1647, is considered. The Gordons' March–May 1644 service is excluded, only from February 1645 through March 1647 is counted. For Montrose, the period under examination is August 1644 to 30 July 1646. The longest service of a unit of Alasdair/Antrim is thirty-four months; for the Gordons it is nineteen months since they disbanded for six months (3 June-December) in 1646; for Montrose it is twenty-three months. One readily sees a disparity between the devotion of units' loyalty to the different leaders. Montrose commanded the allegiance of twenty-five units for one to six months – a dozen of them for only a month. Many of these forces shifted to and from him, having previously aligned with Alasdair or the Gordons. The Gordons held the fidelity of eight units for seven to nineteen months. Much more impressive than either was Alasdair who could rely on sixteen units for thirteen to thirty-four months. That number could be larger, but the activities of seven units (Edinample's, MacDonalds of Keppoch, Mackays of Ugdale, MacLachlans, MacMillans, MacNeills of Carskey, and Stewarts of Appin), are too uncertain to ascribe longer service. Of the units that served thirteen months or longer – eight (the three original Irish regiments, the Camerons, MacDonalds of Clanranald and Glengarry, MacDougalls and Macleans) fielded 500 or more men. Looking at the Gordons, only the Strathbogie Foot had that longevity and strength. For Montrose, just the Atholl Foot had both attributes. Therefore, only Alasdair led a good-sized force throughout his service.

The following chart shows the ebb and flow of the components of Montrose's army between 1 September 1644 and 13 September 1645. With the exceptions of Alford – fought amid Gordon territory – and Philiphaugh – in which Lowland nobles accounted for over three-quarters of the army, the Irish Brigade and the men Alasdair recruited accounted for the largest component.[21]

21 **Tippermuir** 1.9.1644 order of battle: Irish Brigade 1,100, Keppoch 100, Badenoch 500; Atholl F 800, Kilpont's F 350–500, Struan's 60 – 1,700–3,060 Alasdair 55 percent, Montrose 45 percent, Gordon 0 percent. Foot: 3,000, Horse: 3. Baillie, *Letters*, ii. 225, 233, 262; *Collection of Original Letters and Papers … found among the Duke of Ormonde's Papers*, T. Carte (ed.), 2 vols. (London, 1739), i. 73–74.; Gordon, *Abridgement*, 73-75; Mentieth, *History of the Troubles*, 171–173; Napier, *Memorials*, ii. 149–151; Spalding, Memorialls *Trubles*, ii. 403; *A true relation of the happy success of his majesty's forces in Scotland …* (Oxford, 1644), 7–8. Wishart, *Memoirs*, 56–62.
Aberdeen 13.9.1644 order of battle: Irish Brigade, Badenoch with the Atholl Foot 300 total (Gordon, *Abridgement,* 89 has 100/200 respectively); Horse Troops: Airlie's 40, Gordon's & Hay's c.40, Rollo's 20, 1,214–1,550, Alasdair 78 percent, Montrose 22 percent, Gordon 0 percent. 1,450 Foot, 100 Horse, Baillie, *Letters*, ii. 234, 262; Carte, *Ormonde*, i. 74; *Extracts from the council register of the burgh of Aberdeen, 1643–1747* (ed.) J Stuart (Scottish Burgh Record Society, 1872), 28–29; Gordon, *Abridgement*, 80–84, 89; Spalding, *Memorialls*, ii. 405–407/406–13; *A true relation of the happy success*, 10–12; Wishart, *Memoirs*, 66–69.
Fyvie 10.1644 order of battle: Alasdair – Irish Brigade 800–900, Badenoch 100; Montrose – Atholl Foot 200 (including Struan's 50), Monaltrie's Foot 300; Horse Troops – Airlie's, Gordon's, and Hay's (50), Rollo's for a total of 90 Horse. 900–1,000/1,490–1,590, Alasdair 62 percent, Montrose 38 percent, Gordon 0 percent. Gordon, *Distemper*, 89–91; *Memoirs of Scottish Catholics during XVIIth and XVIIIth centuries*, 2 vols. (ed.) W.F. Leith (London, 1909), i. 297; Spalding, *Memorialls*, ii. 426–427; Wishart, *Memoirs*, 73–75, who calls Huntly's 500 men 'a small party' and states they deserted before the battle, gives Montrose 1,500 foot and 50 horse.
Inverlochy 2.2.1645 order of battle: Irish Brigade, Clanranald 200, Glengarry, Keppoch 100, Glencoe, Badenoch 300, Camerons 300–400, Appin 150/200, MacAllisters, MacGregors, Macleans 12–40; Struan's, Abergeldie's Retinues, MacFarlanes, Mackinnons; Horse Troop – Airlie's 50; Perhaps MacAllisters, 1,250–1,550 Alasdair 84 percent,

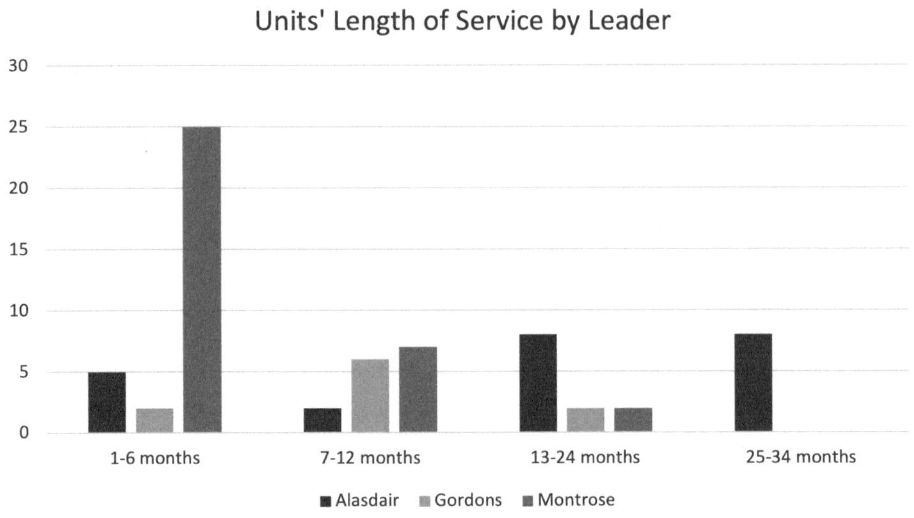

Montrose 16 percent, Gordon 0 percent. Foot: 1500, Horse: 50. Gordon, *Abridgement*, 100–102; Guthry, *Memoirs*, 179; *Memoirs of Scottish Catholics*, i. 321–322; *Ormonde*, i. 75–76; *Rel. Celt.*, ii. 183–185; Spalding, *Memorialls*, ii. 444–445; Wishart, *Memoirs*, 83-85; [Sinclair], *Clan Maclean*, 124–125.

Dundee 4.1645 order of battle: Irish Brigade 800, MacGregors; Lord Gordon's Horse Troop? *APS*, VI, i. 519–521; Baillie, *Letters*, ii. 264; Gordon, *Abridgement*, 112–117; Guthry, *Memoirs*, 183; Spalding, *Memorialls*, ii. 458–463; Wishart, *Memoirs*, 88–95.

Auldearn 9.5.1645 order of battle: Irish Brigade 140+, pt. Clanranald, Glengarry and Keppoch 100, MacAllisters, MacGregors, Macleans; Strathbogie Foot 300–500, Atholl F some, Badenoch co., Monaltrie's Foot 300, Minimore's Foot 300; Mackinnons, Sleat's 400, Horse Troops: Gordon's 160, Aboyne's, Gight's, Newton's, Perhaps: Harthill's, 2,000 Foot, 300 Horse, Alasdair 900 Foot. 39 percent, Montrose 500 Foot +50 Horse 24 percent, Gordons 600 Foot, 250 Horse=850 37 percent, 'Book of Clanranald' in A. Cameron, Religuiae Celticae (ed.) A. MacBain and J. Kennedy, 2 vols., (Inverness, 1892–1894), ii. 187–193; Fraser, *Chronicles*, 296–297; Gordon, *Abridgement*, 121–127; R. Gordon and G. Gordon, *A Genealogical History of the Earldom of Sutherland* (Edinburgh, 1813), 525; Napier, *Memoirs*, ii. 500–501; Spalding, *Memorials*, ii. 473–474; Wishart, *Memoirs*, 98-103.

Alford 2.7.1645 order of battle: Irish Brigade, Clanranald, Keppoch, Glengarry, Appin, MacAllisters, MacGregors; Strathbogie Foot 500; Atholl Foot some, Balloch's co., Minimore's F 200, Monaltrie's Foot 300, Mackintosh co.; Horse Troops: Gordon's 160, Aboyne's, Gight's, Newton's, Rollo's, Perhaps: Struan's Alasdair 800F 35 percent, Montrose 200F+50H=250 11 percent, Gordon's 1,000F+250H=1,250 54 percent 2,300. Foot: 3000, Horse 300. Baillie, *Letters*, ii. 417–419; *Celticae Religuiae*, ii. 192–195; Fraser, *Frasers*, 299; Gordon, *Abridgement*, 128–133; *Memoirs of Scottish Catholics*, i. 348; Wishart, *Memoirs*, 106–112; Gordon, *Genealogical History*, 526.

Kilsyth 15.8.1645 order of battle: Irish Brigade 1,220, Clanranald 500, Keppoch 100, Glengarry 500 & Glencoe 100, Stewarts of Appin, MacAllisters, MacGregors, Macleans 700, MacNabs; Strathbogie Foot 400, Aboyne's Horse, Harthill's, Newton's Horse Troop [400]; Atholl Foot 200, Badenoch some, Monaltrie's Foot 200, Minimore's Foot 200, Ballooch's co.; Horse Troops: Airlie's 50–60/80–100, Gordon's 60–80, Perhaps: Horse

Montrose's Army Components by Leader

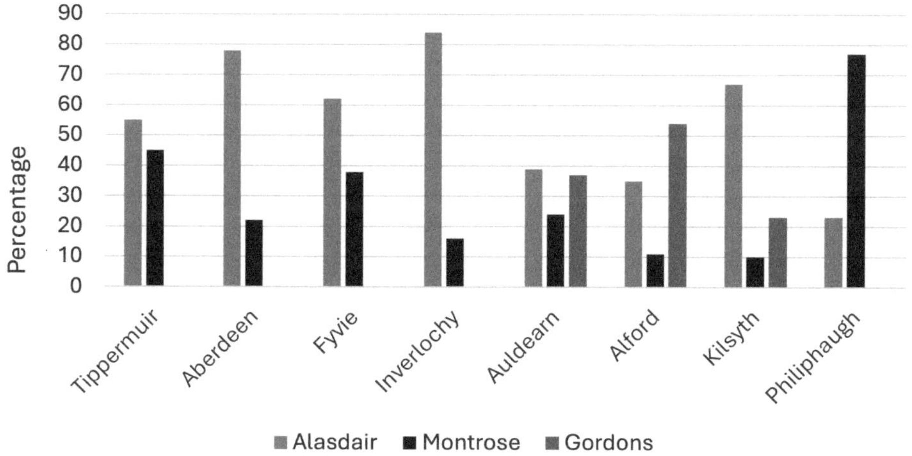

The victory at Kilsyth failed to persuade the former Royalist and future Scottish Engager leader William Hamilton, earl of Lanark, to join Montrose despite a direct request from the marquis. Instead, he refused, disbanded his 1,000 foot and 500 horse, and fled to Ulster.[22] In the 1651 battle of Worcester Lanark, then 2nd duke of Hamilton, would die. Yet in 1645 the earl, despite his Royalist past, found service with Montrose unappealing. Perhaps that says something about the earl, but more likely it reflects an inability to stomach Montrose's allies and their behaviour.

Did Montrose truly have his own army? After the pacification of Lowland Scotland in August 1645, one can see that was scarcely the case. The western clans, promising to return, departed just as the marquis planned his strategic intervention in England, and stayed away. Montrose allowed the Lamont chief to take half the Irish Brigade as his escort for recruiting a regiment in Argyll. Huntly

Troop: Gight's, Foot: 4,500, Horse: 560. Alasdair 3,520F 67 –, Montrose 200 Foot, 160 Horse 500 10 percent, Gordons 800 Foot, 400 Horse, 1,200 23 percent. Baillie, *Letters*, ii. 420–424; Gordon, *Abridgement*, 129–135; *Celticae Religuiae*, ii. 199–201; *True relation … of Kilsyth*, 2–7; Wishart, *Memoirs*,122–125.

Philiphaugh 13.9.1645 order of battle: Irish brigade – A. MacDonnell's Foot & O'Cahan's Foot, 500–400, Horse: Douglas's, Hartfell's (1,500 total), Horse Troops: Airlie's 50–60, Gordon' s & Hay's 60–80, Rollo's; Dragoons: Blackadder's co. Foot:500–400, Horse: 1,700 Alasdair 500F 23 percent, Montrose 1,700H 77 percent. Gordon, *Abridgement*, 156–162; Guthry, *Memoirs*, 202–204; *A more perfect relation of the late great victorie in Scotland* (London, 1645), 2–3; *Three Great Victories* (London, 1645) T1093; Wishart, *Memoirs*, 142–148.

22 Wishart, *Memoirs*, 136.

recalled Aboyne and his forces to the north-east. After the debacle at Philiphaugh Montrose struggled and failed to recreate a potent military force.

The defeat at Philiphaugh and the contrasting objectives of his former allies Alasdair and the Gordons –commanded directly by the Marquis of Huntly – made recreating Montrose's army close to its former strength impossible. In the autumn he managed to raise 1,200 foot and 300 horse. In December, he agreed with Huntly to make a two-pronged attack on Inverness. In January he besieged Inverness with infantry from the Atholl Foot, a company each of MacPhersons and Mackintoshes, and men of Delgatie's and Harthill's retinues. Clanranald, and Glengarry sent some men, while Maclean of Coll sent two sons presumably with clansmen as escorts. From March Seaforth (persuaded by savage quartering), and Reay had men present. Airlie, Arradoul, and Gight the younger provided horse troops. MacDonnell's horse troop and Mortimer's dragoon company inadequately guarded the Spey crossings, which allowed Middleton to cross the river and relieve the siege on 9 May 1646. Rather than uniting with Alasdair or Huntly, Montrose marched around the Highlands, while Seaforth left him and besieged the insignificant tower house of Neil Macleod of Assynt.[23]

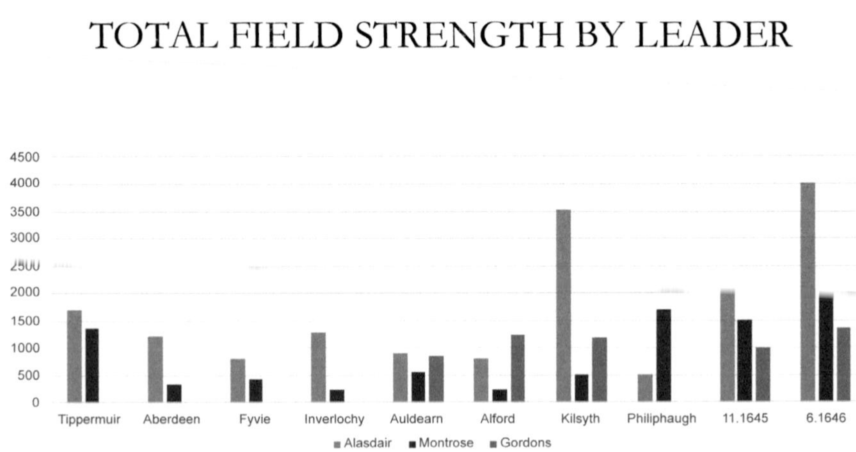

23 Gordon, *Abridgement*, 167–74, 173–84; R. Gordon, *A Genealogical History of the Earldom of Sutherland* (Edinburgh, 1813), 530–532; Wishart, *Memoirs*, 150–157, 160–164,176–178; Napier, *Memorials*, ii. 270–274; Fraser, *Frasers*, 313–314.

The state of the three armies in June/July 1646 contrasted markedly. Huntly, who promptly obeyed the royal command to disband, had a small, balanced force. When it disbanded on 3 June the marquis had 1,000 foot and 240–500 horse. Antrim and Alasdair, who directly controlled Kintyre in Argyll, led 4,000 or more scattered infantry, and no cavalry. The foot consisted of 1,000–1,400 in the Irish brigade (including Antrim's newly arrived foot regiment), about 1,000 MacDonalds and about 2,000 more men from a dozen clans or kin groups. When Montrose disbanded his army on 30 July, he had under 2,000 men. The infantry, perhaps 1,000 men, consisted of the Atholl Foot, the Mackintosh and MacPherson companies, and Harthill's retinue, which also had mounted men. The cavalry, 200–300 men, belonged to Airlie's, Arradoul's, Gight's and MacDonnell's horse troops and Mortimer's dragoon company. The greatest problem for the king, and Montrose, was that the largest anti-Covenanter force in Scotland viewed its objective as the elimination of Campbell hegemony in the western Highlands and the re-establishment of MacDonald power under Antrim, and not the restoration of Charles I's power.

V. Foot: Horse ratios

Montrose's army took months to become a balanced force. From August 1644 to early February 1645, it remained a largely infantry force. At Tippermuir it had three cavalrymen, while at Aberdeen about 100, Fyvie 90, and Inverlochy just 50 troopers on bedraggled horses. Only with the adherence of Lord Gordon (in February 1645) did the number of cavalry increase substantially – with 400 at Auldearn, and 360 at Alford. The army at Kilsyth had over 500 horsemen compared with more than 4,000 foot. Peculiarly, at Philiphaugh his 1,700 cavalry outnumbered the infantry by more than 3:1. Two-thirds of the veterans in that fight were foot soldiers. Afterwards foot predominated with the cavalry mustering about 300 men until it disbanded in July 1646.

Due to the difficult marches of the army, artillery was a rarity. At Aberdeen, the army fielded nine guns captured at Tippermuir. Afterwards the guns were stored in Gordon territory, which led to disputes between the two Royalist factions in 1645–1646.[24] The arrival of four cannon from The Netherlands during the siege of Inverness was a signal event. The loss of the Irish Confederate warships in 1644 seriously handicapped Alasdair's 1645–1646 castle capturing campaigns, because he could not borrow artillery from the ships.

Montrose's longest expedition in Scotland as a Royalist general lasted twenty-three months. For twelve months (52 percent of the period) he managed an

24 Wishart, *Montrose*, 162.

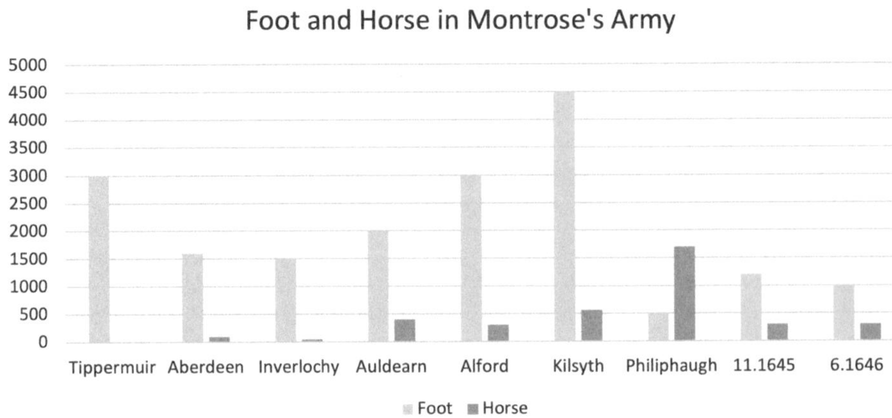

army made of units raised for him and by other leaders. Eleven of those months marked startingly successes that shocked the foundations of the Covenanter state. The twelfth month witnessed the end of the alliance with Alasdair and a catastrophic defeat. Efforts in 1645–1646 to combine effectively with Huntly failed due to disagreements on strategic goals. While Montrose remained in the field for nearly two months (4 June–30 July 1646) more than Huntly, the existence of his army only succeeded in preventing a major Covenanter offensive into Argyll. Historians have wondered why Montrose refused to join Antrim, who would remain in Scotland for months and whose forces only dissipated after a series of defeats in May–July 1647. The answer seems to rest in the king's decision to divide Scotland into different command zones. Entering Antrim's zone would have brought a conflict between the two men due to their divergent objectives. 30 July 1646 saw Montrose disband his army, before sailing to the continent. (His former Irish Brigade men headed west to Argyll, serving there in 1646–1647, and in 1648 in Ireland. Some joined the Mackenzies remaining with them until 1649.) Considering the conflicting loyalties of its units, maintaining a unified force for eleven months marked a major achievement for any general, especially Montrose, who lacked a civilian government to support his efforts.

Appendix I

Units by General

Alasdair and Antrim 27 Units

Irish Brigade 5 Units
Marquis of Antrim's Foot, 6.1646–1647 (6.1646 500–800).[25]
MacDonald's Lifeguard of Foot co., 9.1645–6.1647.[26]
A. MacDonnell's Foot, 3.1644–10.1648 (6.1644 1,030).[27]
J. MacDonnell's Foot, 3.1644–10.1648 (1644 500).[28]

25 NLS, MS 7194, f.2; NRS, PA 7/23/2/49, 50, 52, 54; PA 12/2, 23.6.1647; Commentarius Rinuccinianus; i. 462; McKerral, Kintyre in the 17th century, 69–72; Gordon, *Abridgement*, 203; *Historical Manuscript Commission 11, Appendix pt. 4, The Manuscripts of the Duke of Hamilton* (London, 1887), i. 111–113; Rushworth, *Historical Collections*, 8 vols. (London, 1721–1722), iv, i. 561–562; G. Hill, *An Historical Account of the MacDonnells of Antrim* (Belfast, 1873), 273, 331, 446–448; J.T. Gilbert, *History of the Irish Confederation, and the War in Ireland, 1641–1649*, 7 vols. (Dublin, 1882–1891), v. 264–265, 274, 314, 334, 352; *Ibid*., vii. 347; *Reliquiae Celticae*, ii. 205; Turner, *Memoirs*, 45–48; C. O'Danachair, 'Montrose's Irish regiments' *Irish Sword*, iv (1959–60), 63; J.H. Ohlmeyer, *Civil War and Restoration in the Three Stuart Kingdoms: The career of Randal MacDonnell, marquis of Antrim, 1609–1683* (Cambridge, 1993), 168–179, 183, 187–188, 198–189, 214–217, 219, 227; Stevenson, Alasdair, 224–241, 245, 247–254, 257–258.

26 *Guthry*, 199; Wishart, *Montrose*, 138; Stevenson, *Alasdair*, 107; <scots-Royalist:foot-regiments:alastair-maccolla-s-lifeguard – BCW Project Regimental Wiki (bcw-project.org)> retrieved 8.10.2021 has a history not reflected in any sources known to the author.

27 *A more perfect relation of the late great victorie in Scotland*, 3, 5; Carte, *Ormond*, vi. 71, 73; Gordon, *Abridgement*, 123–124, 129–131, 184–185; *Guthry*, 161–162, 164, 168, 184, 203–204; Memoirs *of Scottish Catholics during XVIIth and XVIIIth centuries*, 2 vols., ed. W. Forbes-Leith ((London, 1909), i. 281; Spalding, *Memorialls*, ii. 385–386, 407-410, 444–445; Wishart, *Montrose*, 55, 68–69, 110, 142–145, 159–160; Cowan, *Montrose*, 210–211, 236–238, 240; Gilbert, *History*, iii. 140; C. O'Danachair, 'Montrose's Irish Regiments', *Irish Sword* (1959–1960), iv. 61–67; J. Ohlmeyer, *Antrim*, 129–133, 137, 139–140, 142–145; Stevenson, *Alasdair*, 103–113, 133, 147–148, 156, 180, 183–185, 241; Stevenson, *Government*, 5; <scots-Royalist:foot-regiments:alexander-macdonnell - BCW Project Regimental Wiki (bcw-project.org)> retrieved 29.9.2021.

28 NRS, PA 7/23/2/49, 50, 52, 54; PA 12/2, 23.6.1647; Carte, *Ormond*, vi. 71, 73; *Commentarius Rinuccinianus*; i. 462; The *diplomatic correspondence of Jean de Montereul and the brothers de Bellièvre, French ambassadors in England and Scotland, 1645–1648*, 2 vols., ed. Fotheringham, J.G. (SHS, 1st Ser. 29–30, 1898–1899), ii. 194, 255; Gordon,

O'Cahan's Foot, 3.1644–10.1648 (1644 500).[29]

West Highland 21 Units

Camerons, 10.1644–2.1646 (2.2.1645 300–400, 3.2.1645 400–500, 10.1645 pt. 600).[30]

Edinample's Retinue, 12.1644–1646x1647.[31]

Kilellan's Retinue, 9.12.1645–6.1647.[32]

Lamonts, 9.1645–4.6.1646 (9.1645 300, 1–2.1646 600).[33]

Abridgement, 123–124, 129–131, 203; *Guthry*, 2434; *Memoirs of Scottish Catholics*, i. 281; Spalding, *Memorialls*, ii. 385–386, 407–410, 444–445; Turner, *Memoirs*, 45–48; Wishart, *Montrose*, 68–69, 99–101, 144–145, 159–160; Cowan, Montrose, 210–211; Gilbert, *History*, iii. 140; C. O'Danachair, 'Montrose's Irish', iv. 61–67; Ohlmeyer, *Antrim*, 129–133, 137, 139–140, 142–145; McKerral, *Kintyre in the 17th century*, 69–72; Stevenson, *Alasdair*, 103–113, 147–148, 156, 180–185, 214–215, 217–218, 229–241, 244 n. 93; <scots-Royalist:foot-regiments:james-macdonnell – BCW Project Regimental Wiki (bcw-project.org)> retrieved 29.9.2021.

29 NLI, Ormonde Papers, 'List of men gone unto the Isles. Sent by the Lord of Antrim to my Lord Ormonde, 15 Nov. 1644'; *Aberdeen*, 28–38; Carte, *Ormond*, vi. 71, 73; Gordon, *Abridgement*, 65–66, 68, 81–82, 123–124, 129–131, 159–160; *Memoirs of Scottish Catholics*, i. 281; *Guthry*, 203–204; *A more perfect relation of the late great victorie in Scotland*, 3, 5; *Reliquiae Celticae*, ii. 185; Spalding, *Memorialls*, ii. 385–386, 407–410, 444–445, 454–455; Stevenson, *Government*, 5; Wishart, *Montrose*, 68, 74, 84–85 especially n. 16, 99–101, 142–145, 159–160; Cowan, *Montrose*, 155, 171, 193, 210–211, 236–238, 240; Gilbert, *History*, iii. 140; C. O'Danachair, 'Montrose's Irish', iv. 61–67; Ohlmeyer, *Antrim*, 129–133, 137, 139-140, 142-145; Stevenson, *Alasdair*, 103–113, 116, 133, 140–141, 147, 156–157, 167, 180–181, 183–185;; <confederate:foot-regiments:col.-manus-roe-o-cahan - BCW Project Regimental Wiki (bcw-project.org)> retrieved 29.9.2021.

30 Gordon, *Abridgement*, 94, 100, 204; *Guthry*, 178; Wishart, Montrose *of Montrose*, ii. 172–174; Spalding, Memorials, ii. 430; Wishart, *Montrose*, 79 n.3; Cowan, *Montrose*, 173, 179, 181–182, 187; W. Forbes-Leith, *Memoirs of Scottish Catholics during the XVIIth and XVIIIth Centuries*, 2 vols. (London, 1909), i. 320–321, 323; A. Mackenzie, *History of the Camerons* (Inverness, 1884), 90–93, 95, 107; Robertson, *Lordship and Power*, 143, 149, 185; Stevenson, *Alasdair*, 141–142, 151–152, 154, 156, 162–163, 215, 217; <scots-Royalist:foot-regiments:camerons – BCW Project Regimental Wiki (bcw-project.org)> retrieved 15.9.2021.

31 Napier, *Montrose*, ii. 172–174; Wishart, *Montrose*, 80 n. 4, 165–166; Stevenson, *Alasdair*, 150.

32 'Documents relating to the massacre at Dunaverty', *Highland Papers*, ii, ed. J.R.N. McPhail (SHS, 1916), 259; Turner, *Memoirs*, 45–46, 239–241; Cowan, *Montrose*, 253; Stevenson, *Alasdair*, 237.

33 *An Inventory of Lamont Papers*, ed. N. Lamont (Edinburgh, 1914), 180–181, 193–194, 209, 222–225, 229–230, 234; Cowan, *Montrose*, 183; H. McKechnie, *The Lamont clan: 1235–1935* (Edinburgh, 1938), 149, 155–159, 162–163, 166–170, 172–175, 187–193; Stevenson, *Alasdair*, 208, 214–215, 217, 226–228; <scots-Royalist:foot-regiments:lamont-highlanders – BCW Project Regimental Wiki (bcw-project.org)> retrieved 16.9.2021.

Largie's Foot co., 10.1645–6.1647.[34]
MacAllisters, 12.1644–6.1647.[35]
MacAulays of Ardincaple, Spring 1646.[36]
MacDonalds of Clanranald, 8x10.1644–9.10.1648 (12.1644 500–800, 2.2.1645 200, 2.7.1645, 15.8.1645 500, 1648 300).[37]
MacDonalds of Glencoe, 10.1644–6.1647.[38]
MacDonalds of Glengarry, 10.1644–9.10.1648 (15.8.1645 500).[39]

34 *APS*, vi, ii. 461; *Reliquiae* Celticae, ii. 207; Synod *of Argyll*, 100; Cowan, *Montrose*, 253; A. MacDonald and A. MacDonald, *The Clan Donald*, 3 vols. (Inverness, 1896–1904), iii. 383–384; Stevenson, *Alasdair*, 215, 230, 235, 257–258.

35 W. Cobbett, *Complete Collection of State Trials* (London, 1810), v. 1391; Cowan, *Montrose*, 253; A. Campbell, *Records of Argyll* (London, 1885), 225–226; MacDonald, *Clan MacDonld*, 403–404; Stevenson, Alasdair 220–222, 235, 237, 240.

36 Stevenson, *Alasdair*, 217-218; <scots-Royalist:foot-regiments:macauleys – BCW Project Regimental Wiki (bcw-project.org)> retrieved 16.9.2021.

37 *APS*, vi, pt. ii. 21–22, 461; Carte, *Original Letters*, ii. 74; Gordon, *Abridgement*, 94, 101; *Guthry*, 169, 172; Wishart, *Montrose*, ii. 172–174; *Reliquiae Celticae*, ii. 179, 181, 191, 193, 195, 197, 199, 201, 203, 205, 207; Spalding, *Memorialls*, ii. 430, 444, *Synod of Argyll*, i. 97–98, 121–122; in September 1646 John Macranald younger Captain of Clanranald the younger and Donald Macranald were excommunicated, *Ibid.*, i. 100, 203; Turner, *Memoirs*, 48–49; Wishart, *Montrose*, 79, 81–82, 114–115, 138, 176, 504; Cowan, *Montrose*, 173, 182, 184, 202, 204, 209, 213–214, 218–220, 225, 243; MacDonald and MacDonald, *Clan Donald*, ii. 328–338; Ohlmeyer, *Antrim*, 214–217, 219, 227; Stevenson, *Alasdair*, 116–117, 140–142, 146, 148–152, 156, 158–159, 161–162, 166, 198–199, 201–207, 209–210, 215, 217, 221, 227, 230, 240, 257–258; Thiess, 'Western Highlands'. 53–54, 144, 149, 151–152, 161, 169–174, 184;< scots-Royalist:foot-regiments:macdonalds-of-clanranald – BCW Project Regimental Wiki (bcw-project.org)> retrieved 26.9.2021.

38 Carte, *Original Letters*, ii. 74; Gordon, *Abridgement*, 99, 101; *Reliquiae Celticae*, ii. 181; Spalding, *Memorialls*, ii. 444; Wishart, *Montrose*, 79 n. 3, 504; Cowan, *Montrose*, 173–174, 178, 183; MacDonald and MacDonald, *Clan Donald*, ii. 203–206; Stevenson, *Alasdair*, 141–142, 145, 151, 156, 158–159, 162, 171, 177,198, 202–207, 209–210, 215, 217, 230; <scots-Royalist:foot-regiments:macdonalds-of-glencoe – BCW Project Regimental Wiki (bcw-project.org)> retrieved 23.9.2021.

39 Balfour, *Works*, iii. 53-5. *APS*, vi, pt. ii. 670–671; Carte, *Original Letters*, ii. 75; Gordon, *Abridgement*, 99, 101, 136, 140, 180; HMC 21: *Hamilton*, i. 113; Mentieth, *History*, 254; Napier, *Montrose*, ii. 172–174; *Reliquiae Celticae*, ii. 181, 183, 193, 195, 207; Spalding, *Memorialls*, ii. 444; *Synod of Argyll*, i. 100, 203; Wishart, *Montrose*, 109, 138, 176, 505; Cowan, *Montrose*, 155, 181–183, 209, 213; MacDonald and MacDonald, *Clan Donald*, iii. 422–427; N.H. Macdonald, *The Clan Ranald of Knoydart & Glengarry: a History of the MacDonalds or MacDonnells of Glengarry* (Edinburgh, 1979)**;** Ohlmeyer, *Antrim*, 188, 214–217, 219, 227; Stevenson, *Alasdair*, 116, 140–142, 151–152, 156, 158–159, 162, 198, 202–207, 209–210, 215–217, 228, 245, 247–248, 258; <scots-Royalist:foot-regiments:macdonells-of-glengarry – BCW Project Regimental Wiki (bcw-project.org)> retrieved 27.9.2021.

MacDonalds of Keppoch, 8.1644–15.8.1645–1647? (1.9.1644 somex100, 2.2.1645 100, 9.5.1645 100).[40]

MacDonald of Sanda's, 2.2.1645–13.11.1647 (Spring 1647 w/MacDougalls 400–500, 24.5.1647 pt. 1,300, 5.6.1647 pt. 300–400).[41]

MacDougalls, 9.1645–6.1647 (10.1645 500, spring 1647 w/ Sanda's 400–500, 24.5.1647 pt 1,300, 6.1647 90+).[42]

MacGregors, 7.1645–5.1647.[43]

Mackays of Ugdale, 9x12.1645–6.1646–6.1647.[44]

MacLachlans, 9.1645–2.1646–6.1647.[45]

Macleans, 12.1644–7.1647 (2.2.1645 12/30/40, 15.8.1645 700).[46]

40 Balfour, *Works*, iii. 271; Gordon, *Abridgement*, 99, 101; Wishart, *Montrose*, ii. 172–174; Spalding, *Memorialls*, ii. 343, 346, 402, 471; Wishart, Montrose, 79, 81–82, 114–115, 138, 176; Cowan, *Montrose*, 155, 173, 181–183; MacDonald and MacDonald, *Clan Donald*, ii. 631–633; Stevenson, *Alasdair*, 116–117, 141–142, 144 n. 38 [but see MacDonald and MacDonald, *Clan Donald*, iii. 420, stating Ranald Og 'died shortly after 1640' and that Donald Glas' son Alexander succeeded him before 1650], 146, 148–152, 154, 156, 158–159, 161–162, 198–199, 201–207, 209–210, 215, 217, 221, 227, 230, 240; <scots-Royalist:foot-regiments:macdonalds-of-keppoch - BCW Project Regimental Wiki (bcw-project.org)> retrieved 28.9.2021.

41 NRS, GD 92.83; Spalding, Memorialls, ii. 445; *Synod of Argyll*, i. 100; Turner, *Memoirs*, 45–46; MacDonald and MacDonald, *Clan Donald*, iii. 391; Stevenson, *Alasdair*, 156, 161, 230, 235–237, 245, 252; <https://wiki.bcw-project.org/covenanter/foot-regiments/archibald-mor-macdonald-of-sanda> retrieved 24.9.2021.

42 'Documents relating to the massacre at Dunaverty', 266–267; *Lamont Papers*, 241–242; Spalding, *Memorialls*, ii. 444; Turner, *Memoirs*, 238–241; MacKechnie, *Lamont clan*, 169–270, 172–174; Stevenson, *Alasdair*, 214–215, 218, 228, 230–237; <covenanter:foot-regiments:macdougall-highlanders - BCW Project Regimental Wiki (bcw-project.org)> retrieved 20.9.2021.

43 Gordon, *Abridgement*, 101; Wishart, Montrose, ii. 172–174, 184–185; *Reliquiae Celticae*, ii.183, 197, 201; Spalding, *Memorialls*, ii. 444; Wishart, *Montrose*, 97 n. 1, 114–115, 138, 165; Cowan, *Montrose*, 175, 181, 197, 213, 225; Stevenson, *Alasdair*, 150, 152, 162, 198–199, 206–207, 209–210; <scots-Royalist:foot-regiments:macgregors – BCW Project Regimental Wiki (bcw-project.org)> retrieved 20.9.2021.

44 Cowan, *Montrose*, 253; Stevenson, *Alasdair*, 189–190, 237, 240.

45 Cowan, *Montrose*, 183; Stevenson, *Alasdair*, 214.

46 NRS, GD. 14/19. 102; PA. 7/23/2/36; PA. 7/23/2/54; PA. 12/1, 17.6.1646 maybe another clan; *APS*, vi, pt. ii. 545–6, 670–671; Carte, *Original Letters*, ii. 75; Forbes-Leith, *Memoirs*, ii. 308–309, 322, 347; *Guthry*, 168–169, 172, 191; *Joint Print of the documents in the causa His Grace John Douglas Sutherland Duke of Argyl …. against Angus John Campbell of Dunstaffnage – Court of Session, First Decision May 12, 1911* (Edinburgh, 1911), 171, 174; Wishart, Montrose, ii. 172–174, 181; 'Papers relating to the Macleans of Duart', *Highland Papers*, ed. J.R.N. MacPhail (SHS, 1914), 333–334; *Privy Council*, 3rd Ser, i. 222–223; *Reliquiae Celticae* ii.183, 195 201, 203; Spalding, *Memorialls*, ii. 444; Turner, *Memoirs*, 48–49; Wishart, *Montrose,* 114, 123–124, 138, 176; Cowan, *Montrose*, 179–181, 183, 185, 202, 213, 216, 218–220, 222, 225, 243–244; Furgol, A Regimental History of the Scottish Covenanting Armies 1639–1651 (Edinburgh, 1990), 163, 224; Hill, *MacDonnells of Antrim*,

MacMillans, 9.12.1645–6.1646–7.1647.[47]
MacNabs, 12.1644–3.1646.[48]
MacNeills (of Carskey), 9.12.1645–6.1646–6.1647.[49]
Stewarts of Appin, 8.1644, 10.1644, 12.1644–2.1645, 4–5. 1645? 7–9.1645, 1645–1646?–6.1647? (11.1644 pt. of 1,500, 2.2.1645 150).[50]

Central Highland Units 1
Badenoch Levies, 8–9.1644.[51]
Garrisons: Ascog Castle 5–4.6.1646[52].
Castle Tirrim 8.1644–1647[53].
Kinlochaline Castle 7.10.1644[54].
Mingary Castle 7.1644–1647[55].

111–113; J.P. Maclean, *History of the Clan Maclean* (Cincinnati, 1889), 166–175, 276–277; N. Maclean-Bristol, *From Clan to Regiment* (Barnsley, 2007) 29–32, 37; A.M. Sinclair, *The Clan Gillean* (Charlottetown, 1899), 181–191, 305, 332–333, 435; [J.C. Sinclair], Historical and Genealogical *Account of the Clan MacLean* (London, 1838), 124–150, 285; Stevenson, *Alasdair*, 151–152, 154, 156, 159–163, 198–202, 204, 206–210, 215, 217, 227–228, 240; Theiss, 'Western Highlands', 161, 208–210, 224, 226, 244–245, 248; scots-Royalist:foot-regiments:macleans – BCW Project Regimental Wiki (bcw-project.org) retrieved 13.10.2021.

47 NRS, GD. 14/19, p. 102; *APS*, vi, pt. ii. 545–546; Stevenson, *Alasdair*, 228.

48 NRS, GD 112/40/2, bundle 'letters 1640–49'; Gordon, *Abridgement*, 96–98, 153–154; *Guthry*, 214–215; *Reliquiae Celticae*, ii. 183; Wishart, M*ontrose*, 114-5, 137-8, 165; Cowan, *Montrose*, 175, 181, 183, 213, 244-5; Stevenson, Alasdair, 149–150, 162, 198-9, 206–207, 209–210, 228; G. Way and R. Squire, *Collins Scottish Clan & Family Encyclopediaa* (Glasgow, 1994), 248–249.

49 NRS, GD. 14/19, p. 102; *APS*, vi, pt. ii. 545–546; Cowan, *Montrose*, 253; Stevenson, *Alasdair*, 214, 228.

50 Gordon, *Abridgement*, 101–102, 135–136, 153–154; Wishart, Montrose, ii. 172–174; *Reliquiae Celticae*, ii. 197; Spalding, *Memorialls*, ii. 444; Wishart, *Montrose*, 113–114, 137–138; Cowan, *Montrose*, 173, 181, 183–185; Stevenson, *Alasdair*, 141–142, 151–152, 156, 162, 199, 206–210, 217; Way and Squire, *Collins Scottish Clan*, 459–461.

51 NRS, SR Moray, ii. 62–63. *A true relation of the happy success of His Maiesties forces in Scotland*, 12; Gordon, *Abridgement*, 74; A. MacPherson, *The Loyall Dissuasive*, ed. A.D. Murdoch (SHS, 1902), 147; Wishart, Montrose, ii. 172–174; *Reliquiae Celticae*, i. 179, 193; Spalding, *Memorialls*, ii. 402; Wishart, *Montrose*, 55; Cowan, *Montrose*, 155, 183, 209; A. Mackintosh-Shaw, *Historical Memoirs of the House and Clan of Mackintosh and of the Clan Chattan* (London, 1880), 334, 334–337 n.1; Stevenson, *Alasdair*,116–117, 127-8; <https://wiki.bcw-project.org/scots-Royalist/foot-regiments/badenoch-levies> retrieved 9.9.2021; <http://www.clan-macpherson.org/scripts/viewmemdata.pl?record=010e_macphersons> retrieved 11.11.2021.

52 Stevenson, *Alasdair*, 226.

53 *Ibid.*, 140, 141, 227, 240.

54 *Ibid.*, 110–112, 115, 124, 137–138.

55 *Ibid.*, 110–112, 115, 124–125, 137–140, 143 n. 16, 153, 155, 195–196, 214, 240.

Duart Castle 12.1644–7.1647[56].
Dunaverty Castle 12.1644–7.1647[57].
Dunyveg Castle 5–7.1647[58].
Kilmun Castle 9.1645[59].
Loch Gorm fort 5–9.1647[60].
Lochhead fort 6.1647–6.1647[61].
Toward Castle 5.1646–4.6.1646[62].

Gordons 13 units

Viscount Aboyne's Horse Troop>Horse, 19.4.1645–3.6.1646, 12.1646–3.1647, 10.1645 300–Horse, 11.1645 pt. 600 Horse.[63]
Arradoul's Horse Troop, 4–4.9.1645–? 14.5.1646.[64]
Badenoch, 2x3–9.1645, 12.1645–3.6.1646, 14.5.1646 co +? 1646–7 2 cos.[65]

56 *Ibid.*, 195–196, 227, 273.
57 *Ibid.*, 235–236, 245.
58 *Ibid.*, 221–222, 230–231, 238–239, 245.
59 *Ibid.*, 213.
60 *Ibid.*, 238.
61 *Ibid.*, 225, 227, 236–237, 240.
62 *Ibid.*, 226.
63 *Aberdeen*, 57–58; Balfour, *Works*, iii. 270–271; Gordon, *Abridgement*, 129–130, 135–138, 143–145, 154–146, 160, 163–167, 171, 173, 182, 188–189, 205; R. Gordon, *A Genealogical History of the Earldom of Sutherland* (Edinburgh, 1813), 536; *Guthry*, 143, 153–154, 160, 184–185, 188–189, 200; Spalding, *Memorialls*, ii. 248–250, 275, 350, 362, 376, 381, 394–395, 430, 469, 474, Wishart, *Montrose*, 97, 101, 106, 109–111, 113–114, 149–151, 162–163, especially note 14; *The Book of Bon-Accord* (Aberdeen, 1839), 76–77; Cowan, *Montrose*, 145–146, 199–200, 202, 204, 209–211, 213–214, 218, 220, 223, 233, 238–239, 250; *Scots Peerage*, i. 101; Stevenson, *Alasdair*, 171, 174, 177, 183–184, 198–200, 202, 204–205, 207, 209–210.
64 *Aberdeen*, 57–58; Gordon, *Abridgement*, 123, 176–177; *Memoirialls of Montrose and his times*, 2 vols., ed. Napier, M. (Edinburgh, 1848–1850), ii. 172–174; Spalding, *Memorialls*, ii. 330, 336; <https://wiki.bcw-project.org/scots-Royalist/horse-regiments/william-gordon-of-arradoul retrieved> 16.3.2021.
65 NRS, SR Moray, ii. 62–63. *A true relation of the happy success of His Maiesties forces in Scotland*, 12; Gordon, *Abridgement*, 74; A. MacPherson, *The Loyall Dissuasive*, ed. A.D. Murdoch (SHS, 1902), 147; Wishart, Montrose, ii. 172–174; *Reliquiae Celticae*, i. 179, 193; Spalding, *Memorialls*, ii. 402; Wishart, *Montrose*, 55; Cowan, *Montrose*, 155, 183, 209; A. Mackintosh-Shaw, *Historical Memoirs of the House and Clan of Mackintosh and of the Clan Chattan* (London, 1880), 334, 334–337 n.1; Stevenson, *Alasdair*,116–117, 127–128; <https://wiki.bcw-project.org/scots-Royalist/foot-regiments/badenoch-levies> retrieved 9.9.2021; <http://www.clan-macpherson.org/scripts/viewmemdata.pl?record=010e_macphersons> retrieved 11.11.2021 .

Blackadder's D co in Fyvie Castle, 1646.[66]

Camerons, Spring 1646 100.[67]

Drum the younger's Horse Troop, c.9.1645–3.6.1646, ?12.1646–3.1647 (2.1646 >30).[68]

Lord Gordon's Horse Troop, c.25.2–2.7.1645 (160, 2.7> Aboyne's Horse).[69]

Marquis of Huntly's Forces, 10.1645–3.6.1646, 12.1646–3.1647 (4.5.1646 1,000 foot and 240–500 horse).[70]

Mackintoshes, 10.1645–3.6.1646 (co. siege of Lethen).[71]

Minimore's Foot, 3.1645–3.6.1646, 12.1646–3x4.1647 (300>200).[72]

66 Gordon, *Abridgement*, 158, 176; Wishart, *Montrose*, 143; <https://wiki.bcw-project.org/scots-Royalist/ents/capt-blackadder> retrieved 3.8.2021; Blackadder was possibly SSNE 22 or 1810.

67 See note 15 Camerons above.

68 *Aberdeen*, 23, 61; Balfour, *Works*, iii. 198, 266; Gordon, *Abridgement*, 48–49, 51–52, 166, 171, 176; Guthry, *Memoirs*, 151, 162–163, 195–196, 225–226, 'Straloch Papers', in *The Miscellany of the Spalding Club*, vol. 1 (Aberdeen, 1841), 33; Spalding, *Memorialls*, ii. 324–325, 330, 332, 335, 338–339, 343–344, 346–349, 352–353, 356–357, 361–362, 369, 374, 379–380, 394–955, 397–398, 400–401, 430, 446, 478; Wishart, *Montrose*, 163; Gordon, *Sutherland*, 532; <http://wiki.bcw-project.org/scots-Royalist/horse-regiments/sir-alexander-irvine-of-drum confuses Sir Alexander with Alexander the younger>, retrieved 3.18.2021.

69 Gordon, *Abridgement*, 129; Gordon, *History*, 200; Guthry, *Memoirs*, 189; *Reliquiae Celticae*, ii. 193, 195; Spalding, *Memorialls*, ii. 447–451, 458–459, 462–465, 467–470, 474; Wishart, Montrose, 87–88, 96–98, 100, 106, 109–112; Cowan, *Montrose*, 188–189, 194, 196, 200, 202, 204–205, 207, 209–211, 233; Furgol, *Regimental History*, 145–146, which states the fate of Gordon's 90–160 troopers is a mystery; <https://wiki.bcw-project.org/covenanter/horse-regiments/lord-gordon> retrieved 1.4.2021.

70 Gordon, *Abridgement*, 166–167, 174–175, 177, 180–182, 184, 187–191, 194–200, 204–205; Gordon and Gordon, *Genealogical History*, 537; Guthry, *Memoirs*, 204, 209, 219, states that Huntly did not disband his army, but that it deserted him 242, 252, 275; Spalding, *Memorialls*, ii. 499; Wishart, Montrose, 157, 160–164, 17583; Cowan, *Montrose*, 239, 243, 245–246, 248, 250; Gordon, *Sutherland*, 536; Robertson, *Lordship*, 136, 138–144; Stevenson, *Alasdair*, 229, 231; <https://wiki.bcw-project.org/scots-Royalist/foot-regiments/strathbogie-regiment> retrieved 12.7.2021.

71 NRS, SR Moray, ii. 62–63; A.M. Mackintosh, *The Mackintoshes and Clan Chattan* (Inverness, 1903), 455; Mackintosh-Shaw, *Historical Memoirs*, 333, 334–337 n.1.

72 *Extracts from the records of the Synod of Moray*, ed. W. Cramond (Elgin, 1906), 125; Gordon, *Abridgement*, 130, 199; Spalding, ii. 413, after the battle of Aberdeen refers to Abergeldie and Monaltrie and 'diuerss vtheris' bringing Highlanders to Montrose's army – Minimore could be one of the others; J.M. Bulloch, *The Gordons and Smiths at Minmore, Auchorachan, and Upper Drumin in Glenlivet* (n.p., 1910), 7–10, 12–13; pers comms from Stephen Langan and Michael Netten of Colonel William Gordon's Regiment of Foot, 2021;< https://wiki.bcw-project.org/scots-Royalist/foot-regiments/william-gordon-of-minimore>; <https://www.skscotsbrigade.org.uk/gordons> retrieved 28.7.2021.

Monaltrie's Foot, 9.1645-3.6.1646, 12.1646–3.1647? (9.5, 2.7.1645 300, 15.8.1645 200).[73]

Skellater's Retinue, 4.1645 (200).[74]

Strathbogie Foot, 2.1645-3.6.1646, 12.1646–3.1647 (2.1645 500, 9.5.1645 500, 2.7.1645 500, 15.8.1645 400).[75]

Garrisons: Auchindoun Castle Garrison 12.1643–6.1644, 4.1645–1643.1647[76], Bog of Gight Castle 3.1645–3x4.1647.[77], Drum Castle 3–5.1644[78], Fyvie Castle 1646–3.1647[79], Kinord Castle 1x2.1646–c.15.5.1646[80], Rothes Castle 1x2.1646–c.9.5.1646[81], Strathbogie Castle 2.4.1646[82], Tilliquhilly Castle? 1646–4.1646[83]

73 *Reliquiae Celticae*, ii. 179; Spalding, *Memorialls*, ii. 235, 346, 413, 433, 454–457; Cowan, *Montrose*, 155, 171, 181, 184, 189–190, 193–194, 204–205, 209–210 discusses Inverey as the possible commander of the Royalist centre at Auldearn, but also mentions MacDonald of Glengarry and Drummond of Balloch as contenders for that role, 211, 213; Stevenson, *Alasdair*, 151, 166–168, 184; <https://wiki.bcw-project.org/scots-Royalist/foot-regiments/donald-farquharson-of-monaltrie> retrieved 20.7.2021.

74 Spalding, *Memorialls*, ii. 435, Stevenson, *Alasdair*, 171.

75 Balfour, *Works*, iii. 291; Gordon, *Abridgement*, 105, 116–117, 120–121, 123–126, 131–138, 154, 156, 163–166, 176, 187–188; Guthry, *Memoirs*, 171, 182; *Reliquiae Celticae*, ii. 187, 189, 191; Spalding, *Memorialls*, ii. 12, 296, 329–332, 338, 343–346, 353, 357, 448, 451, 458, 463–465, 467; Wishart, *Montrose*, 87–88, 96, 99–100, 105–106, 109, 110–112, 114, 118, 153–155; Cowan, *Montrose*, 195, 198, 207, 209, 218, 233; Reid, *Royalist Armies, 1639–1646*, 37; Stevenson, *Alasdair*, 169–172, 177, 180, 182, 192, 197–200, 202, 204–205, 207, 209–210; G. Wimbereley, *Genealogical Account of the Family of Gordon of Knockespock* (Inverness, 1903), 30–31, 33; <https://wiki.bcw-project.org/scots-Royalist/foot-regiments/strathbogie-regiment> retrieved 25.3.2021; <https://wiki.bcw-project.org/scots-Royalist/foot-regiments/john-gordon-of-knockespock> retrieved 12.7.2021.

76 *Diary of Alexander Jaffray*, ed. J. Barclay (London, 1833), 22; Gordon, *Abridgement*, 49, 189; Spalding, *Memorialls*, ii. 296, note 325–326, 330–331, 350, 352–353, 357, 360, 366–368, 375, 404, 469–470.

77 Gordon, *Abridgement*, 199; Gordon, *Sutherland*, 537; Spalding, *Memorialls*, i. 426; *Ibid.*, ii. 465; <https://wiki.bcw-project.org/scots-Royalist/foot-regiments/james-gordon-of-leichston> retrieved 12.7.2021.

78 See Drum the younger note 41 above.

79 Stevenson, *Alasdair*, 141, 179.

80 Gordon, *Abridgement*, 199; Gordon, *Sutherland*, 537; <https://canmore.org.uk/site/33983/castle-island-loch-kinord> retrieved 29.7.2021.

81 J. Fraser, *Chronicles of the Fraser. 916–1674*, ed. Mackay, W. (Scot. His. Soc., 1st Ser. xlvii, 1905), 313–314, his his quote Lewis's character is on 313; Gordon, *Abridgement*, 184–186; Wishart, *Montrose*, 178; Cowan, *Montrose*, 245.

82 Robertson, *Lordship and Power*, 141, 142 n.119, 150, 153.

83 See note 41 Drum the younger above.

Montrose 35 units

Aberdeen Foot, 3.1645-?.1645.[84]
Abergeldie's Retinue, 1-2-?.1645.[85]
Earl of Airlie's Horse Troop, 9.1644-30.7.1646 (9.1644 40, 2.2.1645 50, 8.1645 50-60/80/100, 9.1645 50-60).[86]
Arradoul's Horse Troop, 1-2x5.1646.[87]
Atholl Foot, 8.1644–30.7.1646 (8.1644 800F, 13.9 pt 300F, 12.1644–2.2.1645 some>? 9.5.1645 & 2.7.1645 some, 15.8.1645 200, 9.11.1645 400, 13.2.1646 700, 2–30.7.1646.[88]
Badenoch Levies, 9.1644–2x3.1645.[89]

84 *Aberdeen*, 57–58; Spalding, *Memorialls*, ii. 296, 324, 325–326 note, 332–335, 339, 341, 343, 346, 349, 351–353, 454–455; Reid, *Royalist Armies, 1639-1646*, 15.
85 Spalding, *Memorialls*, ii. 330, 394–395, 413, 430, 443.
86 Balfour, *Works*, iii. 268–271; Gordon, *Abridgement*, 51, 79, 100, 102, 138, 141, 146, 152, 156, 159–160, 162, 168; Guthry, 165, 171, 175, 179, 194, 209, 222–223, 226; *RCGA*, i. 138–140; Spalding, *Memorialls*, ii. 333, 404, 408, 420, 445, 457–458, 462; Wishart, *Montrose*, 63–64, 66–69, 77–78, 85–86; 118, 124; Cowan, *Montrose*, 165–166, 180–181, 183–184, 186, 194, 214–216, 218, 220, 237–238, 248; *Scots Peerage*, i. 124–125, 148, 150; Stevenson, *Alasdair*, 135, 200; <https://wiki.bcw-project.org/scots-Royalist/horse-regiments/james-ogilvie-earl-of-airlie> retrieved 3.15.2021.
87 *Aberdeen*, 57–58; Gordon, *Abridgement*, 123, 176–177; *Memoirialls of Montrose and his times*, 2 vols., ed. Napier, M. (Edinburgh, 1848–1850), ii. 172–174; Spalding, *Memorialls*, ii. 330, 336; <https://wiki.bcw-project.org/scots-Royalist/horse-regiments/william-gordon-of-arradoul> retrieved 16.3.2021.
88 *A true relation of the happy success of His Maiesties forces in Scotland under the conduct of Lord Iames Marquisse of Montrose* (Oxford, 1645), 6–7; Balfour, *Works*, iii. 268–271; Gordon, *Abridgement*, 71; *Guthry*, 161–164, 184, 187, 204, 214, 222–223; Wishart, *Montrose*, 74; ii. 243; RCGA, i. 20, 55, 391, 395, 435; *Reliquiae Celticae. Texts, papers and studies in Gaelic literature and philology left by the late Rev. Alexander Cameron*, 2 vols, eds. A. MacBain and J. Kennedy (Inverness, 1892–1894), (Gaelic and English text of Neil MacMhuirichs history), i. 179, 193; Spalding, *Memorialls*, ii. 444; Wishart, *Montrose*, 52, 55–57, 61, 66, 80, 82, 149–150, 165–166; Cowan, *Montrose*, 151, 156, 159–161, 183–184, 209–211, 213, 241–244; Stevenson, *Alasdair*, 117–118, 121, 131, 137, 156–157, 169, 198, 206–207, 216; <scots-Royalist:foot-regiments:patrick-graham-of-inchbrackie - BCW Project Regimental Wiki (bcw-project.org)> retrieved 10.9.2021.
89 NRS, SR Moray, ii. 62–63. *A true relation of the happy success of His Maiesties forces in Scotland*, 12; Gordon, *Abridgement*, 74; A. MacPherson, *The Loyall Dissuasive*, ed. A.D. Murdoch (SHS, 1902), 147; Wishart, Montrose, ii. 172-4; *Reliquiae Celticae*, i. 179, 193; Spalding, *Memorialls*, ii. 402; Wishart, *Montrose*, 55; Cowan, *Montrose*, 155, 183, 209; A. Mackintosh-Shaw, *Historical Memoirs of the House and Clan of Mackintosh and of the Clan Chattan* (London, 1880), 334, 334–337 n.1; Stevenson, *Alasdair*,116–117, 127–128; <https://wiki.bcw-project.org/scots-Royalist/foot-regiments/badenoch-levies> retrieved 9.9.2021; <http://www.clan-macpherson.org/scripts/viewmemdata.pl?record=010e_macphersons> retrieved 11.11.2021.

Balloch's Foot co. 2.7-9.1645, with Atholl F 1–2.1646, 16.3.1646.[90]
Blackadder's Dragoon co., 9.1645.[91]
Corrybrough's Retinue, 3.1645 (40).[92]
Marquis of Douglas' Horse, 8–9.1645 (pt. 1,500 horse).[93]
Freuchie's Retinue, 19.2–4.3.1645 (300).[94]
Gight the younger's Horse Troop 4.9.1645, 1.1646–30.7.1646 (Auldearn, Alford, Kilsyth? not Philiphaugh, 1646 in Crawford's horse brigade).[95]
Gordon's & Hay's Horse Troop, 9.19.11.1644, 19.2.1645–13.9.1645 (13.9.1644 c.40, 13.9.1645 60-80).[96]
Earl of Hartfell's Horse 8.13.9.1645 (13.9.1645 pt. 1,500 horse).[97]

90 Gordon, *Abridgement*, 130; *Guthry*, 214–215; Wishart, *Montrose*, 109, 134, 165–166, 187–188; Cowan, *Montrose*, 147, 209, 224, 232, 239, 241, 244–245, 251; Stevenson, *Alasdair*, 205, 216.

91 Gordon, *Abridgement*, 158, 176; Wishart, *Montrose*, 143; <https://wiki.bcw-project.org/scots-Royalist/ents/capt-blackadder> retrieved 3.8.2021; Blackadder was possibly SSNE 22 or 1810.

92 Gordon, *Abridgement*, 110–112; Wishart, *Montrose*, ii. 186–187; *RCGA*, i. 271, 283–284; *Ibid*., ii. 422; Spalding, *Memorialls*, ii. 454–455; Cowan, *Montrose*, 193; Stevenson, *Alasdair*, 166–168).

93 Balfour, *Works*, iii. 176, 189, 191, 203, 242, 255, 280; J. Burns, *Memoirs by James Burns, bailie of the city of Glasgow. 1644–1661* (Edinburgh, 1832), 11–12; *The Douglas Book*, 4 vols., ed W. Fraser (Edinburgh, 1885), iii. 330-3; Gordon, *Abridgement*, 145, 152, 158, 160, 162; *Government*, Stevenson, 8; *Guthry*, 169, 196–198, 201–203, 209; Spalding, *Memorialls*, ii. 57, 85; Wishart, *Montrose*, 136–137, 140, 146, 148; Cowan, *Montrose*, 222, 231–232, 234, 236–238; *Scots Peerage*, i. 202–204

94 Guthry, *Memoirs*, 147; Wishart, Montrose, ii. 172-4; Spalding, *Memorialls*, ii. 365, 428, 447, 449–450; Cowan, *Montrose*, 181, 188–189; Stevenson, *Alasdair*, 166–167; <https://wiki.bcw-project.org/scots-Royalist/foot-regiments/james-grant> retrieved 6.4.2021.

95 Gordon, *Abridgement*, 48-9, 94, 135, 176–177, 180; Spalding, *Memorialls*, ii. 321–322, 324–325, 330, 342–343, 347, 359, 374, 430, 448–449; <https://wiki.bcw-project.org/scots-Royalist/horse-regiments/sir-george-gordon-ygr-of-gight (wrongly crediting Gight the younger as a knight)>, retrieved 19.3.2021.

96 Balfour, *Works*, iii. 355, 357–359, 363; Gordon, *Abridgement*, 81; *Government*, Stevenson, 7, 51–52; Guthry, 165, 170–171, 196, 200, 202, 206, 211; Wishart, *Montrose*, ii. 172–174; *A more perfect relation of the late great victorie in Scotland* (London, 1645), 3, 5; *Reliquiae Celticae*, i. 193, 195; *RCGA*, i. 7, 107, 143; Spalding, *Memorialls*, ii. 322, 324-5, 330, 338-9, 341, 347-9, 352, 374, 392, 396, 401, 403–404, 427, 431–432, 448, 453–455; Straloch Papers', 33; Wishart, *Montrose*, 66–69, 74, 106, 109, 118, 120, 169; Cowan, *Montrose*, 147, 165–167, 172, 188, 192–193, 202, 207, 209–10, 218, 220, 223–224, 238, 241; Stevenson, *Alasdair*, 167–168; <https://wiki.bcw-project.org/scots-Royalist/horse-regiments/maj-nathaniel-gordon> retrieved 5.4.2021.

97 *Annandale Family Book of the Johnstones, Earls and Marquises of Annandale,* 2 vols., ed. W Fraser (Edinburgh, 1894), i. cxcii-cc; APS, vi, pt. i. 479, 484, 486, 754; *Baillie*, ii. 314; Balfour, *Works*, iii. 176, 189, 191, 203, 224, 234–235, 241, 255, 285, 287–288, 328; *The Douglas Book*, iii. 330–331; *Government*, Stevenson, 8, 11, 39, 51–53, 56; Gordon,

Harthill's Retinue 9.5.1645? 15.8.1645.[98]
Kilpont's Retinue Late August–c.10.9.1645 (350-500).[99]
MacDonalds of Clanranald 2.1645–9.6.1645 (some).[100]
MacDonalds of Glengarry 2.1645–9.1645 (some).[101]
A. MacDonnell's & O'Cahan's Foot 9.1645 (500).[102]
MacDonnell's Horse Troop 12.1645–30.7.1646.[103]
MacFarlanes 1.2.1645.[104]
MacGregors 12.1644–4.1645.[105]
Mackinnons 1.5.1645.[106]
Mackintoshes 2.7.1645–30.7.1646 (co.).[107]
MacLachlans 1.2.1645.[108]
Macleans (of Coll) (2+).[109]

Abridgement, 145, 162; *Guthry*, 169, 196–197, 200, 202, 206, 210; Napier, *Montrose*, ii. 554; Cowan, *Montrose*, 232, 235; *Scots Peerage*, i. 257, 259.

98 *Analecta Scotica: Collections Illustrative of the Civil, Ecclesiastical and Literary History of Scotland*, ed. J. Maidment (Edinburgh, 1834), 247; Balfour, *Works*, iii. 198; Gordon, *Abridgement*, 186, 204–205; Guthry, *Memoirs*, 256; Spalding, *Memorialls*, ii. 330, 448–449, 475, 477, 505–506; <https://wiki.bcw-project.org/scots-Royalist/horse-regiments/john-leith-of-harthill> retrieved 29.4.2021.

99 *APS*, VI, i. 202; Carte, *Original Letters*, ii. 73–74; Gordon, Abridgement, 73–75; *Guthry*, 163–166; Spalding, *Memorialls*, ii. 403; Wishart, *Montrose*, 56–57, 59–60, 64–66; *A True Relation of the Happy Successes of His Majesty's Forces in Scotland* … (London, 1644), 6-7; *Scots Peerage*, i. 138–139; Cowan, *Montrose*, 160; Reid, *Royalist Armies, 1639–1646*, 36–37; Stevenson, *Alasdair*, 126, 130–131; <covenanter:foot-regiments:lord-kilpont - BCW Project Regimental Wiki (bcw-project.org)> retrieved 12.9.2021. See also Balfour, *Works*, iii. 279.

100 See note 22 MacDonalds of Clanranald above.

101 See note 24 MacDonalds of Glengarry above.

102 See notes 12 and 14 [A. MacDonnell's and O'Cahan's Foot] above.

103 Gordon, *Abridgement*, 176, 184; *Guthry*, 123; Wishart, *Montrose*, 177–178; <scots-Royalist:horse-regiments:capt.-mcdonnell - BCW Project Regimental Wiki (bcw-project.org)> retrieved 24.9.2021.

104 James MacFarlane, *History of Clan MacFarlane* (Glasgow, 1922), 112, 117.

105 See note 27 MacGregors above.

106 Downie, Sir Alexander Mackenzie, and Mackinnon, Alister Downie. *Genealogical Account of the Family of Mackinnon compiled many years ago from authentic records*. 2nd edition, Edward Stanford, London, 1883; D.D. Mackinnon, *Memoirs of the Clan Fingon* (London, 1899), 32–33; T. Maclauchlan, and J. Wilson, *A History of the Scottish Highlands, Highland Clans and Highland Regiments*, ed. J.S. Keltie, 2 vols. (Edinburgh, 1875), ii. 257; <scots-Royalist:foot-regiments:mackinnons - BCW Project Regimental Wiki (bcw-project.org)> retrieved 13.9.2021.

107 See note 45 Mackintoshes above.

108 See note 30 MacLachlans above.

109 See note 31Macleans above.

Monaltrie's Foot, 16.9.1644–1.1645 (28.10.1644 300).[110]
Mortimer's Dragoon company, 9.1645–30.7.1646 (c.125).[111]
Lord Reay's Retinue, 11.1645–9.5.1646, 6.1646.[112]
Rollo's Horse Troop, 13.9.1644–17.9.1644, 6x7.1645-13.9.1645 (13.9.1644 20).[113]
Earl of Seaforth's Retinue, 3.6.1646.[114]
Sleat's Retinue, 5.1645,?.3–30.7.1646 (5.1645 400).[115]
Strathbogie Foot, 9x10.1644 (200).[116]
Struan's Retinue [perhaps a company of Atholl Foot], 8.1644–2.1645, 5–9. 1645? 1646?.[117]
Earl of Traquair's Horse Troop, 4.9–13.9.1645 (120).[118]

110 See note 47 Monaltrie's above.

111 NRS, PA. 12/2, 16.4.1647 David Leslie to Committee of Estates; *Aberdeen*, xviii–xix; Gordon, *Abridgement*, 176, 184–186, 199; *Guthry* 223; Spalding, *Memorialls*, ii. 454; Wishart, *Montrose*, 144–145, 177–179; <scots-Royalist:horse-regiments:john-mortimer - BCW Project Regimental Wiki (bcw-project.org)> retrieved 9.10.2021 and Reid, *Royalist Armies, 1639–1646*, 40, with which this entry disagrees. Mortimer's fate seems uncertain. Stevenson, *Alasdair*, 230, states he was executed. None of his sources in *Ibid.*, 243 n. 62 state that. Cowan, *Montrose*, 283, 291 following Wishart, *Montrose*, 494 has him captured at Carbisdale.

112 Gordon, *Abridgement*, 146, gives Montrose credit for Reay's freedom in 1645; *Guthry*, 143, 170, 195–196, 225–226; *RCGA*, i. 19, 22, 168, 237–238, 263, 305, 341, 369, 532, 556; Spalding, *Memorialls*, ii. 259, 425, 430; Wishart, *Montrose*, 134 n.25, 154–155, 164–165, 176–177, 529; Cowan, *Montrose*, 145, 243, 247–248, 250, 271, 286; Gordon, *Sutherland*, 530, 534; *Scots Peerage*, vii. 167–168; SSNE 93.

113 *APS*, vi, pt. i. 313, 465, 587; Balfour, *Works*, iii. 270–271; Gordon, *Abridgement*, 71, 154, 162, 168; *Guthry*, 161, 164, 206, 208; Symonds, *Diary*, 161; Wishart, *Montrose*, 47, 50, 66-70, 77 n.22, 109, 120, 157–158; Cowan, *Montrose*, 151, 156, 165-6, 238, 240; T.F. Henderson, 'Rollo, William', *Dictionary of National*, ed. S. Lee (Oxford, 1897), xlix. 170; Scots *Peerage*, vii. 195–199.

114 *Act anent recruting the armies* (Edinburgh, 1646), 3; Balfour, *Works*, iii. 296, 350, Fraser, *Chronicles of the Frasers*, 318–319, 334; Gordon, *Abridgement*, 64, 68–69, 85, 109, 121–122, 127, 174–175, 180, 182; *Guthry*, quote 215–217, 220, 236–237; Wishart, Montrose, ii. 265–266; *RCGA*, i. 30, 45, 47, 50, 52, 55, 62, 65, 68, 72, 76, 156, 165-6, 168, 173; Spalding, *Memorialls*, ii. 333, 447–448, 450, 473; Wishart, *Montrose*, 82–83, 176, 179–180, 184, 312, 530; Cowan, *Montrose*, 243, 245–246, 248, 253; Gordon, *Sutherland*, 534–535; Stevenson, *Alasdair*, 112–113, 115–117, 166–167, 216, 228.

115 Wishart, *Montrose*, 176; Cowan, *Montrose*, 155, 243; Stevenson, *Alasdair*, 216, 228, 230; Theiss, 'Western Highlands', 56–57.

116 See note 48 Strathbogie Foot above.

117 Wishart, *Montrose*, ii. 172–174; Balfour, *Works*, iii. 271; *RCGA*, i. 20, 55; Napier, *Montrose*, ii. 172–174, 281; Spalding, *Memorialls*, ii. 343, 346, quote 348; Wishart, *Montrose*, 74; Cowan, *Montrose*, 181, 247, 250; Stevenson, *Alasdair*, 125, 152.

118 Balfour, *Works*, iii. 286, 288–292; Gordon, *Abridgement*, 145, 152, 154, 156–157; *Guthry*, 201–202; Wishart, *Montrose*, 140, 143–144; Spalding, *Memorialls*, ii. 350, 430; Cowan, *Montrose*, 222–223, 231, 234; Scots Peerage, vii. 404–406; Stevenson, *Alasdair*, 210;

Garrisons: Blair Atholl Castle 8.16448.1647[119], Harthill Castle 5.1645–?[120], Kincardine Castle c.1–16.3.1646[121], Pitcaple Castle? –8.1645–9.9.1645[122].

<https://wiki.bcw-project.org/covenanter/horse-regiments/earl-of-traquair> retrieved 4.8.2021.

119 *Government*, Stevenson, 17; Wishart, *Montrose*, ii. 205-6, 238-9, 243, 276; Spalding, *Memorialls*, ii. 472; Cowan, *Montrose*, 193, 200, 207, 239; Stevenson, *Alasdair*, 142, 145, 198, 216.

120 See note 83 Harthill's above.

121 Cowan, *Montrose*, 244–245.

122 J. Davidson, *Inverurie and the Earldom of Garioch* (Edinburgh, 1878), 238, 288–289.

Appendix II

Orders of Battle

Dumfries campaign, order of battle April 1644: Artillery – two guns, two petards, Cumberland and Westmoreland forces – 800 foot, 200 horse in three troops including Governor of Carlisle Sir Harry Stradling's & Sir Philip Musgrave's horse troops, three companies of the Earl of Crawford's Dragoons, and 200 Horse – part of the Earl of Crawford's Horse (including Frances Dalzell's/Mistress Persone's troop and 2–3 others/100 men), and Montrose's troop (100.) Mentieth states a total of 2,000 men, but 1,350–1,500 seems more likely. *True Relations*, 3; HMC *Laing MSS*, i. 214-5; R. Menteith, *History of the Troubles of Great Britain*, trans. J. Ogilvie (London, 2nd edn 1738), 163–164; Napier, *Memorials*, ii. 127, 130–132, 144; Wishart, *Memoirs*, 44–47, 362–363; *True Relations of the Happy Success of the Marquis of Montrose* (Oxford, 1645), 1–3; M. Fraser, *The Rivals, Montrose and Argyll and the Struggle for Scotland* (Edinburgh, 2015), 120.

Northeastern campaign, order of battle 9 May–4 July 1644: Artillery –6 guns. Baillie, ii. 196; Menteith, 164; Napier, *Memorials*, ii. 135–137, 145; Somerville, *Memorie of the Somerville's*, 2 vols. (Edinburgh, 1815), ii. 288-331; *True Relations of the Happy Success of the Marquis of Montrose*, 3–4; *Thurlow State Papers*, (London, 1742), i. 35–36; Wishart, *Memoirs*, 44–47, 362–363; Foot: 2,000; Horse: 500, Earl of Crawford's Horse (including Frances Dalzell's/Mistress Persone's troop and two others), Marquis of Montrose's troop, Earl of Crawford's Dragoons (three companies), Somerville, ii. 297, or 1,500 H+D from Durham and Northumberland under COL Robert Clavering, *True Relations*, 3; <royalist:foot-regiments:sir-robert-clavering - BCW Project Regimental Wiki (bcw-project.org)>, which states Clavering commanded a foot regiment at Sunderland in May as well as a horse regiment at Morpeth, <royalist:horse-regiments:sir-robert-clavering - BCW Project Regimental Wiki (bcw-project.org); <https://wiki.bcw-project.org/scots-Royalist/horse-regiments/marquis-of-montrose,> retrieved 2.8.2021.

Tippermuir 1.9.1644 order of battle: Irish Brigade 1,100, Keppoch 100, Badenoch 500; Atholl F 800, Kilpont's F 350–500, Struan's 60 – 1,700/3,060 Alasdair 55 percent, Montrose 45 percent, Gordon 0 percent. Foot: 3,000, Horse: 3. Baillie, *Letters*, ii. 225, 233, 262; *Collection of Original Letters and Papers … found among the Duke of Ormonde's Papers*, T. Carte (ed.), 2 vols. (London, 1739), i. 73–74.; Gordon, *Abridgement*, 73–75; Mentieth, *History of the Troubles*, 171–173; Napier,

Memorials, ii. 149–151; Spalding, *Memorials*, ii. 403; *A true relation of the happy success of his majesties forces in Scotland …* (Oxford, 1644), 7–8. Wishart, *Memoirs*, 56–62.

Aberdeen 13.9.1644 order of battle: Irish Brigade, Badenoch with the Atholl Foot 300 total (based on their earlier ratio 114/186); Struan's 50; Horse Troops: Airlie's 40, Gordon's & Hay's c.40, Rollo's 20, 1,214/1,550, 78 percent Alasdair, 22 percent Montrose, 0 percent Gordon. 1,450 Foot, 100 Horse, Baillie, *Letters*, ii. 234, 262; Carte, *Ormonde*, i. 74; *Extracts from the council register of the burgh of Aberdeen, 1643–1747* (ed.) J Stuart (Scottish Burgh Record Society, 1872), 28–29; Gordon, *Distemper*, 80–84; Spalding, *Memorialls*, ii. 405–7/406–13; *A true relation of the happy success*, 10–12; Wishart, *Memoirs*, 66–69.

Fyvie 10.1644 order of battle: Irish Brigade 800x900; Foot – Monaltrie's 300, Horse Troops – Airlie's, Gordon's and Hay's, Rollo's, total Horse 90, Retinues – Struan's 50, – 800x900/1,240–1,340, Alasdair 67 percent, Montrose 33 percent, Gordon 0 percent. Gordon, *Distemper*, 90–91; *Memoirs of Scottish Catholics during XVIIth and XVIIIth centuries*, 2 vols. (ed.) W.F. Leith (London, 1909), if. 297; Spalding, *Memorialls*, ii. 426–427; Wishart, *Memoirs*, 73–75.

Harrowing of Argyll 12.1644–1.1645 order of battle: Irish Brigade, Clanranald 500x800/Clanranald, Glengarry, Glencoe, Keppoch, Stewarts of Appin, Camerons 500, MacAllisters, MacNabs; Atholl Foot some, Monaltrie's Foot 300, Badenoch 300, Struan's, Abergeldie's R; HT: Airlie's; Perhaps: Arradoul's Horse Troop, Rel Celt. ii. 183 for MacNabs and MacGregors

Inverlochy 2.2.1645 order of battle: Irish Brigade, Clanranald 200, Glengarry, Keppoch 100, Glencoe, Badenoch 300, Camerons 300x400, Appin 150/200, MacAllisters, MacGregors, Macleans 12–40; Struan's, Abergeldie's Retinues, MacFarlanes, Mackinnons; Horse Troop – Airlie's 50; Perhaps MacAllisters, 1,250/1,550 Alasdair 84 percent, Montrose 16 percent, Gordon 0 percent. Foot: 1500, Horse: 50. Gordon, *Abridgement*, 100–102; Guthry, *Memoirs*, 179; *Memoirs of Scottish Catholics*, i. 321–322; *Ormonde*, i. 75–76; *Rel. Celt.*, ii. 183–185; Spalding, *Memorialls*, ii. 444–445; Wishart, *Memoirs*, 83–85; [Sinclair], *Clan Maclean*, 124–125.

Dundee 4.1645 order of battle: Irish Brigade 800, MacGregors; Lord Gordon's Horse Troop? *APS*, VI, i. 519–521; Baillie, *Letters*, ii. 264; Gordon, *Abridgement*, 112–117; Guthry, *Memoirs*, 183; Spalding, *Memorialls*, ii. 458–463; Wishart, *Memoirs*, 88–95.

Auldearn 9.5.1645 order of battle: Irish Brigade 140+, pt. Clanranald, Glengarry and Keppoch 100, MacAllisters, MacGregors, Macleans; Strathbogie F 300/500, Atholl F some, Badenoch co., Monaltrie's F 300, Minimore's F 300; Mackinnons, Sleat's 400 HT: Gordon's 160, Aboyne's, Gight's, Newton's, Perhaps: Harthill's, 2,000 Foot, 300 Horse, Alasdair 900 Foot/39 percent, Montrose 500 Foot +50 Horse/24 percent, Gordons 600 Foot, 250 Horse=850/37 percent; 'Book of Clanranald' in A. Cameron, *Religuiae Celticae* (ed.) A. MacBain and J. Kennedy, 2 vols., (Inverness, 1892-94), ii. 187–193; Fraser, *Chronicles*, 296–297; Gordon, *Abridgement*, 121–127; R. Gordon and G. Gordon, *A Genealogical History of the Earldom of Sutherland* (Edinburgh, 1813), 525; Napier, *Memoirs*, ii. 500–501; Spalding, *Memorialls*, ii. 473–474; Wishart, *Memoirs*, 98–103

Alford 2.7.1645 order of battle: Irish Brigade, Clanranald, Keppoch, Glengarry, Appin, MacAllisters, MacGregors; Strathbogie F 500; Atholl F some, Balloch's co., Minimore's F 200, Monaltrie's F 300, Mackintosh co.; HT: Gordon's 160, Aboyne's, Gight's, Newton's, Rollo's, Perhaps: Struan's Alasdair 800F/35 percent, Montrose 200F+50H=250/11 percent, Gordon's 1,000F+250H=1,250/5 percent 2,300. Foot: 3000, Horse 300. Baillie, *Letters*, ii. 417–419; *Celticae Religuiae*, ii. 192–195; Fraser, *Frasers*, 299; Gordon, *Abridgement*, 128–133; *Memoirs of Scottish Catholics*, i. 348; Wishart, *Memoirs*, 106–112; Gordon, *Genealogical History*, 526.

Kilsyth 15.8.1645 order of battle: Irish Brigade 1,220, Clanranald 500, Keppoch 100, Glengarry 500 & Glencoe 100, Stewarts of Appin, MacAllisters, MacGregors, Macleans 700, MacNabs; Strathbogie Foot 400 & Aboyne's Horse, Harthill's, Newton's HT [400]; Atholl Foot 200, Badenoch some, Monaltrie's F 200, Minimore's F 200, Balloch's co.; Horse Troops: Airlie's 50–60/80/100, Gordon's 60–80, Perhaps: Horse Troop: Gight's, Foot: 4,500, Horse: 560. Alasdair 3,520F/67 percent, Montrose 200 Foot, 160 Horse 500/10 percent, Gordons 800 Foot, 400 Horse, 1,200/23%. Baillie, *Letters*, ii. 420–424; Gordon, *Abridgement*, 129–135; *Celticae Religuiae*, ii. 199-201; *True relation ... of Kilsyth*, 2–7; Wishart, *Memoirs*,122–125.

Philiphaugh 9.1645 order of battle: Irish brigade – A. MacDonnell's Foot & O'Cahan's Foot, 500/400, Horse: Douglas's, Hartfell's (1,500 total), Horse Troops: Airlie's 50–60, Gordon's & Hay's 60–80, Rollo's; Dragoons: Blackadder's co. Foot:500/400, Horse: 1,700 Alasdair 500F/23 percent, Montrose 1,700H/77 percent. Gordon, *Abridgement*, 156–162; Guthry, *Memoirs*, 202–204; *A more perfect relation of the late great victorie in Scotland* (London, 1645), 2–3; *Three Great Victories* (London, 1645) T1093; Wishart, *Memoirs*, 142–148.

Argyll 1645 Irish Brigade 600+garrisons, Alasdair's LGF co120, Clanranald, Glencoe, Glengarry, Keppoch, Kilellan's R, Lamonts 300, Largie's F co, MacAllisters, MacDougalls (OCT 500), Mackays of Ugdale, MacLachlans, Macleans, Macmillans, MacNabs; Perhaps: MacAllisters

Argyll 1646 Irish Brigade—J. MacDonnell's, Alasdair's LGF co, Clanranald, Glencoe, Glengarry, Camerons pt. 600, Appin, Kilellan's R, Lamonts (into June), Largie's F co, MacAllisters, MacAulays (Lagganmore), MacDougalls (L), MacGregors, Mackays of Ugdale, MacLachlans, Macleans, Macmillans, MacNabs (to MAR); Perhaps: MacAllisters

Argyll 1647 Irish Brigade—J MacDonnell's, Alasdair's LGF co, Clanranald, Clencoe, Glengarry, Sanda's (RP&DC) and MacDougalls (SPR 400x500), Kilellan's R (Dunaverty/DC), Largie's co (RP), MacAllisters (Skipness into June), MacDougalls (RP>DC), MacGregors (into May), Macleans, pt Macmillans Perhaps: Mackays of Ugdale, Maclachlans,

Anti-Estates/Glasgow 9.11.1645 Atholl F 400; 250 MacDonnell's HT & Mortimer's D co, Lord Lewis Gordon's HT

Huntly's 4.10.1645–3.6.1646 Huntly's (14.5.1646 1,000F & 240-500H)

1645 1,500 F, 300–500H, Badenoch 1 co., Mackintosh co, Camerons (SPR 1646 100), Minimore's F, Monaltrie's F; HT Drum's (FEB-3.6.1646), Newton's

Siege of Inverness 1645–9.5.1646/30.7.1646 Atholl F (after 13.2); retinues: Delgatie's, Harthill's, Reay's, Seaforth's, Sleat's, Mackintosh co., MacPherson co., Macleans of Coll 2 sons+?; Clanranald & Glengarry some; Horse troops: Arradoul's, Gight the younger's, on Spey guard to 8.5.1646 250H A. MacDonnell's & O'Cahan's as 2HTs – MacDonnell's & Mortimer's; HT: Crawford's Banff command into FEB 1646: Arradoul's (w Huntly by May, perhaps as early as FEB), Gight's, MacDonnell's, Harthill's, Mortimer's D co; 31.7.1646 Foot: Atholl F, Mackintosh co, Retinues: Sleat's, Struan's; Gight's HT, MacDonnell's HT, Mortimer's D co; *Garrisons* Blair Atholl

Moray 12.1645-3.6.1646 Badenoch

Siege of Assynt Castle: Seaforth, Reay's

Aberdeen 14.5.1646 1,500 F & 500H, Badenoch, Mackintosh co, Monaltrie's F, Strathbogie F; H: Aboyne's, HT: Arradoul's, Drum's, Newton's, *Garrisons:* Auchindoun Castle, Blackadder's D, Bog of Gight

Banff 12.1646-3.1647 1,500 F, 400–500H, Badenoch 2 cos. H: Aboyne's, HT Harthill's; Perhaps: Minimore's F, Monaltrie's F; Garrisons: Bog of Gight, Auchindoun, Lesmore, Loch Kinord, Strathbogie and Wardhouse Castles

Ireland 1647 Irish Brigade, Alasdair's LGF co, Glengarry

Ireland 1648 Irish Brigade, Clanranald 300, Glengarry